A Postmodern Psychology
of Asian Americans

SUNY series, Alternatives in Psychology

Michael A. Wallach, editor

A Postmodern Psychology of Asian Americans

Creating Knowledge of a Racial Minority

Laura Uba

State University of New York Press

Published by
State University of New York Press, Albany

For information, address State University of New York Press,
90 State Street, Suite 700, Albany, NY 12207

Production by Judith Block
Marketing by Patrick Durocher

Library of Congress Cataloging-in-Publication Data

Uba, Laura.
    A postmodern psychology of Asian Americans : creating knowledge of a racial
minority / Laura Uba.
        p. cm. — (SUNY series, alternatives in psychology)
    Includes bibliographical references and indexes.
    ISBN 0-7914-5295-6 (alk. paper) — ISBN 0-7914-5296-4 (pbk. : alk. paper)
    1. Asian Americans—Psychology. 2. Asian Americans—Race identity. 3.
Postmodernism—United States—Psychological aspects. I. Title. II. Series.

E184.O6 U23 2002
155.8'495073—dc21   2001032202

10 9 8 7 6 5 4 3 2 1

Contents

Illustrations

Figure

Preface

How can we know about Asian Americans?[1] Psychology's response has been a modern, empiricist one: We can know by relying on scientifically gathered data and logical reasoning about that data. That position has been based on psychology's adoption of the scientific method which basically grew out of the metaphysical and epistemological assumptions of the Reformation, Renaissance, Enlightenment, and Scientific Revolution. The tradition of treating the scientific method as sine qua non to knowledge has given this method a largely unquestioned status among psychologists. However, tracing the roots of that tradition provides a grounding for assessments of whether that method, as currently used in psychology, provides the most meaningful way to learn about Asian Americans and psychological issues relevant to them.

The Enlightenment has been customarily portrayed as a period of intellectual efflorescence revealing the epistemological basis for objective understanding of reality. However, Western philosophy and science did not develop in a social vacuum: Many of the assumptions underlying modern science have nonscientific grounding in religious beliefs, social disruptions, political orientations, and rationalizations.

Religious beliefs in an orderly physical and human universe established by God implied that just as everyone in Dante's Inferno was placed where he or she deserved, so everyone in society was in his or her deserved place: the bourgeois and the peasants, the believers and the infidels, men and women, the colonizers and the colonized, and white people and people of color. St. Paul's (Romans 13) declaration that rulers were ordained by God was a rationale not only for the divine right of kings, but more broadly for sanctioning the status quo. Pantheism reinforced the idea that what is, should be, as all are parts of God (Toulmin, 1990). Social hierarchies, for instance, were considered legitimate reflections of God's plan, omniscience, omnipotence, and benevolence (Griffin, 1989).

Coupled with religious beliefs about man's duty to have "dominion" over God's creations and the assignment of man to the role of rational, objective overseer, such assumptions were conceptual bases for much of the colonialism of the time. A corollary to the Biblical idea of human dominion over nature and other creatures was that civilized men were meant to save and have dominion over people of color (Toulmin, 1990). Consequently, white men thought of themselves as naturally entitled to speak for the latter and obligated to determine and restrict how those said to have an inferior social status could behave. Indeed, Western scholars thought, God had destined the social and intellectual colonization of some people. Such thinking was subsequently used as a rationale, for example, in the colonization of the Philippines. In a parallel way, males were deemed destined to rule females, who were to be used, submissive, and deprived of voice about their views. Women were regarded as inferior, weak, and childlike while people of color were considered all those plus animalistic. The perspective of the colonizers was elevated over the perspectives of the colonized; the voices of the colonized, it was assumed, could be safely ignored because they do not add to understanding. Like colonialists, intellectual explorers thought that they could understand less exalted people (i.e., the ignorant, people of color, and females) better than those people could themselves.

The modern era and modern science developed in that attitudinal environment. Although no longer as chauvinistic and imperious as men of that time, most researchers today in some ways still assume they know more about their human study participants than the latter know about themselves, impose meanings and explanations on their behaviors, and listen to the latter only from the former's perspective and for the former's purposes. Rather than ask respondents what accounts for their behavior, researchers raised on those assumptions and methods usually limit responses to a particular set of categories and then assume that they can see connections between influences and behaviors that respondents cannot identify themselves. This approach contributes to homogenizing portrayals in which the complexity and multiple meanings of experiences are swept aside so that people can be viewed only in the inquirer's terms.

The definitions, views, and assumptions of psychological methods used to study Asian Americans were historically developed by Europeans and European Americans.[2] Like colonialists, white scientists traditionally thought of themselves as just people, normal for the human species, and that assumption has probably contributed to the belief that the views of (white) Enlightenment scholars were natural, neutral, and objective.

Currently, we still see that many white Americans, albeit without the same colonialist intent, regard people of color as "others" and themselves as simply people. For instance, when black Americans are pictured on greeting cards, the cards are regarded as being for black customers; but when white people are pictured, the card manufacturers intend the card to be for everyone. Likewise, in psychological research, the European Americans upon whom the research is disproportionately based are still regarded simply as normative humans.

Just as females had been viewed as orbiting around or the opposite of males (Tavris, 1991), a glance at introductory psychology books today demonstrates that in psychology European Americans are to some extent treated as the center of the psychosocial universe with marginalized minorities as orbiting satellites around them and their behaviors—indeed, the behaviors of humans around the world—are explained in comparison to research on European Americans. That social order and dichotomous white-nonwhite categorizations are reinforced by that repeated comparison to white Americans. As with females' behaviors that differ from those of males, Asian Americans' behaviors and attitudes are presumed to be in need of explanation to the extent that they differ from those normative white Americans. Studies of people of color commonly focus on how they are distinguished from European Americans in (exotic) culture, (deficient) acculturation, and (separate and marginalized) minority status.

In research on Asian Americans, the contrasts have been exaggerated by long-standing Orientalism, a concept Edward Said (1978) used to characterize French and British colonialist attitudes toward people of the Middle East. Orientalism was characterized by a belief that the Orient—a romantic, exotic place supposedly populated by naturally feminine and passive people who valued hierarchical, traditional authorities—was antithetical and inferior to the democratic and individualistic orientation of the West. That myth was an ideological basis for subjugation of the colonized in Asia. That colonialist explanatory perspective also embraces the pretense that power relations, economic roles, and racial politics and hierarchies are irrelevant to the behaviors and experiences of Asian Americans (K. Chan, 1996).

From the perspective of postcolonial theory, which contests the ideology underlying ethnocentric, Western imperialism, many portrayals and ways of treating people of color today resurrect colonialist views of the "other." Colonialist interests emphasized views of the "other" in terms of their ability to upset or sustain the existing distribution of power (and may be paralleled in some psychological research on high-achieving Asian American students occupying slots in coveted colleges, for example).

From that perspective, a desire to establish a hegemonic perspective that protects the status of those in power sometimes hides behind the search for knowledge (Foucault, 1969). As a societal institution, even science is most responsive to the interests of those in power (Ritzer, 1997). If modern science's claims of authoritative, objective perspective were ripped of their emperor's clothes, and objectivity and validity were exposed as caricatures, then the values and hegemonic interests governing science would be exposed (Denzin, 1995). Moreover, by pointing out how power and ideology operate in discourse and how social, temporal, and historical locations bear on behaviors, knowledge can be reconstructed in a way that points out oppression and transforms society in ways that increase justice, fairness, and racial and ethnic harmony.

Just as ignoring colonialist influences on science would be naive, however, focusing only on the colonialist underpinnings of descriptions of Asian Americans would be reductionist (Sumida, 1998). Other assumptions and concepts of modern science form a framework that also guides psychological research. Reanalysis of those assumptions and concepts shows that science's assumptions and methods are not simply and objectively *the* ways, much less the best ways to know about people.

The book title's reference to the postmodern alludes to our current postmodern era which, many scholars have posited, began roughly at the end of World War II as intellectual discourse shifted away from the premises of modern science and its underlying cultural practices and as the marketing and consuming of commodities, mass media images, and multinational capitalism began to dominate. The title is also meant to imply that postmodernism, an intellectual orientation increasingly displacing modern premises in disciplines from architecture to sociology, offers a useful approach for psychology and for understanding Asian Americans' behaviors and experiences.

In this book, I take postmodern perspectives; but I do not adopt all forms of postmodernism—indeed, I could not simultaneously adopt all forms because some of their ideas are contradictory. For example, while some postmodernists dismiss empiricism as useless, others think that it might be appropriate in some circumstances. I do not align with the so-called skeptical postmodernists who claim that rationality should be discarded; however, I think that scholarly rationality need not be limited to formal logic. In some cases, rationality could take a back seat to other values, such as compassion, that would give us a fuller understanding of an issue, event, or concept. For instance, it might be rational to say that a person dying and in pain should be kept alive because continuing research means that the possibility of a breakthrough cure and emergency Food and Drug Administration approval always exists; but valuing compassion more than rationality might sway a person to try to relieve the person's pain by letting him or her die.

I describe global similarities among the multitude of strands of postmodern thought. Generally, scientific postmodernism rejects the idea that conclusions can be proven to be objectively accurate.[3] Postmodern perspectives call attention to the neglected, peripheral, rejected, tenuous, disjointed, and repressed—be they ideas, perspectives, issues, or studied people.

They imply that understanding the variety and complexity of a group like Asian Americans entails identifying the assumptions behind descriptions and explanations of their behaviors and hearing the meanings they ascribe to their behaviors, experiences, and situations, unconstrained by modern scientific methods alone.

Postmodernism is no panacea to the difficulties of psychological investigations, nor does it masquerade as one. This book is replete with paradoxes: It contains generalizations about postmodernism, superimposing a unity and cohesion to various strands of postmodern thought even though different proponents of postmodernism offer varied and sometimes conflicting views. The claim that statements are constructions rather than actual representations is itself a contradiction because it assumes that the claim, a construction, reflects reality (Rosenau, 1992). You may well see contradictions (only some of which I recognize) in the postmodern positions I take.

Some people interpret poststructuralist and postmodern perspectives as implying there is no place for psychology at all. This book does not go in that direction. However, I do try to destabilize some psychological truth claims to show "how little we really know [and that] much of what we do know is pure [arbitrary] linguistic convention" (Rosenau, 1992, p. xiii).

I describe scholarly and popular psychological characterizations as epistemic cultural acts. The public's psychological outlooks are germane because in a democratic country, research's ostensible goal is not merely to provide knowledge for scholars and therapists, but also to affect the public's understanding and behavior. I also consider public use of psychological concepts, explanations, and characterizations as a way of exposing and examining "the cultural domination of the existing Euro-American knowledge base . . . [and, hopefully, thereby promoting actions] capable of resolving injustices and creating a more equitable society" (Hune, 1997b, p. 323).

Simultaneously, psychological research on minorities could, along with feminist psychology, lead psychology toward forming a new postmodern field that embraces a multitude of quite different perspectives on experiences, behaviors, and interpersonal relations. Currently, as Bevan (1991) noted, "too many psychologists hug the intellectual shoreline . . . content to paddle quietly in their own small ponds . . . [But] the big questions about [the world] will never be answered if scholars simply attend to the comfortable little questions" (p. 481).

Although postmodern analytical approaches, often antithetical to the kind of tightly knit presentation normally produced within systematic, modern frameworks, might occasionally make the following a postmodern pastiche — a "collage hodgepodge patchwork of ideas or views [that] denies regularity, logic, or symmetry [and] glories in contradiction and confusion"

(Rosenau, 1992, p. xiii)—this book's organization is designed to provide a discussion of postmodernism's wide applicability to psychological concerns. Because psychological research has been modeled after the science of the modern era, I begin by making an inevitably controversial postmodern foray into analyzing some of the ontological and epistemological assumptions behind modern psychology's research conceptualizations and practices. In Chapter 2, I provide a brief summary of postmodernism, with an emphasis on its relevance for psychology. Chapter 3 identifies privileged variables and broad, modern assumptions behind psychological research, particularly those relevant to the study of Asian Americans. In the remaining chapters, I take a postmodern perspective to analyze major concepts in portrayals of Asian Americans, including race and culture (Chapter 4), acculturation and assimilation (Chapter 5), and ethnicity and identity (Chapter 6). I end (Chapter 7) with a discussion of postmodern methods and the issues and new roles for psychologists that postmodernism opens. Although I focus on psychological portrayals of Asian Americans, those portrayals reflect larger conceptual and methodological problems in psychological research generally.

Uncited first-person quotes are from students' term papers; I thank the students for giving me permission to quote from them. I also thank the Asian American Studies Department for institutional support, Drs. Bevra Hahn and Nancy Sicotte for their abilities and willingness to deal with the hassles of enabling me to work, the Editorial Board at SUNY Press, and my family for myriad other forms of support.

CHAPTER 1

Modernist Epistemology

Describing what psychology tells us about a minority group like Asian Americans commonly takes the form of summarizing characterizations produced by various psychological studies (e.g., L. Lee & Zane, 1998; Sue & Morishima, 1982; Uba, 1994a). However, to judge those characterizations, consideration must be given to how they are circumscribed by underlying ontological and epistemological assumptions and interpretive practices that psychology, as a social science, shares with other sciences.

Modern Epistemology and Science

Psychology-as-a-science grew from Western philosophy; therefore a brief reminder of science's philosophical roots provides an ontological and epistemological framework for analyzing psychological characterizations and the extent to which science's assumptions are appropriate for psychology.[1] A review of the centuries-long goal of discovering the foundations of reality, epistemology's move from a theological to a secular center, the promise of rationality, and the possibility of scientific knowledge lays the groundwork for a discussion of key metaphysical assumptions.

Assuming that the most basic characteristics of reality[2] are unchanging, Western scholars have long sought constant metaphysical truths and transcendent meanings beyond the particular. They have searched for ultimate, indivisible, fundamental, or absolute entities, laws, or powers that, while requiring no explanation of themselves, are foundations for other explanations (Slife & Williams, 1995).

In the Middle Ages when transcendent knowledge (of what is beyond direct experience) was regarded as God's sole province and an aspect of

1

God's essence, scholarly investigations and explanations were grounded in theology. However, fifteenth- and sixteenth-century humanism, marking a return to the pre-Christian standard of people[3] as the measure of all, set the stage for human-focused science; and the Reformation's argument for direct communication between an individual and God elevated the role of the individual to truth-finder with access to foundations. As the secular, intellectual activity of individuals challenged the imposed conclusions of theological and papal authorities, the medieval metaphysics, distinguishing between God and world, was displaced by a modern ontology, dividing existence into the human mind and the world external to it (Faulconer & Williams, 1990b; Polanyi, 1946/1964).

In addition to outlooks growing from the Reformation, changes in European society during the Renaissance, and Scientific, Industrial, and French Revolutions, along with concomitant faith in the social promise of human rationality, prompted the elevation of human understanding. The concurrence of heightened rationalism and modern prosperity seemed to justify the linkage of rationality, truth, and progress (Racevskis, 1993). The Biblical claim that "man" was created in God's image, coupled with *Genesis'* granting of dominion to Adam, was read to mean that humans are almost godly in their dominion. Whereas at one time, Christians and Islamics searched for intellectual coherence in depictions of reality that glorified and enhanced appreciation for God's creation of nature, the Scientific Revolution spurred a practical agenda for scholars with goals formerly thought to be solely God's prerogatives—control, prediction, and explanation—which are sustaining goals in psychology (Manicas, 1987; Toulmin, 1990).

By combining Cartesian doubt with Lockean empiricism and waving away both theology and philosophy as the sources of answers to their questions (Polkinghorne, 1983), Enlightenment scientists advocated Baconian scientific knowledge gained by using reasoning and carefully measured observations to test explanations against evidence. Knowledge gained in this way would be characterized in a way that formerly distinguished the divine: constant, absolute, and transcendent (Faulconer & Williams, 1990b). In what I refer to as the "modernist science" that grew out of such metaphysical assumptions and epistemological movements, judgments about intellectual conclusions would hinge on how those conclusions were achieved (Toulmin, 1972).

Positivism, a combination of mathematical logic, inductive principles, and (David) Humean empiricism laid out in Auguste Comté's (1798–1857) *Positive Philosophy* and John Stuart Mill's (1806–1873) *System of Logic*, was a set of principles defining the scientific method and epitomizing modernist science (Barrett, 1967). Positivists believed that following those principles would lead to certain, logical knowledge and general conclusions. However, many scholars, including Comté, Mill, and the Vienna Circle of linguistic philosophers, denied that psychology could be a science (Manicas, 1987; E. Nagel, 1979; Robinson, 1976; Slife & Williams, 1995). The latter, for example, declared that all true sciences must explain in terms of formal deduction from a general law and a set of conditions, which was a standard psychology could not meet (Polkinghorne, 1988).

Nevertheless, reflecting the scientistic belief that any field of inquiry can produce objective knowledge by using scientific research methods (Spretnak, 1997), psychology developed from the belief that following scientific procedures would reveal foundational, metaphysical truths about human behaviors and their meanings. While linked to philosophy in Germany, it labeled itself an empirical science in the United States in the years before and following World War I. As psychology became increasingly an American endeavor, it was increasingly defined by its empiricism (Manicas, 1987): Highly controlled studies came to be regarded as the most legitimate way to collect data. In arguments over whether psychology was a positivist endeavor or a nonscience, proponents of the latter position did not promote a coherent alternative and positivism established its discursive hegemony in psychology.

Partly due to the belief that all sciences should use the same hypothetical-deductive methods and partly born of a desire to have the cachet of science,[4] psychology has modeled itself after physics (Faulconer & Williams, 1990b; Kockelmans, 1990). However, to the extent that physical and natural sciences' assumptions about "the nature of truth and the world . . . are not true of the human world and of human phenomena, then the scientific methods based on those assumptions [might] not be appropriate for studying people" (Slife & Williams, 1995, p. 175).

There is neither a logical nor an empirical reason for assuming that methods used in one disciplinary domain or level of analysis should necessarily be appropriate for another. Hypothetical-deductive methods, for instance, have not worked equally well in all sciences (Kockelmans, 1990). Some sciences, such as astrophysics, still produce well-grounded interpretations without being primarily experimental sciences; like most other scholars before the eighteenth century, Isaac Newton relied predominantly on reason (Robinson, 1976). Nevertheless, psychology has insisted on being an experimental science and has primarily used the null-hypothesis-testing technique of the physical and medical sciences. (See Appendix A for a brief summary of psychological research methods.)

The scientific assumptions and methods underlying those sciences gained credence because they were useful in battles against dogmatism and research based on them undeniably provided technological and medical advances; but more than a century of psychology has neither identified comparably precise regularities nor produced comparable levels of control, prediction, and understanding. At most, psychology has found intriguing patterns with multiple exceptions (Richardson & Fowers, 1998). Yet it has continued with the premises of modernist science and so I refer to it as "modernist psychology."

Modernist Scientific Assumptions

As groundwork for this chapter's analysis of the appropriateness of modernist assumptions for psychology, consider the metaphysical ideas psychology has appropriated by molding itself to modernist science's positivist standards and first premises, which still form psychology's bedrock. Four of the key ontological and epistemological premises have been: knowledge reflects the unadulterated imprint of reality; the reality studied by scientists is stable and ordered by laws; parsimonious explanations are best; and the scientific method provides an accurate, objective foundation for knowledge.

The Unadulterated Imprint of Reality

Growing out of the medieval view that the metaphysical world is of timelessness, God, and things rather than perceptions was an assumption about reality and the nature of things in the world (Barrett, 1967). That assumption, the *metaphysics of things*, holds that things are constituted of inherent "qualities, properties, or categories [that] either directly or indirectly determine what the things are" (Williams, 1990, p. 145): Those properties and relationships among them presumably exist independently of any human understanding and determine meaning and knowledge (Spretnak, 1997).

A twin assumption is modernist science's *correspondence theory of truth*: In keeping with the Aristotelian notion that reality is apprehended (i.e., directly understood for what it is without interference), this theory holds that knowledge or truth is found when concepts correspond to what exists "out there" in an objectively knowable reality that is ontologically independent of our creation of it (Manicas, 1987). Much as a signet ring imprints wax, reality allegedly stamps understanding of the world on the mind. Accordingly, knowledgeable people are those who have accurate representations of the world in their minds, molded "and 'enformed' by reality through . . . careful observation and reason" (Faulconer & Williams, 1990b, p. 16).

Based partly on the Newtonian belief that rational laws governed reality, modernist science has held that the world and the relationships among things in it are rational. Therefore, reasoning about empirical data is thought to allow access to knowledge of the material world in its sense-transcendent forms—as concepts, qualities, properties, meanings, categories, and regularities.

Reality is Lawful, Orderly, and Stable

Tied to characterizations of the world as rational is a second key metaphysical assumption, modernist science's belief that reality is characterized by an ultimate order and stability which has, at its seed, logically deducible principles (Faulconer & Williams, 1990b; Polkinghorne, 1990; Toulmin, 1972). The belief in order was epistemologically descended from the medieval view that God created a stable, orderly, hierarchical nature running according to divine and, Aristotle and St. Thomas Aquinas added, unchanging principles.[5] A desire for order and stability was further piqued during the religious wars of the Reformation.

Whereas medieval human experience was explained primarily by one's relationship to God or temporal manifestations of divine truth (Cahill, 1998), by the late seventeenth century some Enlightenment scholars thought that human behaviors, like the movement of planets and other aspects of the natural world, should be understood in terms of transcendent, enduring, universal, underlying governing laws (Polkinghorne, 1988, 1990).[6] This view was bolstered by René Descartes' argument that the basis for knowledge was in the timeless and abstract rather than in the particular, timely, and concrete (Toulmin, 1990). Phenomena, then, were regarded as manifestations or instances of those ultimate, self-evident, indubitable, timeless, noumenal, abstract foundations or first principles (Cassirer, 1951; Toulmin, 1990); those organizing principles purportedly account for the conditions under which events occur and the relationships between apparently disparate events or conditions (E. Nagel, 1979). Consequently, Carl Hempel, the father of a radically empiricist brand of positivism, logical positivism, tempered science's charge by arguing that the goal was to find those covering laws—broad, if not universal, relationships among variables, empirical laws, or regularities that explain a wide range of phenomena and the conditions that support or limit the appearance of regularities (Barrett, 1967; Kockelmans, 1990; Slife & Williams, 1995).

Accordingly, psychology tried to discover expected, causal and necessary relationships arising from lawful, consistent properties and relations (R. Williams, 1990). Today, however, it focuses more on regularities than on universal truths, in part because of its lack of success in discovering the latter.[7]

Parsimonious Explanations are Best

Contributing to the predilection toward claiming the discovery of orderly regularities, a third metaphysical assumption of modernist science has been Ockham's Razor, named after William of Ockham (c. 1290–1349), and later reformulated by Newton in Book III of *Principia* and as C. Lloyd Morgan's

(1852–1936) Law of Parsimony. That rule states that the best explanations are those that require the fewest hypothetical constructs, assumptions, structures, or forces. Not surprisingly, the frequent result of following this rule has been that after a series of studies, researchers concede that "The role of [some variable, X] is much more complex than previously conceived" (e.g., Lien, 1994, p. 237).

The reductionism that has resulted is particularly unsatisfying in psychology, perhaps because people normally perceive so much uniqueness, complexity, and ambiguity in human behavior. Explaining a pebble falling from a cliff in terms of gravity, for example, is often considered adequate but such an explanation for a person falling from the cliff would not because gravity would not provide enough useful information or be sufficiently intelligible (Bauman, 1978). It would fail at a task shared by myth and science—producing descriptions and explanations that help people make sense of themselves and the world (Madison, 1988).

Scientific Method Provides Objective Foundations

A fourth key premise of modernist science concerns how the scientific method itself is regarded. Although it is a type of theory designed by philosophers and predicated on ontological and epistemological assumptions, such as beliefs about what constitutes knowledge and what empirical data mean (Slife & Williams, 1995), the scientific method has been treated as a single, unchanging, authoritative system of ideas. That system is characterized as fixed principles of universal rationality and impartial methods that provide more accurate and sophisticated representations of a rationally structured, internally consistent reality than can ordinarily be achieved (Polanyi, 1946/1964; Spretnak, 1997; Toulmin, 1972).

More specifically, the scientific method is purportedly a timeless, rational, systematic, dispassionate, and value-free way by which scientists can objectively observe events, experiences, and behaviors without affecting what is observed (Gergen, Gulerce, Lock, & Misra, 1996; Hollinger, 1994). It is thus distinguished from the subjective—which has been branded irrational, biased, and self-indulgent—and from other ways of knowing that are self-conscious of the role of human perspective in the construction of knowledge (Keller, 1985). The scientific method, modernist science claims, enables scientists to access reality's ontological foundations and produce unalloyed, unadulterated, apodictic knowledge—the absolute, objective, infallible, foundational knowledge philosophers sought for centuries.

To summarize, one of the key assumptions of modernist science has been the idea that knowledge is produced when the mind apprehends properties or meanings "out there" in the world: Meanings are inherent in stimuli and independent of knowers who simply discover those meanings. Other key premises have included the belief that the world is composed of stable and transcendent structural foundations, notably universal laws and regularities, which can be discovered and objectively known by using the scientific method. By employing parsimonious explanations and the scientific method, scientists presumably can access the highest form of knowledge.

Psychology clings to a self-ascribed identity as a science and uses that identity to give its research findings heft. However, judging psychological "facts" and interpretations based on whether they were produced in a way congruent with an a priori definition of science is arbitrary and authoritarian (Feyerabend, 1970). Has the scientific method, like Bacon's idols (e.g., tradition and habitual ways of thinking), been undeservedly "worshiped and endowed with authority" (Slife & Williams, 1995, p. 171)?

Problems Modernist Science's Metaphysical and Epistemological Assumptions Present

The long-standing, self-satisfying, convenient tendency to view contemporary perspectives as the rational, natural, and mature efflorescence toward which the history of ideas has been headed all along encourages the belief that the current framework is the most apt (Robinson, 1976). But are modernist assumptions appropriate for social sciences?

The appropriateness of psychology modeling itself as a modernist science can be judged by analyzing and evaluating modernist assumptions and comparing those assumptions and corresponding methods with psychological concerns. Do they fit? Reconsidering the four, aforementioned assumptions of modernist science reveals flaws in modernist metaphysics and ways in which modernist science is an inappropriate model for psychology.

The Meaning of Facts

The epistemological appropriateness of the modernist science model can be evaluated in terms of how modernist science views facts, or the relationship between reality and knowledge. Notwithstanding the correspondence theory of truth's implication that facts speak for themselves, "simply there for everyone to see . . . somehow fully transparent to the attentive mind, indubitably given" (Schrag, 1990, p. 66), data themselves cannot be the firm foundation of objective knowledge. Observation and experimentation alone only provide sensory data.

The interpretation of data determines their meaning. That is, data have meaning and are considered to be "facts" only when they are interpreted (e.g., described and classified) and assessed based on nondata, such as onto-logical, epistemological, and methodological presuppositions or criteria, in-cluding research goals, reason, and purported value neutrality (Schrag, 1990; Slife & Williams, 1995; Zelditch, 1992). Consequently, any demonstrated "fact" is already laden with interpretation, such as decisions about whether a description or interpretation constitutes a fact (Glynn, 1990). Knowledge is constructed in the context of assumptions.

The logical fallacy of affirming the consequent supports the misimpression that empirical methods alone can tell us the meaning of facts: Researchers create a hypothesis, test it, and if the results are in keeping with the hypothesis, the reasoning behind the hypothesis is said to be confirmed. Empiricist epistemology has led to the belief that "if we can demonstrate something we believe, . . . there must be something true about the way we are thinking" (Slife & Williams, 1995, p. 196). However, empirical methods can only ascertain whether interpretations of data, events, or behaviors are consistent with a point of view, a prediction, or suppositions; they cannot prove which interpretation is correct and what reality is.

Scientific "facts" are considered "simply facts" only in the context of exclusionary, normalized, taken-for-granted scientific practices and thinking habits (Schrag, 1990). For example, according to modernist science's refer-ential, representational theory of meanings, language—whether used to refer to concepts; characterize people, situations, events or relationships; or describe behaviors, attitudes, and experiences—is a neutral, shared, unproblematic, unobtrusive, clear way of communicating (Keller, 1985; Polkinghorne, 1990): Words have a fixed, reflective relationship to the world and sensations (Faulconer & Williams, 1990a). As misinterpretations demonstrate, however, words and other signs such as symbols and gestures, do not have unambigu-ous, fixed meanings. Even when asking a factual question, researchers can-not be sure of the meaning of a respondent's answers without investigation. To illustrate, a Vietnamese American recalled:

> I was in the sixth grade when this boy asked if I wanted to "go steady." I told him the only way we would have a relationship was if it were "secret" one. He wasn't sure exactly what that meant and neither did I but I guess it was a pretty well kept secret because from that day on we never spoke again.

Researchers would probably misinterpret an affirmative response to a ques-tionnaire item asking whether she had gone steady. By failing to appreciate the role of language in the understanding of behavior, psychology in general has not closely scrutinized its commitment to the metaphysics of things (R. Williams, 1990).

The ambiguity presented by language points to a broader issue: Data can always be interpreted in different ways, so knowledge is eternally provisional and uncertain (Polanyi, 1946/1964). No word about the world is last or final; and all statements of meaning must be tentative (Faulconer & Williams, 1990b).

Nevertheless, the multiplicity and instability of meanings have not been widely examined in part because, as a social institution, psychology limits whose meanings are considered. The researchers' voice is typically amplified over that of the respondents studied; so in effect, researchers are placed in an echo chamber that drowns out the tautological nature of what they "find" or, more accurately, "produce." Scholarly interpretations in terms of underlying structures, for instance, are regarded as evidence of the reality of the structure; the failure of others to perceive those structures is treated as evidence that the structures are hidden. Researchers create explanations in terms of transcendent, deterministic regularities they assumed when they ran their statistical analysis (Slife & Williams, 1995).

More basically, modernist psychological explanations have at their foundations mismatches between psychology's metaphysical assumptions and its concerns, between its methods and its subjects, and between the types of interpretations modernist science expects and the findings psychology produces. They are based on the belief that objectivist interpretations predicated on modernist ontology apply to psychological events and concerns. That modernist world view has been that there are two separate worlds: one objective, beyond experience, functioning according to universal laws, and existing independently of people; and the other subjective, including people's thoughts, feelings, consciousness, and motivations (Bevan, 1991).[8] Although psychology's area of interest is largely the latter, scientism has led to its adoption of a scientific method designed to uncover the former.

The result has been that psychology has narrowed and distorted its subject of interest to fit modernist scientific parameters and transformed psychological facts into events with objectified meaning. The Enlightenment model of science held that primary qualities, such as number, can be known, whereas secondary qualities, such as experiences of color or sound, are too tainted by subjectivity to be known scientifically. Accepting this epistemology, psychology concentrates on primary qualities or, by using operational definitions,[9] tries to transform secondary into primary qualities.

When applied to psychology, the modernist subject-object ontology of the physical sciences inadequately reflects the effects of the interrelationship between the subject and object for the meaning of facts. "Because the realm of meaning exists in a different ontological mode from the physical reality through which it can be represented, we cannot know it using the same procedures we use to know the physical realm" (Polkinghorne, 1988, p. 159).

Even more than in physical sciences, psychology's realm of reality does not have objective meaning that researchers can simply pluck from events because of the role meaning, consciousness, and communication play in human affairs. For example, readings of context affect ascribed meanings. A seventeenth-century atom would presumably behave the same way as a twenty-first century one, but the same cannot be said of people: Human behaviors are vitally embedded in and creating historical, cultural, political, interpersonal, phenomenological contexts in ways that atoms are not. Claims of detachment pull a shade over the contingency of meanings, conditions, and perspectives (Racevskis, 1993). Understanding human behaviors requires appreciation for how they are situated in a realm that emerges from interaction rather than researcher-imposed, a priori meaning.

Accompanying the mismatch between physical and social sciences' ontological realms has been a mismatch between the goals for which the scientific method was established and psychology's goals. From Descartes to Kant, science's concern was presumably to uncover causally determined objects, processes, and mechanisms. However, instead of being causally determined, human consciousness, thought, behavior, and experience are, to a great degree, "intentional, purposive, free, temporal, historical, and reflexive" (Kockelmans, 1990, p. 79; Toulmin, 1990). Indeed, the meanings of human behaviors frequently relate to the fact that the behaviors did not have to occur and that other behavior options were available, but not chosen (Slife & Williams, 1995). Whereas modernist social science often tries to demonstrate causation, most behaviors are not triggered by causal stimulus conditions but by meanings ascribed to stimuli. Although people are situated in a meaning realm, social science usually does not directly study the meanings people ascribe, often relies on decontextualized questionnaires and selectively simplified notions of context, and underappreciates demand characteristics, a study's situational features that push people toward particular behaviors.

Modernist methods continue to "impose meaning on data in an *a posteriori* fashion, leading away from direct investigation of human experience and its meaning" (R. Williams, 1990, p. 144). By holding that all meaningful problems are empirical and casting off any metaphysical considerations as twaddle with no place in psychology, positivism denies the humanity behind behavior (Manicas, 1987; Polanyi, 1946/1964; Popper, 1968; R. Williams, 1990).

For such reasons, between 1890 and 1920, Wilhelm Dithy, Wilhelm Wundt, Edmund Husserl, Max Weber, and William James led a backlash against positivism and asserted that modernist science ignored meaningful experiences and belief systems that distinguish humans (Polkinghorne, 1983). Dithy, for example, argued that in contrast to physical sciences, human sciences should seek understanding through interpretations of meanings

(Meacham, 1999). However, the dominance of positivism has muffled the epistemological alternatives of those previous antimodernist movements.

That dominance also shores up the seeming legitimacy of a modernist scientific framework for psychology. Because assumptions and decisions determine operational definitions, restrict the types of answers that can be found, and channel subsequent interpretations, study results seem to support and justify underlying assumptions. The adoption of an ontology "determines what is counted as an event; data can't correct or falsify the ontology because all data collected within the perspective can be understood only in its terms" (Gergen, 1988, p. 29). Therefore, claims of validity arising from the use of the scientific method and scientific equipment are masks for interpretations based on particular assumptions (Denzin, 1995).

Modernist social science uses self-legitimating criteria to justify its metaphysics and methods (Lyotard, 1984): It is logocentric, a self-referential and self-satisfying system of thought that claims legitimacy by pointing to a connection between its representations and an external reality that cannot be independently substantiated. Even though the scientific method itself cannot be scientifically validated, science is a framework that assumes its own validity (Rosenau, 1992).

In addition to producing logocentric versions of valid research, marrying into conceptual boundaries of modernist ontology and epistemology frames and restricts the types of questions asked. Rather than declare itself a science because it posed questions that required scientific methods to resolve, empirical psychology initially decided to use scientific methods and then posed questions based on what could be studied using tried and not-so-true positivist methods (Robinson, 1976). For instance, it usually asks questions that can be answered in quantifiable terms. However, when behavioral science's research methods and orientations are inappropriate for humans, they deflect investigators from what is important about humans and what makes them interesting (Slife & Williams, 1995), such as the different ways people experience events and the meanings they ascribe.

Regularities

Assumptions about orderly regularities governing the domain of interest have also taken psychology down a conceptual and methodological path that is not altogether appropriate for the study of human behavior. Broadly speaking, they have led to a bias toward explaining behaviors in terms of ontological order. More specifically, from mechanistic psychological explanations to homogenizing research methodology and portrayals and simplistic explanations that overlook meaning, manifestations of the bias permeate psychology.

When psychology began to develop its identity as a science, mechanistic, Newtonian world views dominated. Despite post-Newtonian discoveries in physics undermining rampant mechanistic assumptions and showing nature as a network of relations and transient patterns in an interdependent dynamic world, psychology continued to search for mechanisms in social reality. Posited structures and processes, for example, have often been cast in mechanistic terms. Behaviorists have searched for mechanisms to explain behavior; cognitive theorists have proposed mechanistic gates and filters; and Freud argued that urges build up in us, producing pressures that, if unrelieved, trigger particular behaviors. Linking structural causes and effects, deterministic thinking is rationalized as merely matching a deterministic nature (Barrett, 1967; Gergen, 1985).

Despite the absence of compelling reasons for believing that causal laws should be the fundamental basis for psychological explanations (Faulconer & Williams, 1990b), psychologists search for such laws or for universal regularities. Their modernist assumptions about order create a bias toward interpretations supporting that contention. For example, assumptions about orderliness have been a basis for some to regard varying behaviors as merely superficial manifestations of directly unobservable, yet underlying, transcendent laws or regularities in psychological and social structures, processes, and relationships (Ritzer, 1997; Slife & Williams, 1995). Even though nature can be orderly without being ruled by unchanging laws (Toulmin, 1990), some psychologists, particularly behaviorists, have gone so far as to translate expectations of ontological order into interpretations of "facts" or events as logocentric laws.

The tendency to interpret events in terms of ontological order is also manifested in the wide net psychologists cast in their search for regularities across a range of cultures, circumstances, and species. Many psychologists who study the behavior of rats, for example, are not interested in rats per se, but in behavioral patterns among rats that, in an orderly world, might have parallels in humans. People frequently are not even of direct interest; what is of interest are the hidden influences and principles presumably controlling behaviors or group differences, of which individuals are just manifestations. As the most popular introductory psychology textbook claims, *"It is the resulting principles—not the specific findings—that help explain everyday behaviors"* (D. Myers, 1998, p. 32).

Another manifestation of the presumption of regularity is that theories customarily do not include cultural variables because regularities found in the United States, constituting less than 5% of the world's population, are initially presumed to exist everywhere (Betancourt & López, 1993; S. Sue, 1999). A result of applying modernist metaphysics to psychology has been that people are regarded as roughly interchangeable. Demographic characteristics, such as race, gender, and class, are viewed as factors that account for mild variation around a normative human (Meacham, 1999). Apparently, that normative human is conveniently American—convenient because most psychological research is done by Americans on Americans (S. Sue, 1999). The resulting essentialism, in which differences are treated as unimportant variances from universal processes, has made difficult explanations of behavior in terms of agency, choice, hopes, meanings, reason, radical change, or emergent forces (Lennert, 1997; Polkinghorne, 1983).

Like the physical world, the psychological realm is not only presumed to be orderly; it is presumed to be mathematically so. Mathematics is thought to be a language that matches, expresses, and finds preexisting, logical relationships among naturally existing, transcendent dimensions or properties of reality, constituent elements of a behavior, and links between characteristics and behavior (Barrett, 1967; Hoshmand & Polkinghorne, 1992; see Taylor, 1970). Thus, science accepts an alternative to falsehood and apodictic knowledge: assertoric knowledge, whose truthfulness, while supported by evidence, is stated in terms of varying degrees of probability.[10]

The conceptual delineation of behavioral patterns is not a problem per se. However, it is problematic when statistics are used to imply a mathematical precision to the underlying concepts or when those behavior patterns are said to indicate an unadulterated foundational order existing independently of the cognitive construction of those patterns. Characterizations of order are also problematic when, in the search for noumenal order, modernist methods, assumptions about a fundamental, metaphysical order, and the desire to gather data tapping into it stack the research deck so that considerable variation is reduced to gross similarities. For instance, forced-choice questionnaires or psychological tests require respondents to adjust and squeeze their responses into the tests' formatted response options, thereby codifying complex behaviors into simple categories and imposing similarity on the responses of diverse people.[11] If those assessments do not produce enough order or statistically significant results, psychologists might collapse multiple response categories into a simple dichotomy, thereby imposing a bifurcated order on behaviors to produce the assumed ontological order.

Also reflecting a predilection toward explaining in terms of regularities and perhaps a mechanistic world view is the tendency to attribute the same meaning to ostensibly similar behaviors and overlook whether the behaviors should be considered varied manifestations of one behavior or completely different behaviors. For example, in a nod to Ockham's Razor, the basis for seemingly similar behaviors is ascribed to the same components, processes or demographic variables. Researchers treat behaviors as expressions of basic, unchanging characteristics or essences (Ritzer, 1997).

Contributing to the emphasis on finding regularities, homogenizing investigative methods are used even at the expense of systematically overlooking complex, changing, and particular behaviors and the varied, disorderly appearances of everyday experiences (Polkinghorne, 1990). Rather than be defined as experiencing people who construe their lives and events or as people whose consciousness, agency, and behavior are mutually defined instead of mechanistically related (Meacham, 1999), people commonly are, in effect, defined as a compilation of demographic variables, such as ethnicity, age, and sex. These defining characteristics are too often treated as conditions triggering behaviors or people as media through which structural elements or principles direct behaviors. For example, researchers would classify both of the following sisters simply as Korean despite the possibly very relevant differences described by one:

> When I was six years old, my mom died. My father put my sister and I into an orphanage. Korean people treated us very badly because we were orphans. I felt different from them.
>
> My sister and I were adopted by two different American families four years ago. Fortunately, we live close together so we can see each other frequently. But many things have changed between us. When we lived in Korea, our way of thinking and acting were very similar to each other but now they are very different.
>
> Even though my sister lives in America, she tries to be a part of the Korean culture and community here. She does not want to deal with the American culture. . . . I want to reject the Korean culture and accept the American culture. . . . Because people rejected me in Korea. . . . I try to isolate myself from the Korean community. For instance, whenever I meet Korean people at church or at school, they ask me what my family is like. Sometimes, I feel ashamed that my sister and I have to live in different families and that we were adopted by American families, not Korean families.

Echoing medieval and Enlightenment biases toward order, reductionist descriptions and explanations obscure such individuality whereas listening to respondents reveals complexity which would challenge notions of behaviors as being the result of (an implicitly) deterministic ethnicity. Such reductionism draws an epistemic veil over varying relationships among different, changing individuals and a changing, multifaceted world (Toulmin, 1972). Nevertheless, in a move traceable to Cartesian emphases, modernist science dispatches variant values, feelings, and interpretations in the quest for regularities and thereby passes over the heterogeneity Diderot regarded as characteristic of nature (Anchor, 1967).

One element of a Rembrandt self-portrait, such as the use of dark colors, cannot be extracted and regarded as the painting's essence because much of the meaning of the Rembrandt—what makes it art—is in the relationship among elements or pieces. Likewise, we cannot assume that how a researcher characterizes a sample captures the essence of that sample any more than we can assume, notwithstanding the standardization of Thomas Hobbes' focus on material cause, that recognition of an efficient or material cause, such as the use of color, is defining.[12]

Yet psychologists frequently categorize people in terms of some characteristics (independent variables) and then compare behaviors to see whether the characteristics predict behaviors (dependent variables). That tactic sometimes makes as much sense as trying to understand a piece of music by counting the number of its G-chords and comparing that number to the number in other works or using the occurrence of G-chords to predict the incidences of particular contrapuntal moves.

The application of modernist assumptions about ontological order in the physical realm has different consequences in the realm of human affairs. A search for regularities in the characteristics of cumulonimbus clouds does not have the same consequences as order-emphasizing interpretive practices that produce homogenizing portrayals, if not stereotypes, of people.

Contributing to the problem of the mismatch between modernist assumptions and psychological concerns, adherence to Ockham's Razor has too often been translated into simplistic explanations. While avoiding unnecessary assumptions can help to produce well-grounded conclusions, parsimony should be contingent on the complexity of the issue at hand. Parsimonious explanations of people's behaviors, which may seem to require fewer assumptions than complex ones, might not produce more accurate, clear, or compelling explanations. For example, insofar as additive explanations for behaviors are more parsimonious than more complex, organismic ones, Ockham's Razor introduces a bias toward the former (Pepper, 1942). More generally, a bias toward the simple, additive, stable, linear, easily quantifiable, and mechanistic distracts from emergent, synergetic psychological effects and the way experiences and complex behaviors come into being, develop, intensify, subside, and pass away (Schrag, 1990).

Extending this predilection toward interpreting behaviors in terms of order, even research results that seem to conflict or undermine assumptions about regularities are customarily explained in ways that uphold expectations of orderliness: Researchers frequently cite the possibility that the people studied were unusual in some way or that strictly scientific methods were not followed. Metaphysical and epistemological assumptions about transcendent, cross-situational behavior patterns are not seriously questioned and the possibility of alternative, useful interpretations and multiple truths is downplayed (Tanaka, Ebreo, Linn, & Morera, 1998). The ways in which the social world might be more dynamic and fragmented than currently assumed in psychology are minimized (T. Young, 1991).

In practice, adoption of modernist assumptions about order have had another consequence: What has not fit neatly into an orderly perspective has typically been treated as noise (Bütz, 1995). For example, the implicit publication requirement that a classification system account for almost all studied responses encourages vague, encompassing classification models.

This treatment of the extraneous is part of a larger pattern in which, all too often, psychology regards complexity and situational variability as variance or superfluous nuisance to be controlled, eliminated, or studied at "another" time. Again we see a lack of fit between modernist orientations and psychology: Often, attempts are made to reduce behaviors and participatory, interpreted, rich, and historically, culturally, and socially situated lived experience to a more fundamental relationship or structure by controlling for extraneous variables. However, the attempt to control for a wide array of variables is akin to trying to describe the basic ingredients of a turkey casserole by deleting reference to (or controlling for) spices, noodles, and sauces. The result is not a scientifically clean depiction of a turkey casserole or the essence of turkey casserole. What is left is just turkey.

Given the complexity and temporality of human experiences and behaviors and people's freedom to vary their behavior, psychological characteristics, experiences, and behaviors cannot be reduced to one or two variables while others are "controlled," except as a conceptual fiction. All relevant variables for all members of a sample cannot even be identified and empirical psychological studies cannot produce assertoric much less apodictic certainty that the effect of only one variable has been parsed. When modernist research uses statistical or experimental controls to find foundational regularities in the effects of a variable such as gender, they assume that the same variable is being controlled—in effect, that the variable has the same meaning for different individuals. However, the meaning of characteristics is not simply inherent in them. Despite attempts to control for extraneous variables in a simulation of "all-things-being-equal," situations, individuals, and moments are never equal except as part of a fantasy about transcendent orderliness. In practice, statistical control usually amounts to the conceptual removal of variables.

While purporting to tell us about behavioral tendencies, modernist psychology tells us how researchers, seduced by modernist assumptions, have constructed interpretations of behaviors which were triggered using positivist methods. The multiple, simultaneous layers and meanings of behaviors and experience are overlooked. Complex, changing, holistic behaviors and experiences have become ineffable.

Scientific Objectivity

As the foregoing has suggested, assumptions undergirding the scientific method are, in many ways, not a good fit with psychology. Another aspect of the modernist ontology that is a problematic foundation for psychology is the belief that the scientific method produces objective knowledge of reality (Polkinghorne, 1990).

The pretense of scientific objectivity hides a tautological logocentricity (Keller, 1985): Any proof of the objectivity of scientific findings is contingent on acceptance of modernist assumptions (Fontana, 1994) rather than contradictory premises outside the paradigm. Although modernist science assumes that researchers trained in the scientific method can find an Archimedean standpoint from which they can objectively observe reality, when people experience the world, they do not—and, in fact, cannot—experience a separate, detached, objective world or objectively know their own behaviors or experiences. Humans have no way of transcending their own brains and consciousness to independently know an objective reality. As Einstein's theory of relativity demonstrated, "there is no place to stand that is no place; we are inevitably caught in the very world we are describing and so are inevitably subject to its hold on us" (Sampson, 1999, p. 50). Although some people regard science as a sanctified nowhere, enabling scientists to be positioned without really standing anywhere and to view the world from that nowhere position, it represents one among many possible views.

Therefore, contrary to scientism's tenet, science is not the lone standard of knowledge and reality. As Feyerabend has argued, "it is an illusion to think . . . there is or must be a permanent, neutral matrix to which we can appeal that will tell us once and for all what is to count as better and worse . . . argument" (Bernstein, 1983, p. 72).

Claims of neutrality are socially grounded. "The pretense that science is objective, apolitical, and value-neutral is profoundly political because it obscures the political role that science and technology play in underwriting the existing distribution of power and society" (Hubbard, 1988, p. 13).

Claims of objectivity, as in research that supposedly judges behaviors by objective criteria, are efforts to pass on constructions as simply reflections of reality. Examinations of behaviors purportedly from the perspective of the culture in which the behavior occurs are, likewise, equally parodies because they usually imply both that a culture has a singular perspective that is not simply an artifact of a homogenizing characterization and that researchers can separate themselves from their own background, which would be a prerequisite to taking on the views of those from another culture.

Like the discussion of the meaning of facts implied, to claim science is objective is to deny it is a human activity and to pretend that it is separate "from the life experiences, intentions, values, and world views of the persons who create that science" (Bevan, 1991, p. 477). As developers of hypotheses, creators of operational definitions, conductors of studies, and interpreters of statistical analyses, social scientists are not "passionless automatons . . . holding mirrors to reality" (Gergen, 1988, p. 43). Indeed, they cannot be. Representations of the world, including the meanings or knowledge scientists create, rely on sensory input and interpretations, not sensory data alone. Well-known psychological research on perception illustrates that stimuli are interpreted rather than apprehended and that perceptions do not simply record what exists "out there" (see Figure 1.1).

Even if scholars had objective data or descriptions, they would not be able to make sense of them objectively. Because human knowledge is based on experiences and available ideas, which are themselves based on interpretations influenced by time, culture, and other situated experiences, the interpretation of the data would reflect the interpreter's concerns, culture, interests, attitudes, experiences, assumptions, values, social position, and commitments and those of the community (Richardson & Fowers, 1998).

The interpretation of the data would also reflect more intuition than might be apparent in a textbook description of social science research or journal articles (Bevan, 1991): Although repelled as mere subjectivism, intuition, a subordinated representation of what is not said, often acts as the "tacit coefficient of a scientific theory" (Fuller, 1995; Polanyi, 1946/1964, p. 10). When theories and research findings are consistent with one's own interpretations, values, and outlooks, they seem especially convincing or self-evident (Keller, 1985); when they are counterintuitive, they are frequently doubted and efforts are made to find flaws in the study's method or logical missteps in the conclusions drawn.[13] Even statistical analyses can be based on subjectivity: In cluster analysis, for example, researchers select statistical criteria for groupings and create conceptual labels for each group.

Therefore, not only is rhetoric based on ideologies, but so are modernist psychology and constructions of reality (Bevan, 1991). Researchers' paradigmatic world views and scientific, social, political, and linguistic practices affect which phenomena are deemed worthy of study; how issues are depicted and questions are formulated; which methods are regarded as appropriate; which variables are studied and which are controlled; which data are considered significant; and which types of descriptions or explanations are considered adequate, appropriate, useful, satisfying knowledge (Hare-Mustin & Marecek, 1990; Keller, 1985). Thus, while empirical findings and ratio-

FIGURE 1.1   What White Triangle?

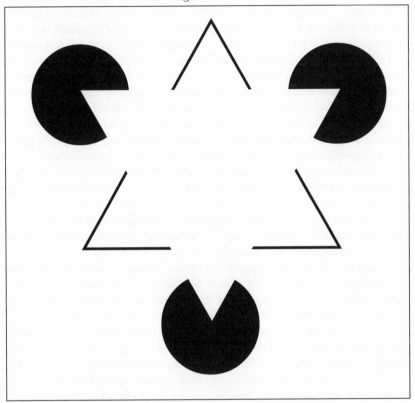

Perceptions do not simply reflect inherent characteristics of stimuli. For example, we are likely to perceive a white triangle superimposed on a background because of our familiarity with triangles. The triangle appears to be defined by lines and to be a brighter white than the background, but covering the lines surrounding the white triangle reveals no difference between the white of the triangle and the background. Illustration by and with the permission of Jerome Kuhl. Source: *Scientific American* Offprints #570, Subjective contours, 1976, p. 2.

nality might be the brick and mortar of a study's conclusions, they alone do not account for them.

Because any experience can be punctuated in various ways and events can be linked in multiple ways producing different meanings, the way a person investigates a subject matter affects what is "found." Niels Bohr's demonstration that light seems to be particles or waves, depending on the measuring equipment and language used to describe it, illustrates a broader point: Because measuring instruments and methods are based on assumptions, imply perspectives, and promote the valuing of particular data, they cannot produce independent, neutral interpretations (Hare-Mustin & Marecek, 1990).

Rhetoric. Science's lack of objectivity casts its traditional disparagement of rhetoric in a new light. Tracing back to Platonic and Aristotelian arguments against rhetoric for its reliance on appearance as opposed to truth and reason, rejection of rhetoric as sophistry became part of the scientific model (O'Neill, 1998). An implicitly dichotomous relationship was assumed: Science's raw truth and rationality–*cum*–empiricism trumped rhetoric, which was dismissed as empty, manipulative technique merely suited to swaying audiences and perpetuating opinion rather than identifying fact. More specifically, science has contrasted rhetoric to rational, scientific activities by noting that: rhetoric uses imprecise language and tropes, such as metaphors and metonyms, whereas scientific language's precise descriptions and operational definitions are neither figurative nor ambiguous; rhetoric is designed to convince particular audiences whereas science is presumably accessible and convincing to all who are rational (Racevskis, 1993); rhetoric convinces by relying on opinion and emotions whereas science convinces through impartial evidence and logic; and rhetoric aims for the pragmatic whereas science aims for truth (O'Neill, 1998).

However, science's sharp, hegemonic distinction between truth and rhetoric is unwarranted. As the use of careful reasoning and supportive evidence to persuade, and not merely flamboyant oratory, rhetoric is neither irrational nor groundless. Without necessarily obviating each other, rhetoric, reason, and data are all tools used to construct meanings and knowledge. The claim of a clear distinction between psychology and rhetoric hides modernist psychology's favoring of some forms of rhetoric over others which, in turn, restricts the acceptable sources of knowledge and forms of arguments by limiting what is regarded as knowledge to the replicable and generalizable (Carlston, 1987; Slife & Gantt, 1999).

Whether a description or explanation of behaviors is accepted as convincing and true and therefore functions as knowledge does not depend just on the use of the scientific method. Because knowledge is socially defined, that acceptance also turns on the rhetoric used to support particular interpretations. Therefore, empiricism and rhetoric are not at odds: "Empirical efforts complement but do not replace rhetorical practices, the rhetorical analysis illuminates but does not invalidate empirical pursuits" (Carlston, 1987, p. 156). Instead, rhetoric can be reinforced by reasoned handling of empirical data.

Rhetoric and science are so intertwined that the adoption of a metaphor of knowledge, a rhetorical move, can affect how researchers try to gain knowledge (Lakoff & Johnson, 1980). For example, knowledge is often regarded as a structure built on a foundation of agreed-upon cornerstones or first premises. New data are interpreted in terms of established knowledge frameworks, such as theories: Data that fit the framework are said to support it; data that do not fit are thought to show weaknesses in it or, if particularly powerful, make theories fall apart. In contrast, if knowledge were viewed in terms of a different metaphor, such as the creation of a meal, nothing might be dominating; data might be viewed in terms of what they add, how they relate to other elements, or how they change the whole.

Behaviorism's ascendency pushed aside the rhetorical devices of early psychologists such as Wundt and James who examined philosophical issues and provided reasoned, discursive constructions of meaning. Nevertheless, psychological discourse still embodies rhetorical decisions and is replete with rhetorical devices (Bazerman, 1987; Feyerabend, 1975; see Zeller & Farmer, 1999). Even science's claim that it is a fact-finding activity is a rhetorical device; the very denial that science uses rhetorical devices is a rhetorical description (O'Neill, 1998). The prestige and authority of science are used for rhetorical effect. Sometimes psychotherapists are taught cross-cultural methods of establishing their credibility to increase their rhetorical influence. Rhetorical skills, such as the ability to convince others of the meaning data will have and portray one's credibility, contribute to successful grant applications. Scientific reports present interpretations of facts in a way (e.g., "This study shows . . . ") designed to influence the audience by implying that facts are speaking for themselves and conclusions are unambiguous and natural. When psychology journal articles have, as American Psychological Association (APA) guidelines stipulate, a "results" section presenting statistical analysis and a "discussion" section presenting the author's interpretation of those results, the pretense is that results are objective findings that are independent of interpretations. But, as is implicitly acknowledged in the introduction to articles, the author's interpretations are guiding the research from the beginning. Early editions of the APA style manual dictated the use of third-person, passive voice, and sparse language as ways of adding to the seeming objectivity, and, therefore, modernist legitimacy, of psychological research.

Like claiming a person is getting his or her 15 minutes of fame without questioning the legitimacy of the original "truism," describing people's behaviors in modernist terms without questioning the underlying assumptions of that framework can produce lots of instances in which behaviors are explained in those terms while shedding little light on whether those explanations are appropriate. Science's traditional authority has often deflected such questioning. Consequently, in general psychology continues to rely on a modernist scientific metaphysic that, in many ways, is inappropriate for addressing psychological issues of interest or providing a comprehensive understanding.

Rather than claim that scientists have direct ways to study the world the way it is, as realism would, a moderate form of positivism holds that science can help us formulate constructs to explain regularities in the world

(Slife & Williams, 1995). Instead of treating identified regularities as patterns existing "out there," they might be viewed as useful, constructed interpretations. For those meanings or interpretation to be socially effective constructs, they must be relayed to others in a convincing manner; thus, both discourse and rhetoric must play a role.

Scientific Tradition.   In the 1950s, Bertrand Russell and Alfred Whitehead nourished a paradigm shift from a reliance on axioms as the basis for timeless, universal knowledge to an acceptance of multiple scientific methods for scholars in different sciences trying to adapt to varied and changing situations and problems (Toulmin, 1990). In the 1960s, many scholars rethinking social theories, primarily critical rather than scientific theories of social life, converged on a focus on the role of language and discourse (Lennert, 1997). Various disciplines, such as sociology, have participated in the resulting discourse. However, the vast majority of psychologists have not responded and have continued with psychology's modernist investigative goals and methods in the apparent belief that "there must be a horse in there somewhere."

When dealing with new problems, "Every succeeding generation [of scientists] is sovereign in reinterpreting the tradition of science. With [that sovereignty rests] responsibility [and] lasting effects on the tradition of science" (Polanyi, 1946/1964, pp. 16, 60). Psychologists have choices. While hypermodern views lament the problems of modernism, postmodernism,[14] an epistemological outlook discussed in the next chapter, represents different assumptions, alternative ways of investigating people's behaviors, and new perspectives on human behavior and the meaning of being Asian American.

CHAPTER 2

Postmodernism

People have at their disposal various languages "with which and through which [to] try to understand the world" (Slife & Williams, 1995, p. 195). No one language is best; each helps us understand from a particular perspective; and, notwithstanding modernist science's self-acclaimed status as a metanarrative (or grand narrative)—a widely shared cultural story, perspective, or belief capable of characterizing, subsuming, and assessing all other discourses or explanations (Fraser & Nicholson, 1990)—each language obscures. Nevertheless, modernist science's claim of access to final, objective, unambiguous knowledge is powerful because it is widely accepted and totalizing, that is, purportedly complete. That power is used to mute other voices (Osajima, 1995a). Like ideologies linking history and progress, Panglossian illusions, and other metanarratives, modernist science imposes homogenizing explanations over differences, which are dismissed as incidental variations, and it marginalizes or omits other foci and interpretations (Lennert, 1997; Osajima, 1995a).

The Hegemony of Empirical Psychology

While offering no independent basis for claiming complete and inherently supreme truth status, modernist science casts itself as *the* fundamental basis of knowledge; sets standards for judging truth claims, meaning, acceptability, and legitimacy; and denounces nonscientific, everyday observations and reasoning as primitive, prejudiced, and illegitimate (Lyotard, 1984). Research psychology has committed and restricted itself to that epistemology, those standards, and their attendant emphases, rules, and interpretive habits. Insofar as empiricism has been almost equated with science, research psychology generally ignores variables, phenomena, and experiences that cannot be studied empirically and translated into numbers; and it restricts itself to investigations and categorizations of relatively easy-to-observe behaviors from which directly unobservable processes might be inferred (Unger, 1988). It has privileged—that is, highly valued and given particular attention to—the overtly acting over the experiencing or meaning-creating person and testing over discourse.

However, as in a piece of fabric, constituted of threads and thread interstices in which no one thread can be isolated and identified as the most important or telling thread, no one perspective can completely account for behaviors or experiences (Faulconer, 1990). So psychology need not be defined by empirical methods or bound by inappropriate metaphysical and epistemological assumptions any more than it was inextricably bound to Wundt's nineteenth-century use of introspective methods. Psychology's polysemic roots in the word *psyche*—meaning self, mind, consciousness, and experiencing person—and *logos*—meaning word, discourse, reason, structure, study, theory, and science—point to the possibility of broadening psychology's methods and realm of concern (Schrag, 1990). Multiple combinations of meanings could identify psychology's subject matter. It is (past) time for psychology to reconceptualize the field, its assumptions and methods.

Over the last few decades and in various disciplines, alternative epistemologies have been examined and employed, notably in two overlapping, postmodern conversations (Polkinghorne, 1990). A general conversation, carried on by Michael Foucault, Jacques Derrida, Jean François Lyotard, and others, describes the futility of seeking any one epistemological foundation that assures certain knowledge, denies creators have the final word on the meaning of what they produce, and challenges conventional ideas about meaning and structure (Denzin, 1994). Participants in that conversation have provided postmodernism many of its identities: For example, Foucault, drawing from Nietzschean ideas, argues that the will to truth and knowledge are interwoven with the will to power; Derrida emphasizes linguistic analysis and the critical, deconstructive reading of texts; and Lyotard attacks metanarratives, sees a multiplicity of ways of producing knowledge (Kellner, 1988), criticizes science for simply generating piles of studies augmenting the power of the already powerful without shedding much light, and advocates social sciences that seek the dissensus of new ideas rather than consensus (Ritzer, 1997).

Multiple, varied, and sometimes contradictory orientations have been subsumed under the appellation of postmodernism (see Griffin, 1989; Ritzer, 1997). The variety has reflected different lines of thought (e.g., Derrida compared to Lyotard) as well as the application of postmodern ideas to different domains, such as art and architecture.

Of particular interest here is another, related conversation concerning postmodernism and the philosophy of science. Postmodernism has challenged epistemological tenets of modernist science, such as the belief in an objectively knowable, referent reality; the faith that positivist data, born of questionable assumptions, provide an unassailable foundation; and the contention that psychological knowledge must be about a modernist foundation or scientifically articulable (Hollinger, 1994; Rosenau, 1992). With the notable exception of feminist research, psychology is largely either unfamiliar with postmodernism or resisting it; in other fields, however, postmodernism has been leading to broad reassessments of epistemological foundations, to critical analysis of the first premises of scientific investigation, and to the use of alternative, nonpositivist methods.

Inasmuch as I simply want to discuss postmodernism's gist as an alternative to modernist psychology and a framework for subsequent discussions of psychological portrayals, the following synopsis of some of postmodernism's premises identifies common threads running through its varied forms. After contrasting premises of modernist science and postmodernism and describing the latter's investigative methods, I discuss criticisms of postmodernism and briefly glimpse at ways in which psychology is already unintentionally leaning in postmodern directions.

Three Contrasting Premises

One way to locate postmodernism is to contrast its premises to those of modernist science. Accordingly, the two approaches could be compared in terms of some of modernist science's premises: Knowledge is achieved by identifying foundational principles or regularities inherent in reality; knowledge is objective, singular, and stable; and language is a neutral and transparent way of expressing knowledge. (See Table 2.1.) I describe ways postmodernism's take on those premises better fits psychology.

The Foundational Versus the Local

As described in the previous chapter, the modernist belief in an orderly reality grounded in knowable, foundational principles has been the basis for psychology's search for laws or behavioral regularities and inductive generalization of research findings. In effect, the people studied, often regarded as the product of forces having consistent effects, are conceptually treated as though they are carriers of behavioral tendencies existing independently of our views of those behaviors.

TABLE 2.1   A Comparison of Modernist and Postmodernist
Assumptions

Dimension	Modernism	Postmodernism
Knowledge	Objective correspondence with reality	Constructions based on intertextuality, *différance*
Knowable	Universal principles underlying fixed order	Contextualized, particular
Study participant	Object of study	Participant in creation of knowledge
Objectivity	Possible using scientific method	Impossible
Constructs	About the ontological	Fictions, constructions
Language	Transparent means of communicating	Mediates what is known

In contrast, postmodernism assumes no ontologically foundational principles or unequivocal metanarrative and rejects Hegelian hopes for metanarratives unifying knowledge (Kupferberg, 1990), making its relationship to Enlightenment beliefs akin to atheism's relationship to deism. It seeks knowledge of more specific narratives about complex, dynamic, interweaving forces, reasons, and spontaneous effects not limited to causes or laws (Keller, 1985).

Why this move away from metanarratives? One answer is illustrated by a common postmodern analogy about a chess game, which is without foundational or universal meaning. When chess players create a game of chess, the meaning of the game before the players does not transcend those players; it is being created by the players in that particular situation (Faulconer, 1990). Likewise, when we read a poem, we are in the "midst of its meaning" (Polkinghorne, 1990, p. 111). Consequently, rather than search for universal relationships between variables, postmodern analyses explore the genealogy of meanings.

Postmodern social scientists take the parsimonious view that meaning—such as the meaning of a chess piece's position or a poem—is inherently contingent; so they emphasize the contingent, particular, indeterminant, and imprecise (Hollinger, 1994; Racevskis, 1993). A postmodern psychology, shifting lived experiences to the foreground, would explore the ways in which behaviors and their meanings are tied to dynamic social, material, cultural, and historical processes and conditions (Gavey, 1989; Griscom, 1992;

Racevskis, 1993), including the interactions of socially located people with varied interests, values, and traditions (Sloan, 1992).

The resulting knowledge about a behavior, cognitive process, person, or group will be complex, heterogeneous, and local—specific to people situated in time, history, situation, culture, social relations, personal development, and awareness. Any characterization of a group would be in the process of being transformed.

Singular and Objective Versus Constructed Knowledge

The equating of knowledge with the identification of foundations inherent in reality is linked to a second premise of modernist science: Because knowledge is of a reality with presumably fixed, foundational properties or singular meanings, as per the correspondence theory of truth and the metaphysics of things, one representation of reality is accurate. In keeping with the metaphysics of things, modernist psychology typically treats behaviors, such as interview responses, as though they have fixed meanings. Superficially similar responses are treated as though they have the same meaning for different people. For example, the answer "I don't know" is regarded as having one meaning even though it might indicate an attempt to avoid answering a question (Ying, 1989), the question has never been given any thought, or a deep-seated and long-standing uncertainty.

From a contrasting postmodern perspective, however, meanings cannot be fixed because people tie events, situations, people, and concepts to different phenomena, standards, and concepts. For instance, when asked whether they are outgoing, people use different reference points, such as locales or comparisons to different people. At one time, an individual might base a response on a recent or cognitively accessible situation, but at another time average his or her behaviors. Accordingly, while resisting the temptation to treat consciousness and subjectivity as new foundations or to reify (i.e., give interpretations and constructs ontological status), postmodernism regards interpretive acts as an epistemological basis for meaning and, therefore, knowledge (Polkinghorne, 1990).[1] Social events and other phenomena still actually occur "out there": They are not socially constructed fantasies. However, they do not have intrinsic meanings. The absence of direct access to reality leaves us with readings of reality (both by the study participants and researchers) and the construction of knowledge.

Critics argue that social constructionism, one form of postmodernism, is flawed because it claims all that exists is nothing more than a shared cognitive construction. They note, for example, that although Hamlet would not have existed without Shakespeare, gravity, not being a mere social construction, would exist even if Newton had never lived (Dembart, 1994).

However, the criticism is undeserved because social constructionism is not claiming that gravity is a constructed fantasy; what is constructed is the interpretation of gravity in scientific terms as an eternal law rather than, for example, in animistic or spiritual terms as the pressure of God's thumb.

Postmodernists regard psychological descriptions or explanations, whether in study participants' self-reports, by researchers, or by casually interacting people, as narratives that impose organization and create versions or readings of events, situations, people, and chaotic, multifaceted experiences (Slife & Williams, 1995). Rather than being viewed as modernist reflections of an independent reality, they are viewed as translations, story lines, or fictions (which, in this case, does not mean false or created out of whole cloth [see Vaihinger, 1924]). As such, studies do not merely set up the opportunity for neutral facts to speak for themselves: Study conclusions follow from meanings study participants invoke and meanings researchers ascribe after they construct operational definitions, collapse categories for statistical analysis, and interpret what research "finds." A study on the effects of gender and race on occupational prestige, segregation, and earnings illustrated this constructive process: It found that "when different occupational characteristics are examined jointly, a different picture appears than when they are examined separately" (Xu & Leffler, 1996, p. 120). Likewise, when various ethnic groups are treated as one for statistical purposes because of small sample sizes, one result may be found whereas when they are categorized into separate ethnic groups, quite different results can be found (e.g., Uehara, Takeuchi, & Smukler, 1994).

In such ways, scientific narratives are constructed and no one perspective, even a scientific one, provides unadulterated knowledge. Instead, knowledge is created through an unending dialectic process—a methodical switching of perspectives in which assumptions are examined, hidden antitheses are exposed, understandings are compared, and any temporary synthesis is returned to the process (Kockelmans, 1990).

Thus, postmodernism's root metaphor is that knowledge is created, much as the meaning of a book's text is based on a created interpretation. Accordingly, the meaning of a psychological "text"—a phenomenon, concept, way of thinking, emotional reaction, questionnaire response, situation, cultural practice, statement, subject, issue, or behavior that can be critically analyzed—comes from interpretation. This outlook, therefore, turns attention less towards social influence as the product of people's stimulus properties or their ability to reinforce or punish and more toward social influences on the meanings people create about each other, situations, and themselves, and in jointly created experiences (Slife & Williams, 1995). Therefore, rather than search for simple stimulus-response regularities because of a psychologist's empiricist assumptions and training, a postmodern analysis might examine the meanings ascribed to behaviors with reference to multiple texts, such as past and foreseeable relationships between the people involved.

The texts brought to bear are crucial in the creation of meaning and knowledge. Any text implicitly, and sometimes explicitly, presupposes and refers to other texts whose meanings make the text intelligible (O'Neill, 1998). For example, the behaviors of a member of a minority are interpreted in relation to other texts, such as the interpreters' self-concepts, what the interpreters may already think about that minority, or their reading of the situation in which the person is behaving. The varied and multiple texts invoked add to the complexity and instability of meanings and the impossibility of producing definitive meanings. Just as the significance of a chess piece is in its relationship to other texts (e.g., strategy options) a player associates with it, the meanings of facts, behaviors, and descriptions are unstable, as are generalizations based on them.

Basic to postmodern epistemology is the idea that even a seemingly whole and unitary concept is established by its difference from other, perhaps repressed or negated, concepts (Scott, 1988). Every text's meaning is created in reference to traces of otherness and *différance*—implicit or explicit difference or contrast with what is absent (Hollinger, 1994).

Consequently, when we read texts, such as a person's behavior or responses to a questionnaire, we interpret without benefit of knowing what they fully mean; final and determinant meaning must be absent because of the intertextuality of meaning. Because meanings are constructed in relation to an interminable number of texts and relate in always changing, multiple ways, *différance*, then, also refers to the eternal deferment of final meaning (Hollinger, 1994). Accordingly, postmodernism, rooted partly in Nietzsche's attack on objective systems of knowledge and Heidegger's critique of Western metaphysics (Denzin, 1994), is ready to displace any conceptual system based on a foundation purporting to establish certain and final meaning (Polkinghorne, 1990).

Postmodernism does not stop at the doorstep of that intertextual instability and complexity. Instead, postmodern studies expose the constructive nature of claims of truth or interpretations of behaviors, address how meanings are created and transformed, and explore their social significance by asking questions, such as:

> how, in what specific contexts, among which specific communities of people, and by what textual and social processes has meaning been acquired? . . . How do meanings change? How have some meanings emerged as normative [while] others have been eclipsed or disappeared? What do these processes reveal about" [the sources and operations of power?]. (Scott, 1988, p. 35)

One reason for postmodernism's focus on power is that power affects which texts and narratives are typically privileged, how knowledge is created, and what is regarded as knowledge (Foucault, 1969). Power "works indirectly *through* knowledge" (Lennert, 1997, p. 67). Indeed, beyond overt domination, much of a group's power comes from its ability to produce meanings that can be used to threaten, pressure, lobby, quiet, or provoke. Much as the *pensionado* system was a colonialist tool designed to help anchor U.S. culture and views into the Philippines and thereby reinforce and secure U.S. colonialism there, depictions of knowledge become a means by which power is subtly exercised and an acquiescent attitude is insinuated. The long-standing linkage of power and the ability to represent interpretations simply as facts or knowledge has frequently led to powerful individuals or groups, such as colonialists, newspaper editors, television newscasters, and members of a dominant group, developing a sense of entitlement to define reality.[2]

Which narratives are the powerful likely to promote? As is suggested by postmodernism's sibling, critical theory, people in power often advocate descriptions of reality that make their status and oppressive relationships seem natural:[3] Many will disparage challenges to myths about equal opportunity and meritocracy; defend the just world hypothesis, which holds that good and bad fortune are deservingly distributed; and claim that God only gives people as much as they can handle. The acculturated subaltern frequently and without thinking adopt and reiterate those views, which have been relayed simply as facts.

Behind dominant narratives about the nature of reality and what constitutes knowledge is usually the masked exercise of power; under the guise of rationality and progress are self-serving ideologies (Dowd, 1991; Gottdiener, 1993). Truth claims are sometimes dressed up as straightforward eyewitness observation. Doing so halts discourse and legitimates the repression or exclusion of other views. For instance, some people claim privileged knowledge about the United States during World War II because they were alive at the time, as though everyone in that situation formed the same, deterministic, or singularly logical interpretations. But they do not have a corner on valid presentations of that time because their knowledge of that period is constructed, as is the knowledge of those born after the war.

Like colonialism, truth claims are also presented as simply reflecting neutral rationality (Racevskis, 1993). However, countering claims that simple rationality supports narratives, postmodern explorations of knowledge expose the hidden values and politics governing descriptions of people, explanations for behaviors and events, and claims of validity. They show that what passes for truth is frequently determined by those in power who manipulate narratives to serve their own interests (Denzin, 1995; Rosenau, 1992).

Those explorations require a heightened consciousness because the reiteration of privileged narratives and their representation as simply facts can hide their constructive nature. For example, the repeated use of the label "political correctness" to disparage deference to the feelings of others, particularly a minority, or the term "playing the race card" to disparage racial narratives, can add an air of legitimacy to characterizations while ignoring the often oppressive usage of the terms.

The power to reinforce dominant views is exacerbated in what postmodernism regards as today's hyperreal society, characterized by representations, images, illusions, or simulations that are difficult to distinguish from reality (Baudrillard, 1983; Rosenau, 1992). (Postmodernists are aware of the inconsistency in referring to comparisons to reality.) The hidden suppositions behind simulations, including psychological tests, and the boundaries between appearance and reality make the simulations look like especially convincing factual representations.

Exposing favored narratives, their links to power, and their lack of objectivity is also difficult because of prevalent social myths and ideologies. For instance, postmodernism, like critical theory, argues that the myth of objectivity often hides the privileging of some narratives and the role of power in claims of knowledge, including scientific narratives (Racevskis, 1993). Reminiscent of a magician's misdirection, the myth directs attention away from hegemonic values, intentions, and effects. As described in the previous chapter, social scientific truths are tied up in ideologies based on particular, signifying, rhetorical practices (Ward, 1995). For example, the promotion of touchstone rationality and value neutrality are values behind modernist psychology's façade of scientific neutrality. When social scientists lay out research findings as simply facts, apart from underlying assumptions and behind the shield of following scientific protocols, they augment the mystique and power of their knowledge claims.

Much of the power of scientific narratives rests with a rhetorical authority socially assigned to scientists as fact finders. Although those who know scientific procedures are supposedly anointed with the ability to produce knowledge, behavioral scientists could instead be viewed as people who have just learned to interpret behaviors in prescribed ways. Their narratives, like metaphors, have become "as if" explanations for behaviors.

For instance, as in several studies of the past 50 years, a study of children between 3- and 10-years old tried to measure racial attitudes. Children were shown colored squares and asked, "'What do you think of when you see the color brown (or other selected color)?' and 'How does the color brown (or other selected color) make you feel?'" as though their answers would reveal their racial attitudes rather than how the children momentarily felt about colored squares (Liu & Blila, 1995, p. 147). The researchers tried to assess the children's self-concept by asking them to choose a picture or a doll that looked like they did, apparently regarding any racial match as "correct." Given the variety within any race, however, the children might have accurately responded that a particular photographed person had bangs, a nose, or ears like they did and regarded those characteristics as more important than skin color. But the researchers apparently did not consider alternative meanings and assumed they knew "the" meaning of any answer. Their power was exercised in their operational definitions and interpretations.

In analogous albeit less egregious ways, researchers generally pose survey, test, and interview questions and impose their own interpretations (or those of the psychometrician who created the test) on the responses. Customary questionnaire formats deprive respondents of the opportunity to freely express their rich, conscious, complex interpretations of themselves, events, and situations, describe contingencies, or say "both" to true/false questions or "a and c" to multiple choice questions. Those paper-and-pencil methods are akin to trying to determine a dream's story line or decipher the meaning of a dream by making statements about the dream and asking the dreamer for "true" or "false" responses. The researcher's created narratives might not even be recognizable, much less meaningful, to the dreamer because the restricted response options eviscerate much of the meaning of an experience or behavior. Likewise, when the American Medical Association lobbies and privileges psychiatric over psychological narratives on insurance payment schedules, it controls discourse. In such ways, power is exercised over knowledge, whether by privileging some narratives rather than others or by restricting whose voices are heard. By contrast, disrupting dominant frames of reference—by exposing the previously neglected, repressed, marginalized, subjugated, supposedly insignificant, and deferred—would reveal how particular narratives are linked to power.

The knighting of only select people as capable of accessing truth denies people without the scientific shibboleth the wherewithal to have their views legitimated. The hegemonic privileging of a researcher's narratives restricts consideration of multiple meanings and makes it difficult to recognize that the privileged narratives are constructions rather than truth.

Postmodernism maintains that the ability to ascribe meaning is not limited to one creator—neither God, author, nor scientist. After all, the meaning of reality, like the meaning of being part of an ethnic or racial group, is not contained in any one, complete and final narrative construction of reality; no single method, not even the scientific method, is always superior (Edmondson, 1995); and no one interpretation exhausts meaning. Meaning arises in discourse.

Because intertextual knowledge is inherently unstable, discontinuous, changing, and constantly reconstructed (Rosenau, 1992), postmodern investigations search for multiple, temporal, unstable truths rather than *the* truth. For example, the meaning of a divorce changes as it undergoes reinterpretations and is never finally and completely explained because the present and past are always seen through the lens of the ever-changing present. Consequently, a postmodern study would examine multiple, interrelating narratives. Because each narrative simultaneously and necessarily highlights and ignores, elevates and silences, and reveals and conceals, researchers might initiate lengthy counter debriefing dialogues in which they ask respondents to provide feedback on the researchers' interpretations of respondents' questionnaire answers or explore why respondents describe experiences, events, motivations, and beliefs in one way instead of another to more fully understand their meaning.

Thus, postmodernism is poststructuralist in its denial that texts have fixed, self-evident meanings and that causes of behaviors must be grounded in a priori foundational categories (Scott, 1988). Although it is not synonymous with poststructuralism, it is also poststructuralist in its denial that the meanings of words necessarily correspond to things (Taylor, 1970).

Neutral Versus Destabilizing Language

A third difference in the premises of modernist science and postmodernism concerns the significance of language—broadly including words, gestures, symbols, images, meanings, and signs. The modernist treatment of language as neutral and transparent (and, therefore, as warranting little attention), contrasts with postmodernism's view that language plays a central, transformative role in the creation and representation of knowledge and the shaping of experiences (Denzin, 1995).

From the latter point of view, we never know about or even refer to things-in-themselves; all knowing about reality requires some translation, as in the act of perceiving or describing in words. Knowledge cannot be taken outside a discourse system because it exists in and by means of language, and is shaped by discursive conventions (Richardson & Fowers, 1998). Epistemologically, in the beginning there is the word and the word is used by humans to create, describe, and mediate interpretations that provide meaning and produce knowledge.

However, as the work of Wittgenstein (1963) and poststructuralists suggests, language does not have a direct correspondence to a sensory experience or a referent or noumenal world (Barrett, 1967); representations of reality—such as statements about categories, events, and relationships—are mental constructions that do not provide pure, transparent descriptions of the referent reality that is external to the mind (Rosenau, 1992). Thus, variables do not necessarily have any ontological status other than as constructs and finding relationships between variables or constructs does not necessarily have any ontological significance.

As symbols of thoughts and experiences, words are inadequate, leaving inexpressible residue and *différance* (Bauman, 1978). Whereas the conventional modernist view of language is that articulated thoughts are clearly understandable by members of a linguistic community, Derrida's view, in keeping with the earlier discussion of intertextuality, emphasizes that language is composed of signs referring to what is absent and is subject to misinterpretation. Every time we grab a thought, that thought has unclear, changing connections to other thoughts: What is articulated is swimming in traces and meanings of other thoughts and experiences so ephemeral and hidden that speakers are not even fully aware of the meanings of what they have said (Denzin, 1994). "Signs always have traces of other signs," like remnants of crossed out words (Ritzer, 1997, p. 120; Spivak, 1974). Even what appears to be a simple, declarative statement has undeclared meanings. For example, saying that a 20-story high-rise has no thirteenth floor is accurate and understandable only given particular linguistic and cultural conventions. Language is replete with surplus meaning (e.g., "race" has meaning beyond its denotation); metaphors have traces of other concepts; and meanings vary from person to person as words evoke varying associations in different people.[4] Scrutinizing the signification process exposes language's destabilizing effects on claims about the meaning of research findings and the limits of knowledge based on arbitrary linguistic conventions (Rosenau, 1992).[5]

In an illustrative study of the epistemic implications of language, women used a Likert scale to describe themselves in terms of a series of characterizations presented to them, such as "I am passive," and then described the definitions they had in mind for key words such as "passive" (Landrine, Klonoff, & Brown–Collins, 1992). While African-, Asian-, European-, and Latina–Americans did not differ in their responses on the Likert scale, they defined key words like "passive" and "feminine" differently: White American women usually thought of "passive," for example, as "being laid back and easy-going" whereas the women of color thought of it as "not saying what I really think." Had participants' responses only been filtered through the researchers' operational definitions and interpretations, as is typical, the conclusions about the women would have been inappropriate. Indeed, the researchers reported that they heard definitions they had not previously considered. Nevertheless, identity measures, for instance, inquire about "ethnic pride" without seeking meaning and contextualization. By contrast, postmodern psychological analyses shed light on the ways in which both signs and the structures they represent do not have fixed properties or stable referents (Denzin, 1994); propensities toward psychologism, the renaming of processes, events, behaviors, and reasons in psychological terms; and the consequences of habitually substituting causes for reasons, which creates ontological entities, such as memory, in place of activities, such as remembering (R. Williams, 1990). (More detailed postmodern discussions of the role of language can be found in literary criticism.) Thus, postmodern studies include the analysis of language; local, unstable intertextual meanings; privileged perspectives; and relationships between power and discourse.

Postmodern Methods

A psychology starting with postmodern premises would have different goals than mainstream psychology does now. For instance, it would seek analytically rather than mathematically assertoric knowledge, examine meanings ascribed to behaviors, and define validity differently.[6] Several methods serve those goals.

Deconstruction and Hermeneutics

Derrida advocated deconstruction, one way postmodernism displaces, analyzes, and creates knowledge.[7] Deconstruction is an attitude toward and a method of questioning assumptions; examining the seams and cracks in theories, concepts, and methods; and seeking new interpretations consistent with stimuli (Sarup, 1989). I hope to demonstrate in this and succeeding chapters, when I deconstruct various psychological practices and concepts, that deconstruction entails:

- disrupting seemingly natural conventional meanings and identifying the limits of claims of knowledge;
- exposing the ideology behind imposed meanings, produced "facts," and versions of reality as well as disassembling social and theoretical myths underpinning knowledge claims and ascribed meanings (Hollinger, 1994);
- unraveling what is not apparent in a statement or concept and showing that what is privileged is determined by what is absent;
- identifying concepts, assumptions, and meanings that are taken-for-granted and privileged as well as those that are unprivileged, marginalized, silenced, and suppressed;
- uncovering hidden anomalies and contradictions inherent in any attempt to understand human experiences by exposing

counterexamples, contradictions, and paradoxes rather than smoothing them over (Ritzer, 1997);

- stripping oppressive constructions and undermining dominant discourses to expose hegemonic intentions (Handler, 1992);
- exposing false choices;
- revealing the multiplicity, ambiguity, contingency, and instability of meanings (Handler, 1992);
- inverting dichotomies by pushing the superior out of its privileged perch to reveal multiple opposites and uncover narratives that binary oppositions obscure (Sarup, 1989);
- highlighting the complexity and diversity of local, specific, contextualized human experiences (Slife & Williams, 1995);
- demonstrating the ways in which meanings relate to other texts and are based on *différance* (Dickens & Fontana, 1994);
- inspecting the contextual nature of what has been regarded as true and the way contextualization changes the meaning of findings;
- showing the historical, cultural, and social purposes behind dominant constructions and how and why some narratives have been excluded while trying to extricate ourselves from given, misleading portrayals and the force our time in history has on our thinking (Bruns, 1987); and
- weighing the usefulness and consequences of alternative constructions and developing new frames of reference.

The point about dichotomies is based on the observation that many narratives are grounded in hidden dichotomies in which one element is typically dominant over or prior to the other in an explanation. A deconstructive analysis might begin by noting the implications of dichotomies, such as past/present; mind/body; knower/known; truth/falsehood; masculine/feminine; strength/weakness; self/other; privileged/silenced; whole/part; rational/irrational; good/evil; same/different; present/absent; private/public; central/peripheral; subject/object; universals/particulars; etic/emic; and fact/belief (Faulconer, 1990; Rosenau, 1992). Such reasoning, said to be a common artifact of Western cultures (Bower, 2000), needs to be examined because when characterizations of situations, people, issues, or concepts are viewed in terms of polarities, the result is unnecessarily limited, false choices, and caricatures that conceptually distort and overshadow complexity (Morawski, 1990).[8] Deconstruction, Derrida argued, can expose the arbitrariness of boundaries and the alternity behind any sign (Ritzer, 1997).

Deconstruction purposefully undermines, reverses, and displaces binary, fixed oppositions that derive their meaning from their socially established contrasts. It might invert dichotomies, evaporate the boundaries between binary pairs, or show them as supplements of each other to clarify overlooked problems or reveal alternatives. For example, research finding that Asian Americans are more likely than white Americans to be self-effacing, deferential, and willing to assume blame is customarily interpreted in terms of Asian cultural values (e.g., Connor, 1975; Fenz & Arkoff, 1962; Weisz, 1989). If we reconsider those findings by treating the white Americans' behaviors as the ones to be explained, we might conclude that, compared to Asian Americans, white Americans are likely to assume a superior position, not give in, and avoid blame. Instead of recycling vague cultural explanations, such an interpretation would raise new questions, including "Why might white Americans behave that way?" and "What does this finding tell us about how Asian Americans and white Americans are socially, economically, and politically situated?"

Thus, in exploring such inverted dichotomies, deconstruction is subversive, digging beneath the surface of social relations and behaviors and uncovering buried, oppressive patterns. Like rhetorical analysis, it can provide insight, discern duplicity, or demonstrate that what has been taken as fact is metaphorical (Bruns, 1987).

Hermeneutics,[9] the study of interpretations, offers another, related way of reconfiguring psychology into a postmodern discipline. An undercurrent of postmodernism, it closely scrutinizes texts and actions to find specific, contextualized, hidden meanings (Rohmann, 1999).

Like phenomenology, hermeneutics strives for knowledge about life as it is lived. Like approaches taken by Heidegger, William James (K. Schneider, 1999), Taoism, and Buddhism,[10] it tries to begin with the fullness of the original experience before detachment, abstraction, and division of figure and ground, as when one aspect of an experience becomes the figure against the background of the rest of experience; hermeneutics then tries to understand parts in relation to wholes. It is similar in that way to phenomenological accounts that examine the unique, local, contextualized, and private meanings of and feelings about experiences without reducing them to structures and elements (Slife & Williams, 1995). It produces qualitative examinations of the richness of human experience and the irreducibility of its meaning. For example, it directs attention to intentions, beliefs, feelings, moods, imaginations, and desires which, because they are not directly manifested in overt behavior, are not customarily accessed by those using empirical methods (Kockelmans, 1990; Richardson & Fowers, 1998). Hermeneutics further bolsters interpretations of behaviors and social events with examinations of contextualizing, sociohistorical meanings (Fowers & Richardson, 1996) and ways in which knowledge is historically conditioned.

Hence, compared to the discursive moves and rules forming scientific disciplines (Gergen, 1988), postmodernism offers alternative epistemological starting points for a dialectical discourse and different discursive rules. For example, it contrasts with the modernist scientific protocol, which favors a top-down interpretive strategy akin to putting together pieces of a jigsaw puzzle guided by knowledge of how the final product will look: Before a modernist study is conducted, the meanings of variables are defined and a hypothesized narrative guides the way the results will be interpreted. A handful of other variables or narratives emphasizing other texts might be mentioned as possibly complicating factors, but they rarely undermine the researcher's a priori framework. Contrary to a tradition that authorizes social scientists as fact finders on the grounds that they know how to observe objectively, a postmodern psychology based on a communicative reasoning paradigm would disavow the claim that knowledge can only be based on logical deduction about objective observations[11] and might use a more inductive, bottom-up methodological strategy in which study participants' experiences and behaviors are interpreted in terms of different narratives.

Postmodern scholarship invites dialogue, whether between a reader and text,[12] among interpreters, or among different types of discourse (such as literature and philosophy), each using its own signifying methods. Like other postmodern methods, hermeneutics thus creates knowledge by critiquing, reasoning about, and expanding upon successive interpretations of phenomenological qualities (Polkinghorne, 1983). What one person thinks and relays to others is regarded as a discursive move, as are new or modified descriptions of reality, interpretations, defenses of a narrative, explanations, logical analyses, knowledge claims, metaphysical assumptions about what is, epistemological assumptions what and how we can know, critiques, changes in the direction of a discussion, and efforts to furnish a fact to support a theory (Gergen, 1988). Empirical findings can be brought into the conversation too, as can generally accepted, authoritative or persuasive statements (O'Neill, 1998), but they are never the last word; they are fodder for critical analysis.

Successive interpretations are needed, Derrida argues, because whenever the divide between the self and the unknown is crossed, only traces of the latter are grasped; whenever the unknown seems to be understood, new questions arise. With every act of (temporary) understanding, we have a new cognitive standpoint so the world must be understood again from that new position; the unknown continually reappears and challenges us (Nuyen, 1994); and complete understanding is always deferred. Analytical discourse prevents the heteroglossia of successive interpretations from simply amounting to a sharing of tales by children around a campfire and keeps negotiations of meaning from lapsing into chitchat or arbitrariness.

The critique, evaluation, and negotiation of interpretations of behaviors, events, or situations, and constructions of meaning would not be grounded in a universally shared or formal rationality; nor would questioned assumptions be completely resolved through recourse to an outside source, such as direct observation. As in a jury weighing various interpretations of presented evidence, the produced understanding is subject to change and cannot be predicted by a compilation of participants' views (Manicas, 1987; Polkinghorne, 1990).

Participants might analyze different versions of sometimes thematically similar narratives told by variously situated groups and individuals (Denzin, 1994). In keeping with standpoint theory, efforts would be made to hear the voices of variously located people, particularly the typically marginalized and silenced. Discussants would be sensitized to whose truth, based on which premises, is displayed in which narratives and whose alternative constructions are muted.

Science becomes a social enterprise: It is a good conversation (Bevan, 1991). In contrast, discourse in modernist psychology is all too often halted because authorities, like Superman empowered to see what is not apparent by ordinary means, have apparently given the complete explanation (Faulconer, 1990); ideology masquerades as knowledge; no alternatives are assumed or recognized; and nothing presumably remains to be said.

Evaluating Narratives

By rejecting modernist methodological foundations and logocentric interpretations, postmodernists are left to identify criteria to be used to evaluate claims of knowledge. To accept as valid whatever feels intuitively correct or is commonsensical would not be intellectually serious. Simply accepting narratives study participants tell about their behaviors creates similar problems because they are not necessarily the best interpreters of their own behavior.

Reliance on eventual consensus as a criterion is problematic because, in the continuous challenging of narratives, any consensus would be just a temporary point in a discussion. That consensus also runs the risk of being built on common sense rather than reasoned views and makes consensus another grand narrative (Lyotard, 1988). Apparent consensus may actually be obedience or conformity reflecting differences in proponents' power—particularly, the values and judgments of the dominant—rather than dispassionate analysis (if that is even deemed appropriate for a particular issue). When the people creating the consensus rely on established power-knowledge standards like "majority rules" (Mann & Kelley, 1997), subordinated groups are at risk of being bowled over and the most popular rather than the most appropriate might rule, as the Federalist Papers describe. Yet to abandon criteria altogether and regard everyone's ideas equally would be to sink into a relativistic quagmire from which we would derive neither knowledge of "what is real" nor any purpose to examinations of ourselves and the world.

The Issue of Relativism. Radical postmodernism,[13] sometimes called skeptical postmodernism, is unabashedly relativistic: It holds that since objectivity has been debunked and, consequently, right and wrong views cannot be objectively weighed, there is no truth, ontologically everything begins with human interpretations, and all narratives are of equal value and equally arbitrary (Rosenau, 1992). It leaves us without any hope of having criteria to judge world views (Griffin, 1989). This view, duly criticized for its nihilism, undercuts a basis for scholarly efforts to improve social conditions.

However, most forms of postmodernism do not claim several, equally valid, truths and do not rail against all truth claims. They do not consider relativism to be the only possible alternative to the rejection of scientific objectivism and deny that the absence of a necessary link between signs and the signified leaves the dregs of relativistic definitions and concepts. Postmodernism generally claims that although the meaning of psychological facts, descriptions, or truth claims are contingent on the concepts and language used to construct them (Barbiero, 1999; Buchowski, 1994; Ritzer, 1997), meaning's intertextual contingency does not imply that all narratives are of equal usefulness or validity. Even without unadulterated access to foundational reality, what-is-regarded-as-knowledge, like various signifiers— whether words, research methods, ideas, or theories—can be judged by using various criteria.

Some people counter that various criteria are not needed: Reason alone should be the criterion. However, the easy emphasis on rationality overlooks the fact that, despite cross-cultural differences in what is considered to be logical, the elevation of rationality is commonly based on the assumption that Western reasoning—such as formal logic, a cultural creation—is the only or best type of reasoning (Gergen, 1985; Polkinghorne, 1990). It also minimizes the effects of values, power, timing, ascribed meanings, and favored concepts in determining what is accepted as reason and which statements will be agreed upon as premises. Even rationality is discursively constructed to serve particular perspectives, as Nietzsche argued. Rationality is not even always fairly assessed, as when assumptions that reason and emotion are dichotomous leads to claims that someone (particularly a woman) who is angry must be irrational.

Postmodernism's avoidance of final judgments neither embraces the relativistic position that each person's knowledge is equally valid nor leaves us with tautologies. Although humans do not have access to an objectively knowable, external truth about human behaviors against which to compare ideas, different ascribed meanings can be judged from various frames of reference that can lead to the rejection of any particular meaning. Data can clarify the usefulness of assumptions (Slife & Gantt, 1999); and possible alternative interpretations can be limited by rigorous analysis (Dickens & Fontana, 1994). Postmodern analyses can undermine a relativistic, babbling free-for-all.

Some Criteria. In the absence of an Archimedean standpoint providing an objective, absolutely "best" perspective, any criteria can be interpreted or weighted differently (Bernstein, 1983). Therefore, rather than try to establish a singular criterion, knowledge negotiators would view issues from multiple perspectives. Depending on the question asked, dialectic judgments would be made in terms of varied criteria.

Among the multiple, contestable criteria that could be used to judge narratives are their persuasiveness and the value premises underlying them. Social constructionists emphasize criteria such as credibility, trustworthiness, transferability, and confirmability of interpretations; some feminists emphasize lived experiences, caring, accountability, and praxis; and, because critical theory concentrates on criticism that leads to social transformation, most critical theorists emphasize the ability to produce emancipation (Denzin, 1993). Postmodernists have discussed three additional criteria.

First, the quality of supporting and disconfirming data, evaluated in terms of multiple frameworks, could be a criterion. Inasmuch as people cannot step outside of all premises when they reason, conduct research, or produce narratives, judgments about the quality of the data grounding interpretations might be based on analysis of metaphysical premises and their consequences rather than on descriptions of the scientific procedures followed (see Bevan, 1991). Doing so can help to expose the multiplicity of meanings sometimes hidden by narratives; demonstrate that what is regarded as knowledge is contingent on premises, definitions, and the excluded; and clarify the usefulness and limits of various ontologies. Rather than regard constructions as more or less true, they can be viewed as more or less informed and sophisticated (Guba & Lincoln, 1998).

Rejecting the modernist belief that ideology is incompatible with social science, postmodernism, as a social theory, is admittedly ideological. Its desire to understand and promote a more just social order points to a second criterion—the usefulness of explanations (Lemert, 1991). However, "usefulness" in this context is not synonymous with modernist criteria such as efficiency and control (Rosenau, 1992) and would not include the expectation that accumulated knowledge would lead to universal predictability. Pragmatic analysis could entail offering alternative perspectives for consideration, seeing whether knowledge propositions predict events, and judging the effectiveness of decisions and actions based on particular knowledge or belief premises (Hubbard, 1988; Polkinghorne, 1983). Pragmatic criteria could include narrative fertility and viability in various domains or discursive and intertextual usefulness (Botella, 1995). In this context and shorn of modernist metaphysical and epistemological baggage, research can be useful without being objective.

Interpretations concordant with what else is known are generally more useful than incoherent constructions (Rychlak, 1975): They make the world more understandable. Hence, the usefulness of interpretations is also dependent on their clarity and coherence.

However, that generalization does not assume the existence of a coherent foundational realm nor does it assume that apparent coherence in some areas, such as electricity and engineering, is matched by coherence in the realm of human behavior (Glynn, 1990). Indeed, postmodernism does not expect or superimpose order and coherence in ways modernist paradigms do. While psychology has often treated contradictory findings, complicated causes, disequilibrium, unpredictability, and changes as statistical errors or evidence of methodological flaws, defective theory, or deviance (T. Young, 1991), postmodernism, like chaos theory, expects dynamic variations, twists, and reverses of human behaviors and processes without making chaos a new foundation. It decenters order, stability, determinism, and certainty to highlight marginalized and excluded subtexts (Rosenau, 1992).

In the absence of a permanent, neutral point of appeal in judging which interpretations are best, narratives can also be evaluated in terms of a third criterion, their consequences. What does a view help us to understand? What are the social repercussions and moral implications of created models, theories, and interpretive practices? For example, what are the consequences of favoring rationality over compassion (Morawski, 1990)? How does a knowledge claim oppress? Why have some positions and arguments dominated (Bernstein, 1983)? Postmodernism's subversion of boundaries (Kellner, 1988) raises questions about how social constructions of reality create dynamic boundaries and the social effects of those boundaries.

When knowledge is likened to a system of roads, modernist psychology asks about the correct way to traverse from A to B whereas postmodern inquiries question the consequences of different paths in terms of various criteria—as well as for whose interests this system has been established, why people are traversing those paths, and whether destinations can be reached without using the roadway at all.

Thus, notwithstanding charges that it is relativistic, postmodernism does encourage evaluative criteria. Nevertheless, the framework postmodernism offers has been criticized on several other grounds.

Criticisms of Postmodernism

At times, postmodernism has been facilely dismissed in the form of sarcasm, name-calling, and snide references to "pontificating." It has been attacked with non sequitur arguments that postmodernism represents attempts to settle "old scores" or that some postmodernists "could not recognize, much less solve, a first-order linear differential equation" (Gross & Levitt, 1994, p. 6) as though differential equations are directly relevant to important epistemological challenges or constitute the criterion of scholastic legitimacy.

Physicist Alan Sokals perpetrated a well-known hoax in a sociology journal, *Social Text*, by writing an intellectually empty article on quantum theory and postmodernism. This hoax was reputed to be an indication that postmodernism is nonsensical although an interpretation more consistent with the publication is that the reviewers for that journal did an inadequate job; even Sokals admits as much (MacIlwain, 1997).

Nevertheless, postmodernism has also been duly criticized. (My interest is not in providing a thorough overview of criticisms of postmodernism and responses to it; interested readers can refer to Denzin, 1994; Dickens & Fontana, 1994; Kellner, 1988; Ritzer, 1997; Smith, 1994.) One legitimate complaint is that esoteric postmodern argot can be obfuscating and pretentious, and thereby marginalize and exclude people from discourse and compound misunderstanding arising from the textual contingency of interpretations. The problem is exacerbated by the fact that the relationship among terms and the connection between concepts and the larger postmodern argument are often inadequately explained although that issue could be resolved with a different balance of breadth, depth, editorial page limitations, and reader accessibility.

Another criticism of postmodernism is that it is irrational. Postmodernism's rejection of the reduction of reason to its logical and empirical scientific form has been used as evidence in the indictment of postmodernism as irrational (Bruns, 1987; Kupferberg, 1990). Noting a lack of a singular, pure rationality, however, does not make postmodernism misologic. Postmodernists argue that the prejudice of scientism, dismissing as irrational whatever does not fit the modernist definition of rationality, has unnecessarily impeded the recognition of the limits of reason and ways in which different forms of reason are appropriate for different realms (Hollinger, 1994).

The identification of alternatives to formal logic widens ideas about what constitutes reason beyond the interests and norms with which it has been conflated (Hollinger, 1994; Racevskis, 1993). Rationality is not sacrificed, for example, by the replacement of the "reasonable person" standard with the "reasonable woman" standard in judgments of a victim's behavior in rape cases (see Forell & Matthews, 1999).

Hence, postmodernism scrutinizes the scope, historical effects, and limits of reason (Racevskis, 1993; Ward, 1995): It acknowledges different forms of rationality (Bruns, 1987); analyzes the not–completely–rational investigative habits underlying empirical knowledge (Hollinger, 1994; Racevskis, 1993); examines the ways in which reason enables, constrains, or is insufficient to ensure progress (Hollinger, 1994; Lennert, 1997); recontextualizes ideas; and questions the "ways in which language, power, social factors, and history shape our views about reality, truth, and knowledge" (Hollinger, 1994, p. 177). In keeping with some of the original goals of modernist science, postmodern science values rational analysis and dialectic identification of hidden dogmas and assumptions while still enabling the abstraction of patterns or explanations that can be subject to further, in-depth analysis.

Opposition to postmodernism for a purported lack of rationality sometimes seems to be rooted in hierarchical orientations. Postmodernism has been "denounced" for its seeming lese majesty by linking it with the political left, social scientists, feminists, pluralists, and ethnic studies specialists. As with many criticisms of multiculturalism, exaggerations and misdirections of attention are at the root of claims that postmodernism's decentering invites a cacophony, "makes a 'shrine' of . . . disparate discourses," and emphasizes differences, which undermines integrating possibilities and denies commonality (K. Schneider, 1999, p. 23). Especially in evidence when discourse is demonstrating that a dominant group has been advantaged over others, many calls for emphasizing commonalities seek to quiet identification of those advantages; ignore ethnic, racial, class, and gender differences that affect how those advantages are distributed; and erase the ways in which groups define themselves as culturally unlike the dominant culture (Sampson, 1999). In a similar misdirection, postmodernists' criticisms of social conditions and portrayals of them sometimes are ascribed purely to postmodern epistemology while the social conditions are ignored.

Ironically, one criticism of postmodernism is that some postmodernists have eschewed categories such as class, race, and gender as outdated modernist concepts. As a consequence, those postmodernists overlook many important social issues and lack a counternarrative that could lead to the overthrow of existing oppressive relationships and mythologies of superiority (Hollinger, 1994). Indeed, some forms of postmodernism are nihilistic to the point of discouraging social engagement (Botella, 1995)—by disavowing the possibility of any coherent knowledge, indiscriminately including so many perspectives that social action is precluded, or deferring social action on the grounds that deconstruction results in deferment of final meanings.

However, not all forms of postmodernism share this problem; scholars need not be bound to use some existing forms of postmodernism; and excluding political and social analysis is not necessary to a postmodern psychology (Friere & Macedo, 1995). Postmodernism, encouraging reanalysis, need not end with a form of deconstruction attenuated by value-neutral playfulness, a desire to express creativity, or a search for irony as one might see in deconstructive literary criticism, architecture, or music.

Indeed, postmodernism generally has ties to the emancipatory activism of critical theory. In psychology, deconstruction can be a step toward a broadened awareness that can lead to social action. It can be put in the service of efforts to change public policy beyond mental health service delivery, increase understanding of individuals and groups, and ameliorate discrimination. Oppressive conditions can be exposed by a hermeneutic psychology's interpretations of reality from specific standpoints, in terms of cultures, societies, events, politics, images, human existence, race, class, and gender, and in relation to possible communities (Bauman, 1978; Nuyen, 1994). Postmodern psychologists can help to undermine oppressive relationships and create a more egalitarian society by identifying oppressive relationships; analyzing the oppressive consequences of narratives, including the silencing of narratives; and showing how society oppresses various groups.

Postmodernism has also been criticized for essentializing modernity in terms of the search for order, rationalism, and certainty while "failing to see a variety of different discourses within modernity, different stages of modern thought, competing paradigms and a more variegated conceptual and intellectual field" (Kellner, 1998, p. 77; Toulmin, 1990). Similarly, Jürgen Habermas, from whom some aspects of postmodernism have grown, has criticized postmodernism for denouncing jejune Enlightenment efforts that either have not had the opportunity to be completed or have taken errant steps that were not necessary to Enlightenment premises (Denzin, 1994). Although that is, to some degree, a valid point, such missteps in modernist efforts have not been widely recognized in psychology.

Ironically, similar criticisms have been leveled at postmodernism: Despite the multiple perspectives subsumed under the postmodern rubric, on occasion postmodernism has been treated as one viewpoint and has been criticized for one form or another's incompletely developed position. At times, criticisms apply to particular forms of postmodernism but not to others. Some forms of postmodernism do lack a basis for judging narratives (Ritzer, 1997), for example. Not all embrace communicative reasoning or hermeneutics.

The various forms of postmodernism are sometimes even contradictory (Kellner, 1988). Just as postmodernism generally rejects the notion of one, final truth yet implicitly claims a superior truth status to modernism, different forms of postmodernism each claim to have the right view or approach (Rosenau, 1992; Winter, 1992). Foucault's postmodernism denies permanent, knowable truths about human nature and, like social constructionism, points to the construction of multiple truths whereas one extreme form of postmodernism rejects the possibility of any (even local or contingent) truth.

One strain of postmodernism might initially sound "new age": In place of rational narratives, it advocates narratives that emphasize personal fulfillment, intuition, faith, spirituality, and other concepts reminiscent of humanistic psychology. Although not necessarily irrational, those bases for narratives can be problematic because they might just reflect projection, delusions, or mindless arbitrariness that contribute little to discourse or knowledge. That form of postmodernism nevertheless raises worthwhile questions about practical reasoning and the role of expediency in what is accepted as knowledge.

Various forms of postmodernism also have been criticized for proposing their own metanarratives to substitute for modernist foundations. For example, in light of Derrida's criticism of any social theory that grounds itself in a fundamental standard or a starting point other than a product of *différance* (Dickens & Fontana, 1994), postmodernism has been accused of making *différance* a new, albeit unstable, grounding. Because Lyotard (1984) argues against grounding knowledge in negotiation rather than language, postmodernism has also been criticized for making language a new grounding and treating psychological processes, such as perception, as artifacts of language (Handler, 1992; Polkinghorne, 1990).

As psychology works through and creates a postmodern orientation that addresses its concerns, it need not hyperprivilege signs in the way some postmodernists have; it need not deny that environmental stimuli activate sensory receptors and, in a nondeterministic way, thereby initiate the creation of concepts and classifications in neural pathways. Postmodernism is a work in progress. The very spirit of postmodernism pushes toward continual transformation addressing problems in any narrative, even a postmodern one.

A Postmodern Psychology

Just as many modernist philosophers and scientists denied that psychology could be a science, some postmodernists denounce as useless efforts to establish a postmodern social science. Derrida, for instance, thought that a postmodern social science is impossible because texts in the social world are infinitely interwoven with other texts and irreducibly uncertain (Rosenau, 1992).

Certainly, the knowledge produced would not have the characteristics sought by Enlightenment science: It would not be objective, apodictic, or mathematically assertoric and it would not produce final, foundational psychological truths. Without abandoning rational standards altogether, a wider range of standards beyond formal logic would need to be adopted.

Just as a more rhetorically oriented psychology would not be as far removed from traditional research as it might appear at first glance, neither would one more oriented toward continually interrogating intertextual meanings. Albeit without a postmodern orientation, psychology's modernist discourse is already intertextual: Theories rely on other texts, methods are corralled by reference to traditional texts, such as favored statistical tools and ways of treating study participants, and privileged concepts and tropes used to translate descriptions implicate other texts. My point is not that modernist psychology just needs to tweak the edges of its research to become postmodern; it is that psychology can offer prime territory for postmodern analysis. Furthermore, postmodernism does not constitute a radical diversion from the orientation of William James or the social constructionism of Berger and Luckmann (1967), George Kelly (1955), and constructive perception research.

Most psychologists probably already concede that no single, grand, psychological framework provides completely satisfying explanations for all behaviors and that any explanation inevitably excludes some ideas. They occasionally analyze the applicability of concepts (e.g., defense mechanisms) to particular behaviors without the baggage of the concepts' parental grand (e.g., psychoanalytic) theory. Psychologists already compare competing explanations, and a postmodern psychology would analyze alternative interpretations. Hermeneutic analyses of multiple narratives would provide knowledge that nevertheless transcends the mundane.

Psychology does not need to cling to its self-image as a modernist science, a separate culture from humanities, to justify its scholarly existence. By being postmodern, psychology would not simply be subjective and relativistic, just as literary criticism is not. Working from postmodern premises does not mean that psychology must emphasize kitsch, pastiche, artful presentation, and irony, which are all aspects of postmodernism. However, its goals, methods, definitions, and conclusions would change. A postmodern social science, examining the complex, interrelated, specific, and unique, could provide only tentative, contextualized descriptions and explanations (Rosenau, 1992). Validity would be more like valid interpretations of literature than like logical and mathematical deductions. Some tools of formal science might be used, but as descriptive aids rather than means of predicting and controlling (Polkinghorne, 1990).

Abandoning the metaphysical assumptions of the correspondence theory of truth and the belief that the scientific method has a universal, objective, beatific link to truth does not mean abandoning the quest for useful explanations and descriptions of reality. A postmodern psychology would offer and analyze the premises, coherence, and consequences of different, organizing narratives.

In the next chapter, I use postmodern analytical tools to demonstrate some of modernist epistemology's impact on psychology and its research methods. In subsequent chapters, I discuss privileged variables in psychological portrayals of minorities such as Asian Americans. Those variables are race, culture, acculturation, ethnicity, and ethnic identity. I describe ideological purposes behind uses of the concept of race, decenter readings of culture in terms of various texts, analyze acculturation signs, disrupt conventional meanings of ethnicity, deconstruct modernist assumptions behind ethnic identity measures and models, and, throughout, describe alternative postmodern approaches.

CHAPTER 3

Privileged Methodological Texts and Narratives

When modernist epistemological assumptions have not unduly distorted data and conclusions, empirical research has produced general understandings that have had a beneficial impact on public policy.[1] That research has, for example, demonstrated the need for funding of AIDS-education outreach; illustrated varying outcomes following drug treatments; compared dropout rates from mainstream mental health facilities and those designed for minority communities to show the need for the latter; and identified ethnic differences in beliefs about healthy behaviors, concepts of mental health, and views of psychotherapy, which bear on the delivery of health services. Therefore, useful translations of data, concepts, and interpretations should not be dismissed out of hand with the claim that the modernist psychological research has all been worthless.

Nevertheless, this chapter's postmodern genealogical analysis, exposing and unraveling origins of psychological metanarratives, points to ways conceptual problems created by psychology's adoption of modernist science's metaphysics, described in the first chapter, are often matched by problematic methodological and interpretive moves. It shows the effects of chronically privileging some variables, study participants, and points of view.

Toward that end, general characteristics of the research are deconstructed: I identify meanings that have emerged as normal or implicitly denied (Scott, 1988); uncover negated, muted texts; unveil assumptions behind constructed narratives; expose limits to claims of knowledge; and undermine standard frameworks and meanings. That is, I take the modernist psychological research as discursive narratives in the creation of knowledge and offer postmodern perspectives as discursive responses, which will surely be controversial but will, I hope, spur discursive rejoinders from others, including non-psychologists who employ fragments of psychological research in psychological narratives they build.

Privileged Defining Variables and Texts

In the research, some variables (e.g., age, gender, generation, English proficiency, and country of birth) have been regularly privileged in psychological portrayals of Asian Americans (and Latino/a Americans). As postmodernists like Derrida would anticipate, those privileged variables have often been dichotomies, such as descriptions of study participants as male or female, or foreign- or U.S.-born. Some variables have been hyperprivileged in part because they are easy to assess. For example, the existence of a widely accepted test of acculturation has probably increased the privileging of acculturation.

Acceptance of those privileged variables has been predicated on the belief that the variables simply and naturally reflect who Asian Americans (and Latino/a Americans) are; the privileging of the voices of researchers as authoritative; and the clouding over of the constructive nature of the selection of variables. Rather than indicating the predilections or ego of particular researchers, the privileging of those variables has followed from modernist psychological assumptions and practices.

The concept of "Asian Americans" or "Asian Pacific Islanders," of course, glosses over heterogeneity: It subsumes both diverse groups with varying characteristics, such as predominant language preferences, cultural beliefs, and socioeconomic statuses, and individuals uniquely combining personality characteristics, intelligence, attitudes, experiences, and personal values. So among the effects of repeatedly privileging a few, inadequately differentiated variables to define Asian Americans are homogenized, essentialized, underdifferentiated portrayals. Intragroup heterogeneity, complicating the meanings of statistics showing between-group differences, is easily overlooked (Tanaka et al., 1998).

Skewering the diverse, complex, and normally recognizable can lead to ham-handed public policies detrimental to communities. For instance, when medical school admittance and scholarship policies have essentialized Asian Americans in panethnic terms, deeming Asian Americans generally to be an "overrepresented" group because of the relatively high number of Bharatiya (i.e., South Asian or Asian Indian) Americans, Chinese Americans, and Japanese Americans enrolled in medical schools, they have established policies leading to the systematic underrepresentation of other Asian American groups (Uba, 1994b). In turn, that situation has left some Asian American communities with insufficient numbers of culturally knowledgeable medical service providers.

In addition, group–defining variables are often treated as though they have singular effects on homogenized individuals. That treatment exacerbates the modernist predilection toward rendering people as homes of or conduits through which deterministic variables act.

Characterizations of people in terms of a few variables also seem to accentuate ways in which they are acted upon rather than choose to behave (Ritzer, 1997). Humans are treated like objects with characteristics when their humanity is actually more in their ability to generate meaning and have meaningful experiences (Polkinghorne, 1988). Therefore, the emphasis on demographic variables avoids much that is relevant to psychological functioning.

Privileged Subjects of Study

The privileging of some variables extends to the tendency to draw from particular populations. That tendency is frequently due to practical limitations on researchers. For example, college students, an economically and educationally skewed population, are the most commonly studied group because their participation in studies can usually be obtained easily and for free. To avoid the expensive process of developing translated versions of questionnaires, researchers regularly limit their samples to the English-proficient. (Appendix A discusses other difficulties finding samples and conducting psychological research.)

Such privileging of some populations is widely recognized. Less attention, though, is given to the skewing of samples in studies of minorities: Minority students at colleges with relatively large numbers of that minority are favored to be in such studies because those colleges are most likely to hire psychologists who study that minority and researchers often draw samples from their own campuses. Additionally, the colleges are most likely to have ethnic studies courses from which researchers at other campuses might seek sufficiently large samples of those minority members.

While Asian Americans whose ancestors came from East Asia have been especially likely to be included in samples of Asia Americans, how that privileging may attenuate claims of knowledge about Asian Americans has been largely unanalyzed. That privileging is part of a broader pattern in mainstream psychology, which is overwhelmingly based on white American samples. However, the overdependence on white samples is probably taken for granted because many white Americans (including researchers) view white Americans as simply people. Moreover, the privileging of white samples is supposedly justified on modernist grounds: Psychology is searching for relationships among variables and, amidst metaphysical orderliness, samples are simply interchangeable, generic specimen constituting a basis for generalizations. Ironically, even though science is supposed to be more exacting than everyday knowledge, the APA condones vague descriptions of samples in terms of homogenizing demographic characteristics because, from a modernist framework, more specific descriptions are impractical and unnecessary.

The treatment of study participants[2] as generic types and a sample as representative of others turns again on definitions of participants in terms of essentializing variables. However, as the first chapter described, individuals are even less representative in psychological realms than in other research areas, such as basic chemistry. Demographic and other hyperprivileged classifications become the basis for hyperreal, often static characterizations of individuals.[3]

In contrast, one way a postmodern psychology would mitigate the treatment of a group as generic people would be to engage and distinguish a wide variety in that group and decenter privileged subgroups. In studies of Asian Americans, for example, psychologists might ask "What would we learn if Bharatiya Americans were regarded as prototypical Asian Americans rather than only as another Asian American group?"

More basically, a decentered, postmodern analysis of people as fragmented products of various discourses—in relation to different texts and contingent, rearticulated, social, political, and epistemological relationships (Finlay, 1989; Winter, 1992)—would counter the essentialization. Moving beyond privileged variables and samples and having more specific understandings of samples would create opportunities to examine new research topics (e.g., how minority status is regarded in various socioeconomic communities) and broaden intertextual analyses.

Unprivileged Variables and Texts

Privileged variables become privileged texts in psychological narratives. That privileging leaves other texts unprivileged.

The Different "Other"

One of the unprivileged texts in psychological narratives is postcolonialist theory's concept of the "other." That concept has changed somewhat from its historical roots when white Americans regarded themselves as wholly distinct from nonwhite "others" who were viewed "only in terms of how much they deviated from the illustrious Caucasian standard" (R. Young, 1994, p. 160). The significance of being regarded as the "other" was related to the condescending narratives European royals and aristocrats created about peasant masses, the views colonialists had about the colonized, and the beliefs male chauvinists have had about women. Regarding some people as "other" has been tied to narratives about what is "natural,"[4] such as the supposedly natural subalternity of minorities (except for Aboriginal Americans) in light of vague, "first come, first served" notions, and it has been used to try to justify various forms of discrimination.

As postmodernists like Foucault would contend, assumptions about the "other" continue to serve social, psychological, and political purposes and contribute to biases. Classifications of Amerasian children in Vietnam as "others" is probably one reason that, in the United States, they were not typically referred to as "Americans," despite the U.S. citizenship of their fathers.

The ruts left along the "Other" conceptual trail, long embedded deep in America, can still trip the unaware. Mainstream psychology has portrayed minorities in terms of white Americans, who are typically treated as simply normal humans and the basis for normative standards—not a surprising move given Foucault's view that normalcy is defined by those with power. By and large, minorities and people in other countries have been studied to test the universality of behavior patterns found primarily among European Americans (Gergen et al., 1996; S. Sue & Morishima, 1982). When minorities are not viewed as part of "us" but instead as "other," focusing on how they might deviate from white normality is considered a natural framework. For that reason, some psychologists expect white control groups in studies of minorities but not minority control groups in studies of white Americans (S. Sue, 1999); attempts to explain concentrate on those behaviors that are unexpected because they differ from those of white Americans; and when cultural differences are used to account for the different survey responses of minority Americans and European Americans, they are customarily aimed only at explaining the behavior of the former.

Mainstream psychologists with such an orientation are reflecting attitudes often heard in America generally—where we hear "diversity" being used as a conversational code word for any population that is not singularly white. For example, an all-black group is sometimes called "diverse" but an all-white group is not. When not indicating any recognition that the group of African Americans is diverse, those references to diversity are translations for people of color as "others." Treating various Asian American groups as one may also be hinting at the homogeneity[5] conventionally imposed on "others."

When dominant frames of reference are normalized and any behaviors that cannot be explained by that framework are cast as abnormal, some of the oppressiveness of the concept of minorities as "others" is hidden. Oppression of Africans and African Americans was considered so natural by members of the white establishment before the Civil War, the enslaved's desire to run away from slavery was considered a pathological syndrome, drapetomania, as was talking back, procrastinating or refusing to work, or otherwise not being openly deferential to plantation owners (Landrine, 1988). Surely, had the enslaved not been regarded as "other," their behavior would not have been considered a "syndrome," much less pathological. Psychologists now shake their heads looking back at the history of the behavioral sciences' view of people of color; however, power still provides opportunities to cast one's view of reality as simply impartial knowledge rather than a construction and makes still-existing oppressive relationships even more subtle and difficult to eradicate. For example, a top-selling introductory psychology textbook tries to explain the absence of famed people of color in psychological history by asserting that the reason was that "conventional thought had held that higher education was the exclusive domain of White males" (Wood & Wood, 1999, p. 26)—privileging the "conventional thought" of white men while avoiding the simple acknowledgment of racism and sexism impeding access to higher education for people of color and women. In contrast, hermeneutically analyzing or deconstructing taken-for-granted frameworks helps to expose muted texts and oppressive constructions which, in turn, can lead to emancipatory scholarship.

For instance, a linguistic analysis shows that, paralleling narratives about Latino/a Americans, some narratives referring to the "home nations" of Asian Americans—and meaning nations other than the United States (e.g., Lester, 1994)—reflect and contribute to the assignment of "other" texts to Asian Americans and, as I describe in a subsequent chapter, the treatment of Asian Americans as guests. Narratives referring to Asian Americans as "Asians" and non-Asian Americans as "Americans" (e.g., Jeong & Schumm, 1990; Min, 1995b) do likewise by implicitly excluding Asian Americans from the category of "Americans." Lexical appropriation of the colonialist perspective, as in the statement, "as their number increases in the future, Asian Americans will look less strange than they do now" (Min, 1995b, p. 274), is sometimes used without thinking. Those types of narratives raise questions about how deeply ingrained are white-as-normal narratives, the believability of the implicit promise of dominant acculturation narratives, and the meaning of being Asian American.

Moreover, perhaps as remnants of colonialist attitudes as well as historical establishment concerns about the Eastern and Southern European immigrant "others," many of the traditionally studied variables—including expressiveness, assertiveness, academic achievement, amount of parental supervision, support for elderly parents, and likelihood of conforming—refer to behaviors that might disrupt society's status quo. For example, studies examining whether Asian American families are cohesive might be regarded as valuable insofar as they are used to alleviate unease over whether the minority will present a problem to the status quo in the form of a need for social services.[6]

In addition to homogenization, colonialist attitudes, and concerns about sustaining the status quo, exoticism is sometimes a text related to the otherness ascribed to minorities. In particular, the exoticism ascribed to Asian Americans is sometimes linked to notions about the exoticism of "others." According to Daryl Bem's (1996) theory of the development of sexual orientation, the sexually dissimilar, linked to anxiety and other forms of arousal, are regarded as exotic; and the exotic becomes erotic. In a parallel way, perceptions of Asian Americans as "other" may be one step toward perceptions of them as exotic and, particularly in the case of stereotypes about Asian American women, as erotic. (The link between exotic and erotic is probably a little further removed for Asian American men because their gender introduces a more threatening power element to social relations.)

Thus, otherness may be a de facto privileged text but it and related texts are unprivileged in psychological narratives. Ignoring those texts speaks to a larger issue.

Unprivileged Texts, Simplifying Portrayals

While any narrative will unprivilege some texts, the repeated focus on favored variables, groups, and other texts has pushed to the shadows the chronically unprivileged.[7] Many of the unprivileged variables are just the type one would expect to be overlooked given modernist orientations deemphasizing consciousness, such as study participants' flexibility, experienced ethnic composition of nearby communities, noticed characteristics and interpretations of situations, perceived behavior options, and anticipated consequences of behaviors. Instead of examining the meanings study participants ascribe to situations and, hence, to their own behavior in those situations, researchers frequently assume they know the meanings, which are inherent in the behaviors. Categories and other texts are typically treated as though they have the same static meaning for all, so their varied meanings are unprivileged. For example, study participants categorized as living in a nuclear family are conceptually and statistically often treated as though they are in the same familial milieu. After awhile, chronically unprivileged concepts, texts, and related narratives are so muted or negated that their absence is barely noticed.

To get a sense of how simplifying the unprivileging becomes, consider what is unprivileged in the classic conceptualization of the traditional Asian American family (e.g., E. Lee, 1997). While depictions of traditional families are not knit from whole cloth, the honoring of the concept of "traditional Asian American family" minimizes much of the complexity and variability of families and ignores other narratives (e.g., Uba, 1994a). Characterizations of the traditional, patriarchal, Asian American family, for example, marginalize Filipino/a American families whose "traditional" structure has more egalitarian gender roles. The result is simple, jejune portrayals setting the stage for policy makers to make decisions based on overly broad generalizations. Indeed, policy makers are given little alternative: They look at the numerical data presented to them but are frequently not in a position to judge the ontological and epistemological assumptions underlying them. Chronic privileging of simple prototypes can also contribute to stereotypes, such as portrayals of eldest sons as dutiful and fitting into "the" oldest son role.

The repeated reference to traditional families, implying an unchanging constancy over generations if not centuries, downplays new and emergent influences cutting at the seams of the dominant conceptual fabric.[8] Using this framework, empirical investigations offer little hint to shifts in familial coalitions or how individuals create their family roles through negotiation, as when a Filipina American stopped arguments with her mother by putting call blocking on her telephone and ignoring her mother's pages for a month.

Empirical portrayals of Asian American families typically have centered around variables such as the period in which ancestors came to the United States or level of acculturation. However, more complex and recognizable families would emerge in psychological doppelgängers that also included often ignored family types: stepfamilies; single-parent families; and interracial families, including both those with exogamous couples and Asian children adopted by non-Asian American couples.[9]

Bringing abusive family relationships, such as the following, into scholarly discourse could broaden textual interpretations beyond clinical narratives:

> In the old fashioned Korean view it was very common for parents to discipline their children by hitting. . . . As my brother and I began school and started to behave in ways that were acceptable in the US culture but not in the Korean culture we were hit often. . . . my brother would send me to sleep early and he would wait up to greet my parents home from work. Being older he

tried to protect me by keeping me out of sight . . . but I heard everything. . . . I always kept one ear open for any noise to indicate my parents' arrival. . . . I was always ready for the slightest noise of anger and jump out of bed to . . . stop the hitting. I learned in school that hitting was not tolerated in the US. I didn't understand why this was happening. I knew my father wasn't a bad man and he was nothing like the [abusive] men portrayed in the movies. . . . I thought . . . my brother and I were bad children, but we would never do any of the [wayward] things other American children would do. . . . I still jump to any sounds I hear as I sleep, although I live alone. I can't remember the last time when I had a deep sleep.

As a result of her poor sleep, she had little energy to play and other children teased her, claiming that Asians were too weak to play or that she was uncoordinated and shy. She wanted to talk with someone about her problem but knew she was not supposed to discuss family matters and could not tell relatives because of a language barrier. Asking her parents would have questioned their authority and broaching the subject to her brother was consistently met with the charade that he, being a strong oldest son, was not negatively affected by the beatings.

She identified an issue that transcends clinical discourse:

It seems strange to me how we are suppose to think of the family unit as one entity yet when it comes to . . . problems we are forced to deal with them alone. . . . I knew that my parents hit because they thought it was what they had to do if they loved their children. . . . The more I acted like my peers at school the more my mother hit me. Therefore I tried to become more "Korean."

Such a narrative, suggesting a complexity to ways that generational disparities in behavior standards can be relevant texts to identity, personality, health, and even stereotypes, would hardly be revelatory from clinical perspectives; but those connections have been widely ignored in mainstream research on those topics. Families seem to be dichotomized into fodder for either clinical or scientific studies; in the case of the latter, her family would probably simply be classified as Korean American, nuclear, and traditional.

While some texts are ignored by default or oversight, psychology's institutionalized rules also encourage the negation or glossing over of texts. For instance, to ensure the anonymity of participants, the APA instructs researchers to vaguely identify the source of samples, as in describing them as coming from "a large northeastern university" or an "undisclosed university," as though universities are interchangeable. However, samples could be identified in ways that do not abridge confidentiality rights while still providing hints about the surrounding population and perhaps the economic class of the sample. For example, they can be described in the following ways: "The samples for the study were drawn from three low-income housing areas in Los Angeles, California, within a prescribed area which included the area known as Chinatown" (Becerra & Chi, 1992, p. 37) or study participants were students who "attended a community college in Los Angeles, usually Pasadena City College or East Los Angeles College" (Fujino, 1996).

The systematic withholding of information does not help research consumers to understand the behaviors of study participants. Information about samples is particularly needed in studies of minorities. Some Asian Americans, for example, purposefully go to colleges in the West with relatively large Asian American populations; others purposefully go to colleges with few Asian Americans. Therefore, ethnic identity studies cannot legitimately treat samples from one college or another as the same. Knowing the reasons study participants chose the college they did, the minority group's percentage of the college from which the sample was drawn, the particular city in which study participants live and, therefore, some idea of the size and composition of area minority populations and local interracial relationships would supplement the available texts and help consumers discursively analyze the meaning of behaviors described in research findings. Even on the level of physical matter, "the mere increase in molecular size beyond some 500 atoms [has a quantitative and qualitative impact, leading] to 'new' or 'emergent' properties and 'new' laws of physics" (Bertalanffy, 1969, p. 68): so even from a modernist viewpoint, it should not be surprising that the size of the community and how members of a sample see society and their positions in it can also be relevant to the meaning of human data. A Filipina American illustrates:

> In Hawai'i, my culture, heritage, and language were predominant and very accepted as part of the norm creating a melting pot for the "new" Hawai'i. . . . I felt quite comfortable [and believed] that people were generally accepting of all races.
>
> My arrival to Los Angeles was definitely an eye-opener. Aside from the fact that Los Angeles was a big city and had an enormous population, I began to feel quite [anxious, stressed, and] different . . . I didn't know how to fit in. Each time I was myself (manifesting Asian American characteristics), I was either looked down on or ignored which led to my insecurities towards my physical appearance and communication skills. My role models were hard to find and I was more attentive to the fact that

being [white] American was highly valued as seen through the media, social circumstances, and the business world.

Self-reports like this one illuminate the meaning of her sociogeographic location as well as her location in the intersection of other discourses.

Seemingly due to disciplinary habit, some texts are overlooked and left to sociology and anthropology, thereby sustaining the interdisciplinary divisions that impede the development of more sophisticated understandings. As a consequence, opportunities to clarify the meaning of behaviors are lost; nonpsychologists are left to speak for psychology and apply their understandings of psychological perspectives; and many issues are minimized. For instance, with the exception of research on minorities and women, issues of poverty are usually invisible in psychological portrayals. As a Vietnamese American's description of her family's poverty illustrates, however, poverty is related to psychological issues such as self-concept, family relations, and stress:

> As a result of being foreign-born Asian American, my parents does not have the opportunity to work in a high paying job. . . . they are working as seamstress. They are being paid by pieces. The work are very stressful. They are usually rush to get things done. When they make mistake my sisters and I have to disassemble it. They never get any advancement nor benefits. I never learn how to sew [because they would] make me work for them. There is not enough money working as seamstress. . . . I hate my parents for depending on welfare. Sometime I wish they go get a regular job like . . . other American parents. But how can they [when] they don't know English. Sometime I want my dad to go push shopping carts and my mom to work as a gardener. They don't need English to do that. Than again that will be embarrassing if my friends see my parents working like that . . . I am also helping them out financially. Their public assistance is not enough for food, clothes, and car insurance. . . . I feel sorry for my parents for being in America where there is no future for them. Right now I hope to get my CPA license and find a good job. That way I can buy a house for them. I hope I can find a good job without racism standing in my way.

Much as a dismissive "everyone has problems" cliché grossly distorts differences in the severity and impact of those problems, categorizing simply by acculturation level or race distorts and overlooks their intertextual meanings and local embeddedness in a confluence of other identities and (e.g., political, historical) circumstances.

Modernist psychological parochialism favors particular types of concepts and research questions, leaving others as detritus. Modernist psychologists are more likely to ask quantitative questions such as, "How communicative are Asian Americans compared to non-Asian Americans?" than questions about verbal devices and styles or when Asian Americans' thinking may differ from what they communicate. Regarding people as just embodiments of lawful, transcendent relationships among variables typically overrides phenomenological narratives too. Facing the Rocky Mountains is a different experience, and can lead to different behaviors and attitudes, depending on whether you are admiring their beauty, hoping your automobile can climb Interstate 70, or tumbling down a ski slope. Analysis of quantitative variables, such as the height of the mountains, or categorical variables, such as season, only provides certain types of knowledge, which might not even be meaningful when trying to understand why a person decides to live near those mountains.

To explain behaviors in terms of experiences in lived, changing, temporal, unique, interpreted contexts, creative efforts to balance values and perceived options, intersecting discourses, and intertextual meanings, psychology needs to reconsider unprivileged texts. Doing so will produce psychological narratives that are both wider ranging and more specific than is now standard, as well as more conducive to social action.

Privileged Interpretations

Modernist assumptions, discursive rules, interpretive habits, and dominance are among the factors that affect which texts are privileged and which are unprivileged. A result of chronically privileging some texts and unprivileging other texts is that some interpretations become privileged.

Much as the power interests underlying dominant narratives are frequently hidden, so are unprivileged texts that could expose those narratives' weaknesses and undercut their acceptance. For example, a popular narrative holds that Asian American families tend to have cultural values conducive to their children's educational achievement. In the absence of contrasting texts, the ways in which Asian American familial circumstances are not conducive to high academic performance are hidden, portrayals move away from identifiable families (Hune, 1997a), and privileged interpretations are sustained.

Some narratives tend to be privileged because of sociohistorical outlooks, born of modernist metaphysics and Western values, that underlie theories and practices in both scholarly and popular communities. Consider the concept of personality, commonly defined in the West as the relatively stable, self-contained set of unique characteristics, beliefs, attitudes, values, motives, and behavior patterns that are found in the same person at different times and across situations. This conceptualization reflects and contributes to the general public's psychological narratives so that some Asian Americans interpret their own bicultural behaviors as slightly disturbing. A Korean American who behaves differently with Korean American and white friends, illustrates: "I know . . . my personality in terms of behaviors, attitudes, self-concept, and even values change according to whom I am with. Thus, I wonder which group of my friends or if anyone including myself knows the real me."

Demonstrating some ways in which the reins of Western values have steered the course of personality narratives, humanistic psychology views personality in terms of "authentic" selves "with strong boundaries . . . that can resist influence from outside"; this type of personality is valued over changing selves which, from a Western point of view, might be considered waffling, hypocritical, or pathological (Markus & Kitayama, 1998, p. 65). Inconsistencies, multiple meanings, and situational variability are painted over or viewed as abnormal. Alternative views of personality—as a dynamic creation rather than as a static characteristic, as changing ways of interpreting and behaving, or as a mix of flowing psychological processes—are not considered.

The search for modernist, transcendent regularities has encouraged decontextualized studies that treat the social location of white Americans as standard. For instance, the presumption of a social location that tends to allow a direct relationship between inclinations and behaviors (as would be more prevalent in a powerful group) produces personality narratives that give little attention to the effects of social power on behavior patterns and discrepancies between private values, feelings, or preferences and public behaviors. Investigators typically treat behavior (particularly that of white Americans) as a direct expression of personality, interpret differences between white and nonwhite Americans' personalities in terms of culture rather than power, and ignore circumstances in which preferred behaviors are forbidden (as in "It didn't take me long to stop rebelling against my parents, because I never won") or impeded (as when immigrants with limited English proficiency feel unable to express themselves in arguments with native-English speakers). Moreover, personality narratives are selectively applied: Perhaps because Asian Americans are often viewed as culturally "other" than white Americans, dominant narratives are more likely to describe the behaviors of Asian Americans in terms of vague, yet orderly, cultural effects than individualistic personality.

At the same time, whereas experiments usually emphasize social conditions determining the behaviors of people seemingly without personalities, personality research often assumes that behaviors reflect an individual's (particularly a white person's) desires, values, and personality, and irons out situational variability, inconsistency, and ambiguity. The personality tests upon which research narratives are partially based typically downplay circumstantial exigencies and variations in behaviors, actual interpretations of events and situations, and the changing meaning of a personality characteristic within a constellation of characteristics. Personality narratives also commonly overlook ways in which ideologies affect the treatment of others, as when expectations that Asian Americans are polite promotes polite behavior toward them, which elicits reciprocal politeness that seems to support the stereotype that Asian Americans are polite.

The search for transcendent regularities also steers psychologists away from studies of experiences, such as those reported by a Japanese exchange student:

> After about two months [in the United States] . . . my host father specifically said to me that he wanted to have a sex with me. [His "rationale" was that extramarital affairs were common in Japan.] I was so shocked that I immediately called my local [exchange student] coordinator. [Despite repeatedly telling the coordinator what the host father said, this high school student was told to stay in the home and if anything else happened, the coordinator would then remove her from the home.]
>
> Although my host father admitted what he said to me, my host mother did not want to believe it. She said that I misunderstood what he said because English was not good enough and also because of cultural gap. . . . She said even that I seduced him [and that] my host parents had been accepting foreign students, including Japanese female students, for a couple of years without any problem and there were prettier girls than I in my host father's college if he wanted an affair.
>
> In school, whenever I thought about the problem with my host father not only I felt like crying but also I actually started crying uncontrollably in classes. Other students and teachers misinterprets that I was crying because of getting poor grades in school. I could not tell anybody what was going on. . . . I developed a great amount of self-hatred. Instead of blaming my host father, I blamed myself for not being assertive.
>
> The end of my first home-stay came four months later. My host father became crud again. [I think she meant "crude" but "crud" works too.] He told me that he loved me. He asked me to kiss him, but I refused. He touched my legs so many times

that I was scared by a thought something more could happen. However, his verbal expression shocked me more than anything. He said that he thought about me when he masturbated. Moreover, he tried to explain how he did it, but I tried not to listen to what he was saying.

The search for regularities leads away from consideration of stereotypes, sexism, and power differences *as texts* impacting, for example, how Asian Americans are perceived, what they experience, and which meanings are ascribed to their behaviors. When Asian Americans do not seek therapy in situations like this, their experiences do not bring notice in published discourse. Hence, by chronically adopting a modernist viewpoint and ignoring what does not fit within it, such as experiences, modernist frameworks guide the selection, assessment, and use of concepts in interpretive narratives.

Thus, assumptions, concepts, research methods, and narratives form the mirrored walls of a chamber confirming and supporting each other; the world outside that chamber is barely given a glance. Inside the chamber, the repackaging of the same modernist assumptions and methods, variables, and types of statistical analyses produces similar portrayals of a group or behavior patterns. As a result, findings seem robust, reality seems orderly, interpretations seem to be transparently valid representations, heterogeneity among members of a group is minimized, and modernist assumptions and methods seem justified. Consistent interpretations, composed in the service of modernist expectations and biases, are regarded as signs of validity rather than as indications that the same biases are being imposed in various studies.

Privileged Voices

Biases introduced by interpretive habits are compounded when some narratives ascend to a royal station because they have an authoritative source. In practice, the pronouncement of authoritative facts is often socially restricted to the province of an elite, such as those with a PhD who supposedly have keys to objectivity. Much as when people assume that commentators are insightful, fair, and reasonable, or privilege their assessments over those of the creators of a film, book, or artwork, researchers' interpretations are often privileged over those of the people whose behavior is being interpreted. That privileging becomes problematic when, within the framework of a study, those interpretations become dogmatic statements whose meanings are not open to discursive challenge.

Whereas postmodernism rejects the belief that some appropriately educated people have access to objective truth and casts doubts on the legitimacy of burying and disempowering constructed meanings of a wide array of variously situated people, "the modern discourse [has] attempted to curb the proliferation of meanings, particularly those constructed by the unauthorized 'other' " (Martinez-Brawley, 1999, p. 333). Viewing behaviors only in terms of the researchers' ontologies, values, and interpretive practices is reminiscent of paternalistic, colonialist efforts to justify the failure to listen to the supposedly irrational colonized on the latter's own terms. Even when white persons cast a member of a minority as an expert or spokesperson for that minority, their view—that the minority has a shared consciousness and, therefore, one can speak for all or a particular individual should be the spokesperson—is dominating.

The privileging of researchers' voices is also in force when a study is published. Publication and the prominence and accessibility of the journal in which an article is published often determine whose psychological narratives are heard and disseminated as "true," even more so before articles became prevalent on the Internet. Mainstream psychological narratives are further circumscribed by the format and content condoned and showcased by the similarly educated who review and slant published theoretical, methodological, and interpretive narratives in ways that customarily reflect dominant ideologies and practices and reinforce the walls of that interpretive chamber.

Indeed, the APA's rhetorical standards exacerbate the privileging of reviewers' voices in a modernist echo chamber. To save space in journals, the APA instructs researchers to simply name psychological tests or surveys they administered, for example, even though most readers are not intimately familiar with every questionnaire named. Bedeviled readers must, hypothetically, search for a copy of the test—not an easy task—to evaluate the study. In practice, the appropriateness of the test is not examined in detail by readers and the protocol casts readers in a passive role as observer. The researcher's concepts or interpretations of psychological scales become descriptive or explanatory standards; the missing is unnoticed (Silbey, 1997); descriptive or explanatory concepts, sheathed in psychological acronyms and esoteric argot, are often cast as being beyond the ken of nonpsychologists; discourse is discouraged as negotiation of narratives is invidiously halted; and the remaining, dominating, conventional narratives become ever more powerful. Parallel problems are apparent in the silencing of unprivileged voices in clinical settings.

Privileged Clinical Voices

Clinical psychology as a rhetorical endeavor is in some ways consistent with postmodernism. (See Biever, Bobele, & North, 1998, and Machado &

Gonçalves, 1999, for descriptions of some postmodern therapeutic approaches.) Cognitive, psychodynamic, and humanistic-existential therapies already entail identifying narrative schemata used to interpret events; show how incomplete, biased, and counterproductive narratives affect behaviors; treat language as a catalyst that organizes emotional and cognitive turmoil to promote a clearer understanding of meaning; help clients reconstruct more useful narratives; and identify subtexts.

Even so, to the extent that therapists base their therapeutic conceptualizations and methods on modernist research, they are entangled in its epistemology. Behavior modification therapies, for example, are based on a belief in deterministic relationships between previous responses to behaviors and future behaviors.

Therapeutic relationships are also frequently tethered to modernist assumptions, as when clients believe that psychotherapists have neutral, authoritative knowledge enabling them to see "the" meaning of their behavior. This elevated social position assigned to therapists contributes to the privileging of the clinicians' perspective. When conducting therapy and publishing studies, clinicians find that their classification of behaviors as evidence of psychopathology is usually unchallenged.[10] In light of the social role of therapists as experts or authorities, a client's doubts about a therapist's diagnosis are sapped of much of their credence and challenges may be treated as client transference or a defense mechanism.

Although budding therapists in graduate school are warned about believing they are authorities with *the* Truth about the real meaning of behaviors, the constructive nature of the psychotherapist's voice is frequently not exposed to clients and is, instead, socially regarded as being in tune with the foundational and even the apodictic. For example, trauma has historically been defined from the therapist's perspective rather than from the client's: If the latter deny that an experience was traumatic when the therapist surmises it must have been, the therapist might conclude that the client is repressing whereas if the client describes an experience as traumatic when the therapist does not, the client might be pinned with the label "adjustment disorder" or said to have a pathological desire for attention (Root, 1992).

Over time and in different cultures, the number, conceptualizations, and manifestations of mental disorders have varied (Chung & Kagawa Singer, 1995), reflecting differences in culture, social awareness, types of research, ethnocentrism, and sexism. Nevertheless, by communal agreement or conformity, the world of U.S.-recognized psychopathology is regarded as encompassed by one modernist narrative that objectifies psychological states and reifies forms of psychopathology. As the bible of psychopathology and a hyperprivileged clinical text, the *Diagnostic and*

Statistical Manual of Mental Disorders (DSM) is treated as *the* classification of mental disorders. It is treated as though it mirrors a natural, transcendent taxonomy rather than the current sociohistorical and intellectual location of the developers and users of DSM even though it was not until the current edition that cultural variations were included in the DSM narrative—and as an addendum at that.

Diagnostic labels, whether used by therapists or by the general public when the terms enter common parlance, are shared constructions of experiences or ways of explaining behaviors (Botella, 1998). They are shared largely because alternatives are silenced: As popular discursive forms, DSM constructions encourage focus on some descriptions and explanations and, consequently, build berms against others. Therapists, even more than researchers, face political, economic, and discursive pressures to privilege DSM criteria (e.g., to be paid by insurance companies). Regarding DSM classifications as discursive moves, however, could debunk DSM's rusty foundation and expose its limitations.

Indeed, postmodernism encourages an iconoclastic look at privileged clinical voices because from some postmodern perspectives, psychotherapy is basically a vehicle for promoting society's dominant values, social explanations, and interpretations (Roffey, 1993). For example, clients are frequently induced to define their problematic experiences in socially sanctioned terms (Richardson & Fowers, 1998), such as personal insecurity, that downplay the effects of their lack of power and other structural limitations or appeal to the therapist's orientation. Early twentieth-century efforts to justify racial segregation on the grounds that the (stereotypes about a hyper-) sexuality of black Americans endangered the mental health of white Americans worried about sexual assault demonstrate that narratives about causes of mental disorders have sometimes served political purposes and social prejudices. So too did some 1950s clinicians' claims that increased civil rights would lead to mental disorders among black Americans because of the disruption of a well-defined, denigrated identity and status (Landrine, 1988).

Postmodern Alternatives

Beyond merely encouraging a closer examination of the privileging of some texts and voices, the unprivleging of others, and the way that privileging channels created narratives, postmodernism offers psychology a broadened scope. It offers alternative orientations and methods to address problems of modernist psychological research discussed in this chapter, such as what to do about researchers' privileged texts and voices.

Research participants do not have to be cast in the role of mere data providers, as when they are treated as bigger versions of white rats—mere sources of scores or producers of behavior. Instead, researchers could treat (and some postmodern researchers have treated) respondents as people engaged in signification processes and include their assessments of their behaviors and status in the discourse. (Given traditional hierarchical relationships between researchers and study participants, researchers may need to establish clearly that expansive, nondeferential answers are being sought.)

Postmodern investigators would not limit their intertextual analysis to texts they identify. Rather than replicate power hierarchies in which behaviors are analyzed from the perspective of a knowing researcher testing his or her theory on objectified people, much as a physicist might study a planet, a postmodern psychologist would take more seriously the fact that samples are composed of heterogeneous study participants with consciousness and draw out their explanations of how they think the meaning of their behavior is related to other texts—experiences, concepts, events, and statuses. For instance, a Chinese American, looking back at his mother's violent, bruising, nearly tear-inducing attacks when he was in high school, his concern that disclosing the abuse or crying would not look manly, and his eventual responses in kind might be asked about his experiences in terms of texts such as gender roles, love, persona, and others of his choosing. Inasmuch as cultural texts, such a films, literature, media creations, art, and music, are sites where meanings and ideology are contested (Denzin, 1993), respondents might be asked about cultural texts with which they identify; videotaped behaviors or films by and about Asian Americans might be used as texts to spur discussion and produce more useful, accessible, and meaningful knowledge than is now typical.

The prototypical psychological question, "Why do people behave the way they do?"—which, in modernist hands, has implied a lasting, transsituational, if not deterministic, basis for behavior—and the question, "What does being Asian American mean?" might be answered not in terms of categorizations or relationships between variables, but in terms of the varied, unstable meanings different people create. They would be addressed by identifying simultaneous, intersecting, and dynamic texts and discourses that are twisted, combined, contextualized, severed, and inverted to produce complex and more meaningful portrayals than modernist psychology now provides. A postmodern psychology would look for local and situated, rather than universal, interpretive schemata; and generalizations would be consciously contextualized, partial, and from identified perspectives (Hoshmand & Polkinghorne, 1992).

Not only can the researcher's voice lose its encyclical status, so can another privileged voice, represented by the respondents' first answers. Study participants could be given the chance, perhaps with prompting, to revisit their experiences and offer additional narratives (e.g., relating to different emotions, thoughts, or ambiguities) that were lost in their first responses when they picked one cognitive thread from many. Just as we might think of clearer responses to a physician's question after we have left the physician's office, follow-up responses might more accurately or fully reflect a respondent's views.

Listening to study participants' narratives, however, does not mean simply glorifying the conclusions they draw or hyperprivileging nonacademicians as representatives of the community (see K. Chan, 2000). Inasmuch as popular narratives often have traces of scholarly conceptualizations that have become part of popular culture, such as additive claims that Americanized behaviors or attitudes are selectively appended by the foreign-born without any loss of past identity, researchers have to guard against mistaking the effects of an echo chamber created by the accessibility of and the public's interest in psychological issues for independent perspectives. An intertextual analysis would include both texts study participants recognize as being relevant to their behaviors and other texts.

Researchers might also investigate the disparity between what people articulate and what they mean. For example, when people claim to think that people should "tolerate" diversity, do they mean "tolerate," as in putting up with something unpleasant, or are they using a popular phrase without thinking? When they say, "I could care less," are we safe in assuming they mean they *couldn't* care less? Inasmuch as some people simply reiterate what they have heard others conclude, the narratives need to be critically analyzed: Researchers need to distinguish among narratives that mindlessly echo banalities the respondents have heard others cite (e.g., some psychologisms), those that reflect intellectually impulsive jumps to conclusions, and those that are signs of careful, personal scrutiny. Relationships between the quality of ascribed meanings and behaviors might be analyzed.

Thus, the role of psychologists is not simply to take dictation. Analysis of the voices and linkage to behaviors, attitudes, beliefs and social relations are crucial. Not driven by insular theoretical concerns (Ritzer, 1997), postmodernism encourages hermeneutics, deconstruction, and dialectic and semantic analyses, including the exploration of contradictions in not always rational narratives.

Postmodernism also calls for expanding discourse. To open interpretations to discourse among readers of a study, researchers could provide the exact wording of questionnaires (e.g., on a web page), descriptions of the multiple, perhaps tentative, meanings respondents read into the survey items, and signs of the conditional nature of their textualized answers. For the same purposes, they might provide complete quotations of interview responses and dialogues. Doing so is admittedly time-consuming, but so is research that is not part of an intellectual dialog or that reflects only positivist biases. (Gorman [2000] provides a good example of the use of quotes.) Extensive quotations of hermeneutic discourse about issues are needed because just as respondents highlight some of their experiences more than others, authors—extracting and privileging what they consider relevant, placing quotes, and attaching meaning to them—necessarily manipulate texts and thereby affect readers' ability to evaluate the authors' interpretations. Quotes can also expand discursive opportunities by engaging readers.[11] Similarly, case studies have a potential role as provocative fodder, forming the basis for a contestation and negotiation of the researchers', clinicians', clients', and readers' narratives and new interpretations.

Thus, the interpretations opened to discourse include not only the respondents' but also the researchers'. An analysis might burrow into dominant narratives for new meanings; examine how individuals are seeing themselves; uncover tacit, interpersonal rules and standards; and seek meanings rather than laws as definers of social relationships (Richardson & Fowers, 1998). In examining the seams and gaps in the knowledge produced by research, clinical experience, and personal ways of processing information, a postmodern psychology explores the intertextuality of meanings; the social creation of knowledge; what people regard as useful knowledge; and how discourses, metaphors, and narratives have "street value," that is, applicability to other relations (Gergen, no date).

Consider the concept of banana as an illustration. Although some researchers have mistakenly claimed that bananas are "People who have intimate relationships with two or more cultures" (LaFromboise, Coleman, & Gerton, 1993, p. 395), which is probably a definition more fitting the bicultural or even cultural anthropologists, a more conventional meaning of bananas might be "Asian Americans who show little evidence of (e.g., racial, cultural, minority) sensibilities commonly associated with Asian Americans and disclaim their connection with other Asian Americans." In common parlance, a banana, seeking to emulate invisible white standards of normality, behaves like, identifies with, and wants to be white.

Peeling back the construction of the concept, a postmodern analysis might hermeneutically examine or deconstruct intertextual meanings buried in the concept of banana, such as what Asian Americans think constitutes "behaving like, identifying with, and wanting to be white Americans." How is "behaving white" defined? Moving beyond Supreme Court Justice Potter Stewart's definition of pornography, which types of behavior at what frequency displayed by which people constitute criteria people use to judge who is a banana rather than, for instance, simply acculturated? Asian Americans who behave like, associate with, and identify with white Americans because they married white Americans would not necessarily be bananas. So does "acting white" refer specifically to behaviors that grow from a sense of entitlement and power? If so, what does the use of that label tell us about the user's view of the standing of Asian Americans in the broader society? In discourse with historians, psychologists might also analyze issues such as how colonialization has influenced Filipino/a American attitudes toward "acting white."

Deconstruction shows that the concept of banana is frequently defined in dichotomous terms: "Acting white" is often implicitly opposed by "acting Asian (American)." Many foreign-born Asian Americans might regard behaving in ways they have been taught by their parents as "acting Asian" and might label the acculturated, monolingual U.S.-born as bananas; American-born Asian Americans might be more likely to think that "acting white" is countered by "acting *Asian American*." Exposing different meanings of the concept of banana would point to meanings of being Asian American. That exposure may entail analysis of the relationship between the meaning of the banana label and other psychosocial texts, such as concepts of assimilation, marginality, and biculturalism; available behavioral options; political tools; the defense mechanisms of the labeler; reasons and ways in which Asian Americans behave like, identify with, and want to be like African- or Latino/a-Americans; or ways in which the label "banana" is a racial appellation or a broadly ethnic one.[12]

Thus, notwithstanding some superficial concordance between psychology and postmodernism, the latter marks a radical departure from modernist psychology and cannot be appreciated by simply looking for how it fits into a basically modernist conceptual framework and set of investigative methods. It has alternative goals and offers different methods of analyzing the meanings of behaviors and concepts.

A postmodern psychology would mark a swing back toward psychology's analytical, philosophical roots without abandoning notable reliance on supporting evidence, observations of people's behaviors, or study participants' self-reports. Implying new goals reminiscent of James' evaluation of ideas in terms of social and intellectual consequences, it would be concordant with postcolonial and critical theories. Its broadened scope would call for the application of more practical knowledge about minority communities than is acknowledged or legitimated by modernist psychology.

Although some psychologists study minorities as just another sample in which to test the universality of findings on white Americans, I venture that most psychologists who study minorities do so because they are interested in the latter's experiences and the reasons they behave the way they do. Less wedded to and motivated by the idea that the research should look for universal relationships or their limits, they could be in the vanguard, joining feminists, in tearing psychology from its modernist moorings as well as establishing working interdisciplinary discourses in areas such as sociology, history, political science, and ethnic studies. Those studying minorities could produce more differentiated views that move readers of the research away from global characterizations of them as out-groups and thereby promote cross-ethnic interpersonal skills and interracial understanding.

Psychology, like a culture, creates forms of knowledge and knowledge content (Fuller, 1995). When psychologists studying minorities use standard investigative methods and seek traditional, modernist goals, they too often inadvertently replicate the types of descriptions promoted by the same goals and methods that have marginalized minorities and sometimes produced myth rather than knowledge.

Psychologists do not have to adopt the assumptions and methods that those who dominate psychology would use to study minorities nor do they, as those studying minorities have demonstrated, have to study dimensions that may have grown out of colonialist interests. They could, for example, study the circumstances in which minorities sometimes feel they are not quite fully welcome whereas middle-class white Americans, as a group, have less reason to question their own entitlement in social spaces (Candace Watase, personal communication). They could examine why Asian Americans and black Americans in classrooms frequently do not feel they have the right and responsibility to participate in class discussions, but do in Asian American and Black Studies classes they identify as their own. Is the silence a reflection of the fatalistic acceptance of both a lack of power to affect dominant narratives and a secondary role generated by oppression, as Paulo Freire posits?

Postmodern psychologists have a wide-open field to examine what passes for knowledge about minorities in ordinary conversations, how that knowledge develops and disseminates, and why there is resistance to other views. As Lyotard maintains, knowledge is a commodity that will play an increasing role in competitions for power; so psychological portrayals of minorities will increasingly become proxy fights for the power to control narratives about them. If psychologists studying minorities do not think about epistemic issues, they leave the field open to others to define (Toulmin, 1990) and perhaps to conceptually colonize the minorities they study. Like critical theory, a postmodern psychology can be a basis for emancipatory scholarship.

Although chronically privileging one text over others distorts the resulting portrayals and, as critical theory argues, privileging one form of oppression at the expense of others elides the interrelationships among forms of oppression (Kincheloe & McLaren, 1998), the temporary privileging of one narrative or text can be helpful in analyzing the meaning of minority status or being Asian American and the meaning of related behaviors. By shifting lines that exclude, privilege, and marginalize, issues are seen from multiple perspectives. So the next several chapters deconstruct or hermeneutically treat various conceptual texts—specifically, the concepts of race, culture, acculturation, ethnicity, and ethnic identity—that have been given privileged roles in descriptions and explanations of the behaviors of Asian Americans and that, from a postmodern perspective, form bases for the appreciation of *différance*, heterogeneity, and particularity among minority group members such as Asian Americans.

CHAPTER 4

Constructions of Race and Culture

Race and culture are concepts commonly invoked in both scholarly and popular portrayals of Asian Americans. This chapter looks at their meanings in both social realms. Indeed, a postmodern analysis ultimately oriented toward social action on, for instance, racial fronts, or seeking to produce research benefiting more than the researcher's curiosity necessitates focus on the everyday meanings of relevant concepts. So too does an investigation concerned with meanings of prosaic behaviors as they play out in real situations rather than in a modernist study.

A discourse analysis of race, concentrating on how the concept is used, how words are manipulated in racial discussions, and the effects of that manipulation, affords one way to understand the social significance ascribed to race. Deconstruction—in particular, uncovering taken-for-granted, unprivileged narratives; disrupting conventional meanings by revealing the instability and ambiguity of meanings; and revealing sociohistorical purposes behind constructions—affords a method of analyzing that discourse. Accordingly, in this chapter's deconstruction of race and culture, I examine the absence of a noumenal anchor to the concept of race; the instability of race's meaning; the hidden intertextual meanings behind uses and nonuses of the concept of race; the meanings of being white; the silencing of racial narratives; some of the complexity and ideologies obscured by simplifying uses of the concept; and the concept of culture as a popular text affecting perceptions and as a variable in psychological descriptions.

The Intertextuality of Race

For centuries, morphological characteristics associated with racial classifications were treated as markers of inherently important genetic differences;[1] even now, they are sometimes perceived as naturally occurring—insofar as endogamy is considered natural—and inherently meaningful. Absent grounding in either evidence or reason, the duo pillars of modernist science, race, when it is considered at all, is usually treated as a nominal, mutually exclusive category in psychological research. Yet as a cultural idea used to emphasize a particular set of physically minor differences, it is an unstable social construction—or why else would a person be a member of one race in the United States and, after a plane ride to Brazil, disembark as a member of another race?

The constructed meaning of race is so dependent on the different texts brought to bear, the term *race* is almost homonymic. Consequently, understanding the rich meanings of race entails appreciation for race's relation to multiple, decentered texts, such as ethnicity, and ideologies.

Instability of the Meanings of Race

Absent clear cultural similarities among Korean-, Samoan-, and Hmong-Americans, the grouping of such diverse ethnic groups as "Asian Pacific Americans" appears to be based to some degree on constructed racial similarities.[2] Further suggesting a linkage between ethnicity and racial appearance, many or perhaps even most Asian Americans do not regard Bharatiya Americans as Asian Americans. Inasmuch as the image of Asian Indians is not negative and their historical experiences have not been widely dissimilar to those of many other Asian American groups, the social distance seems to be based on physiognomy. Although Asian Americans are commonly thought to be of one race, differing views of whether Bharatiya Americans are Asian Americans show instability in various Asian American groups' racial identity.

The instability arises because, rather than being inherent in an individual or group, race's meaning and relevance are contested, negotiated, displaced, and transformed in multiple, diverse, changing, temporal, geographic, political, economic, and social sites—as in interpersonal relations, media images, and lexicon. The marriage of an exogamous couple, for example, can create a rippling reexamination and contestation of race's significance among relatives of the couple. Racial identity develops in the context of this instability.

The varying relevance assigned to race also illustrates its unstable meaning. For example, race is assigned much relevance and, therefore, is privileged in characterizations of African Americans whereas the racial ambiguity of Latino/a Americans contributes to a tendency to unprivilege their race and, instead, emphasize their culture. Similarly, race is generally not as privileged as culture in characterizations of Asian Americans.

To many Americans, race signifies a general U.S. social hierarchy of acceptability, with white people at the apex, black people at the nadir, and all others in between. We see, for example, that police harass the black more than the white, and other minority members are typically between the extremes. However, just as the significance assigned to a race is unstable, so too are racial hierarchies: Compared with other groups of color, black Americans are not as underrepresented on network television shows because they constitute a larger market than most minorities do; and many Americans prefer to marry within their own race so that for people of color, marrying white Americans is often not a first choice.

Much of the instability in race's meaning is due to its wide-ranging intertextuality, such as its perceived relation to wealth, power, criminal behavior, and nationality, and the unstable significance of racial-minority status.[3] For example, people are embedded in multiple layers of potential minority statuses (e.g., in school or workplace) or majority status (e.g., within the family). Consequently, a white student who is in the minority at school is likely to develop a different minority identity than an Asian American student who is in the minority both at school and in the larger society; and being one of a handful of Asian Americans in a community is likely to have different effects on social relationships than being part of a substantially sized, local ethnic community some non–Asian Americans perceive as threatening.

Race's meaning is unstable because what it signifies is unstable. The instability and intertextuality of race's meaning become apparent with an examination of what race signifies. One way to identify what the concept signifies is to examine its uses.

Uses of the Concept of Race

A consideration of historical context clarifies some current uses. In that context, *race* has referred "to any general category in nature (e.g., the "race" of fishes), ancestral line (the race of Abraham) or historical identity (the English race)" (Rohmann, 1999, p. 330).

Long linked politically, economically, and morally with Western colonialism, race was regarded by white colonialists and settlers as an indicator that they, as humans, children of God, and rational representatives of civilization, were different from and morally superior to the colonized; by casting the colonized as subhuman, less developed, heathen barbarians, colonialists justified to themselves their colonialist treatment of the "others" (Perlmutter, 1999).[4] For example, they ascribed the illnesses and deaths of the colonized, not to the loss of freedom, germs colonialists brought, merciless overworking, or inadequate health care, but to the racial feebleness of the exploited; when the colonized, poor immigrants, and minorities were forced into densely packed, segregated ghettoes, their crowded living conditions were dismissed as part of the mystery and depravity of "others." Although the oppressed could have explained their plight as an effect of discrimination, colonialists felt entitled to define racial "others" and the meanings of their behaviors rather than listen to how they defined themselves. Claims that protests about injustice were signs of the decrepitation of the subjugated are reincarnated today in the surplus visibility phenomenon in which many, but certainly not all, members of a dominant group regard challenges to their "natural" world view as illegitimate, loud, excessive, and offensive efforts to gain unfair advantage (Patai, 1992).

The concept of race developed as a way to prop up social biases in the name of differences between "others" and "us"—even if doing so required casting Irish and Italians as nonwhite (Kincheloe, 1999).[5] The differences, and thus unpredictability, of others were regarded as threatening (Bauman, 1996).

From 1607 Jamestown to the first U.S. Naturalization Act to racial profiling today, race has been explicitly, officially, and informally used to categorize Americans as citizen or "other." The conflation of race and nationality underlies common interactions in which accentless Asian Americans, like their Latino/a American counterparts, are queried, "What nationality are you?" The response "I'm an American" is usually rejected with a rejoinder along the lines of, "No, I mean *really*—what are you?" Such questions do not merely reflect ignorance of the difference between nationality and ethnicity; they indicate that Asian Americans are being regarded as racially "other" than Americans in a way that accentless white and black Americans are not. Likewise, labeling children as "Amerasian"—a term perhaps first used in Pearl Buck's (1930) "novel *East Wind, West Wind* . . . referring to children of Asian and white American [parents], living in Asia" (Root, 1998, p. 262)—juxtaposes and contrasts identities as Asian and American. In such ways, race is not simply a category; it is also an action—a judgment.

In addition to a historical view of the uses of race as a basis for understanding race's meaning today, the meaning of race can be understood by directly examining its present uses in research and conversation. Those uses constitute signs of race's meaning. Even the method researchers use to assess race seems to affect racial self-identification (Johnson et al., 1997) and signals the sensitivity and complexity invoked by references to race.

On interpersonal and societal levels today, the meaning of race changes with divergent uses of the concept—whether as a defense against charges of racism or a basis for different types of racism,[6] interpretations of behaviors, social distance, or public policies. Race is sometimes used, for example, to try to give oneself credibility in racial discussions. For instance, some white

Americans claim to be disproportionately beleaguered and victimized by racism and favoritism toward minorities (Kincheloe, 1999) as a way of trying to establish their racial narratives. Upon complaining that too big a deal is made of racism, other people who look white try to protect themselves from charges of racism or award themselves credibility on the issue of race by revealing their ancestry includes a bit of some minority. Even though their appearance mitigates many of the sensitizing experiences associated with being a person of color, they use race to try to elevate their own moral, interpersonal, and political currency in racial discourse. Some people make disparaging jokes about a racial group, for instance, and then use their race as a shield when, in a variation on "some of my best friends are . . . " they reveal their own membership in that group. They thereby implicitly try to give a social legitimacy to the joke, signal that they are not racist, and set themselves up as arbiters of offensiveness for the whole racial group. In such ways, the social meaning applied to the concept of race is simultaneously hidden and yet embedded in ideology.

Consequently, appreciating the effects of those uses and ideologies on the construction of racial identity requires analysis of texts that are customarily marginalized: Whose voices are defining the relevance of race; how are various texts and narratives being used to sustain particular ideas about it; and how do different individuals process that input? How are individuals and populations breaking down, moving, transforming, and creating racial boundaries in ever-evolving relationships with other changing groups and texts (Kincheloe, 1999)?

A related basis for some of the instability in race's ascribed meaning is the fact that Asian Americans, like Latino/a Americans, have contradictory racial identities. When race is discussed, racial discourse usually pivots around the binary relationship between black and white Americans. Within those parameters, other groups are frequently ignored, appropriated by one group or another for its own benefit, or left in an ambiguous position. For example, Asian Americans are regarded by many white Americans as the near-equivalent of white when the issue is who might be a desirable neighbor but as law-breaking minorities by racially profiling police officers. Groups that are neither black nor white are part of racial politics, but simultaneously peripheral to it: They are racialized—characterized in terms of race—and deracialized—perceived as people for whom race is irrelevant (Takagi, 1993) or, in the case of the biracial, ambiguous. As one Japanese American confessed, the absence of a social location left her in limbo: "I was trying to be this 'generic' race since I didn't feel really accepted by either side." Her confused racial identity speaks to racial categories that marginalize whoever is not white or black and leaves them to be defined by what they are not.

Stereotypes constitute texts that people use to create meaning, interpret their environment and their place in it, and motivate and justify their behavior. Therefore, regarding racial stereotypes as narrative attempts to define "others" exposes and contextualizes additional uses of the concept of race. Doing so turns racial stereotypes into forums for investigating ideology, differences in power over narratives, and the interpersonal meanings of being Asian American. For example, effeminating stereotypes of Asian American men might be deconstructed in terms of underlying heterosexual rhetoric and reliance on dominant ideologies treating white men as the norm (Xiaojing, 2000).

Deconstruction of the model minority stereotype also exposes an underlying ideology that promotes behaviors reminiscent of characteristics a medieval king might want of his subjects: hard-working, law-abiding, and not likely to upset the status quo. It shows that the concept presumes the standpoint of a dominating individual or group, a set of values, and the entitlement to define model behaviors. Surely, if sophisticated understanding of oppression were a criterion of model behaviors, a dominating group would rarely deserve to be the model much less be in the cognitive position of defining model awareness. Analysis of the power and oppressiveness behind the stereotype as a sign would show how it attenuates allowable behaviors and assigns a tenuous acceptance: Challenge the status quo and the "praise" is replaced with charges of bumptiousness (see Woo, 2000).

Stereotypes frequently serve power interests. For example, casting stereotyped behaviors as somehow natural deflects attention away from other bases for people's behaviors, such as discrimination or poverty. Further hinting at the power issues underlying stereotypes and racial narratives, racially subordinated groups are sometimes not disparaged because of their purported lack of character, but instead resented because of their success: In a contemporary extension of an old viewpoint, those white Americans who regard themselves as simply standard humans sometimes define the successful nonwhite as somehow unfairly superhuman.

Feeding the stereotypes are media portrayals. Examination of media portrayals of racial minorities exposes underlying racial ideology. The exposure of minorities to those mainstream depictions push some toward alienating views of themselves as "others" and, when compounded by the experiences arising from reactions to their race, lessen the likelihood they will view themselves simply as humans.

As Foucault would predict, in addition to creating portrayals of various races, those with power, such as the media,[7] create narratives about the nature of race relations. For example, the emphasis on contentious relationships between African Americans and Korean Americans and the lack of mainstream news reports of Korean Americans in roles other than as combatants against black Americans—such as Korean Americans starting a new business or donating to black community programs, black Americans volunteering to help Koreans prepare for citizenship examinations, or joint musical performances and poetry readings (E. Kim, 1993)—form texts that become foundations for popular, interpersonal perceptions of both groups and, by extension, other Asian Americans as well. Both the issues of power and the standpoint anchoring such characterizations suggest another text bearing on the meaning of Asian Americans' race, namely, the meaning of being white.

The Meanings of Being White

A semiotic approach to understanding the psychological significance of race and the meaning of being Asian American might entail examining what not being Asian American means. Such an examination, considering both the meaning of not being a member of some other minority and the meaning of being white, would counter dominant psychological research narratives and prevalent popular views of white Americans as nonracialized humans.

Consideration might be given to the observation that one of the privileges of dominant groups is the opportunity to be unaware of their own privileged position and the significance of their race.[8] As postmodernism argues, dominance often translates into a sense of entitlement to dominate and define (e.g., knowledge). Protests by minorities, coupled with increases in U.S. minority populations, have challenged that dominance and presumption of entitlement. When white parents (in what sometimes *appears* to be a joking manner) bemoan that their child is the only white student in a class, they are often voicing alarm over their loss of a sense of entitlement to dominate numerically and the comfort associated with dominating. Likewise, claims that a nonwhite group is "taking over" a classroom, restaurant, or neighborhood are fearful voices that the distribution of power will change (e.g., the speaker might be temporarily at a disadvantage) and the speaker's group will have to make accommodations or its sense of how society should be will not be embraced by others. Some white Americans even complain when they do not have the perverse entitlement to use racial slurs some African Americans use to refer to each other.

In a field study demonstrating such a meaning to being white and racial disparities in power affecting interpersonal relationships, Stacy Lee (1996) observed that white high school students had the power to disparage Asian Americans and to establish an explanatory narrative claiming that the disparagement signaled acceptance of Asian Americans; however, Asian Americans did not make counterdisparaging "jokes," which may suggest that the claims of the former were disingenuous and Asian Americans were aware of the power differentials. Historically, minorities who did express a sense of entitlement to occasionally dominate or assume an equal status were considered "uppity"; now, a similar sentiment is manifested in less direct ways.

The degree and ways in which a person feels such a sense of entitle-ment to dominate, define reality, and set social rules affect attitudes, behav-iors, interpretations of behaviors, and, therefore, interpersonal relationships. Variations in the degree to which white Americans have such a sense of entitlement to dominate, though, further complicate the meaning of being white and, therefore, the meaning of being nonwhite.

Silenced Racialized Narratives

Generally, however, since the heyday of the Civil Rights movement, the sense of racial entitlement to dominate and define has been coupled with efforts to downplay racial narratives on the grounds that racial narratives are irrelevant or unfounded. With research in feminist psychology and studies of minorities being notable, albeit marginalized, exceptions, this pattern is seen both in psychological research and in everyday conversations in which be-haviors and attitudes are described or explained.

Mainstream psychology, for example, has given scant attention to racialized views of various American groups, complex racial experiences, differences in perceptions of and responses to racism, ways racial experiences might affect behaviors, reasons people use or do not use racial narratives, ways members of one minority might treat those of another minority group as "others," or ways people do or do not think that their race has affected their lives and outlooks. Upon recognizing the biological overlap among members of racial groups and the arbitrariness of some racial designations, many mainstream psychologists reject race as a valid scientific concept (e.g., Morris, 1998) and thereby feel justified in dismissing racial narratives. That disregard for the significance of race is disingenuous: Even though racial classifications are not always clear much less biologically relevant, race has social ramifications; and despite claims that differences related to race are really some other social differences, the associated social variables are typi-cally unexplored (Betancourt & López, 1993).[9]

Race, gender, class, sexual orientation, appearance, and handicap are windows onto the world. Together, they provide vistas of inequalities and unfairness in opportunities and resources. In society generally, the desire to board up those windows is based largely on a desire not to look at that inequality; at the very least, academia need not supply the nails. On the contrary, moving away from the tunnel vision created by modernist psycho-logical assumptions or presbyopic failure to see issues through new eyes expands viewpoints.

Because racial narratives highlighting unfairness in the distribution of power and privilege can disrupt the status quo, they are more frequently suppressed than cultural narratives outside of scholarly arenas too. The silencing of racialized narratives has taken multiple forms in everyday life. In most "multicultural curriculum" ideas, it has taken the form of sugarcoating or denying racial dynamics by looking at minority groups only as cultural groups and ignoring the relevance of racism. On the rare occasions race and class issues are included, they are customarily mentioned only with regard to minorities, which creates the impression that those issues are only relevant to minorities.

Sometimes people go to sociolinguistic lengths to pretend that race is not a relevant text through a nonuse of the concept. Many people use code words for race, such as "high risk," "multicultural," or "alien," so that racism does not appear to be the basis for their disparagement and devaluation of various groups (Pang & Shinagawa, 1995; P. Williams, 2001). In the United States today, references to "ethnicity," like references to "diversity," are typically used to refer to racial minorities; both terms are used as codes for race or as a way to avoid discussions of race.

When some people cross-dress racial concerns as other issues or attempt to sidetrack the discourse by quibbling about tangential issues to avoid major ones, discourse is restricted in an effort to avoid appearing to be racist. Insistence on the use of Aboriginal American caricatures as "mascots" for schools and teams, for instance, mark attempts to hide the sense of entitlement to dominate behind specious claims that the caricatures honor Aboriginal Americans. The fact that the views of Aboriginal Americans are not respected speaks to that sense of entitlement.

The goal of "celebrating diversity" in a multicultural curriculum provides an example here, too. Because people seldom think of celebrating racism, poverty, and unequal access to opportunities, references to "celebrating diversity," like celebrating a birthday or holiday, cast diversity as a playful, almost trivial, break from the norm. Accordingly, a curriculum designed to celebrate diversity is usually one that ignores the consequential, skirts examinations of bias, focuses on different types of food, or promotes the idea that race is irrelevant by emphasizing cross-racial physical similarity—as though teaching children "you have a nose, he has a nose too" is going to help them get along or undermine interracial divisiveness.

The framing of racial issues in familiar and comfortable terms often has the effect of silencing racial narratives (Mann & Kelley, 1997). For example, too often racial narratives about Asian Americans focus solely on the ways in which they are victims of racism and minimize ways in which they are perpetrators. Some white Americans, claiming unawareness of any elevated status arising from their whiteness, try to delegitimate racial narratives that cast them as other than a neutral, raceless normal. In a series of interviews with exogamous couples, for instance, most of the white American men defined their identity in terms of their humanity or nationality;

rejected a racial identity, which they associated with overt racism and white supremacists; and denied any significance to spousal differences in racial privilege while trying to prevent their wives from exploring their cultural and racial experiences or identities (Pang & Shinagawa, 1995).

This boxing of racial narratives denies their everyday relevance and, like the belittlement of evidence of racism, does not take the narratives seriously. For example, when University of Connecticut, Asian American students suffered racist assaults by other students and brought the problem to the attention of the dean, the only action the dean apparently took was to write a memo saying that the students were "satisfied that their complaint was handled in a serious and solemn manner"—implying that giving them the opportunity to voice their unhappiness was sufficient action (Morse, 1995, p. 349). Similar responses have occurred at other campuses, such as the University of California, Berkeley (Delucchi & Do, 1996). Those translations of racial issues into a pro forma mimicry of concern slyly negate racial narratives.

Another invidious way some people try to sidetrack, delegitimate, and suppress racialized narratives is to disingenuously and rhetorically ask whether racism exists in countries outside the United States—implying that racism in the United States is not really all that bad or that racism is human nature and, therefore, nothing can be done about it.[10] Denial of the legitimacy of racial narratives also commonly takes the form of dismissing the subordinated groups' protestations of unfairness as whining, their efforts to gain equality as offensive, their disparaged goals as unfair, and their tactics as unpleasant (Patai, 1992). Disdain for them is thereby made to seem justified to some eyes.

The ways in which locally created, multiple meanings of race and various racial narratives reflect, identify, inform, and create boundaries of racial identity and affect behaviors and experiences are potentially rich areas for psychology (Omi & Winant, 1994). However, by treating race as an independent variable, overlooking its intertextual meanings, and ignoring the impact of the chronic negating of racialized narratives on how people construct their identities and behave, psychologists plug their own ears, gag themselves, and leave the field to be shaped by others. This move is consequential not only because racial interpretations, along with competing ones, need to be repeatedly reintroduced into psychological discourse; it is important because, in the contestation of the meaning of race, whose voices are heard—determined in large part by social, economic, and political factors—affects the meanings created, particularly in the case of people who simply reiterate ideas they have heard others espouse.

The void left by mainstream psychology's repeated silencing of racial narratives leaves the impression that psychological characterizations can be complete without consideration of race, concedes racial narratives to other disciplines, contributes to the silencing and oppression of minority voices, and by default certifies racial interpretations that are devoid of psychological perspectives. Understandings would be enhanced by analysis of issues such as the situations in which race is considered a relevant text, how the concept is used in social situations, ways in which people are racialized, and perceived response options to racialization.

Culture: Significance From Text

In contrast to race, "culture" has taken on what postmodernism calls a heroic position in both popular and research portrayals of Asian Americans: The concept has been assigned particular significance as a basis for many behaviors, such as academic achievement. Deconstructing or taking a hermeneutic approach to this hyperprivileged text sheds light on why Asian Americans behave the way they do and the meaning of being Asian American in this postmodern age.

Especially in depictions of someone else's culture, as in most operational definitions, the ways in which the meaning of culture is constantly being appropriated and the ways in which culture is an ongoing creation in a continuing, discursive dialectic of text, interpretation, and cultural, temporal, and interpersonal social location is frequently minimized (Bruns, 1987). Instead, cultures and, therefore, ethnic groups as cultural groupings, are commonly distinguished in terms of an unchanging set of defining characteristics with decontextualized meaning: a learned, shared, internalized, set of rules or social constructions; secular and nonsecular beliefs; ways of interpreting behaviors, events, and situations (Bandlamudi, 1994; Fabrega & Nguyen, 1992); styles of interacting; behavior patterns; norms; communication styles; language; symbols; knowledge; expectations; values, and attitudes.

Much as with claims of behavior regularities, the concept of a distinct, coherent culture is predicated on definitions of sameness and difference. That is, like an individual's identity, a culture's identity is constituted by an underlying tension between what signifies sameness and what signifies difference among cultures (Polkinghorne, 1988). The fluid boundaries defining cultural similarities and differences do not simply exist "out there." Rather than being objective, then, descriptions of behaviors as cultural are often based on the identification of objectified similarities and differences (Segal & Handler, 1995).

Today's characterizations of a culture might seem objective, as might attributing cultural roots to behaviors; but that objectivity is bred of modernist illusion. Despite occasionally pointed recognition that American behaviors are cultural too, those behaviors that differ from a (commonly ethnocentric Anglo-American) norm are most likely to be attributed to culture. Even though many behaviors do not have the same meaning when displayed at varied times, in different countries, or by different individuals, only behaviors that differ from that norm are customarily considered cultural.

Also arguing against the idea that cultural explanations for behaviors are objective is the frequent adhibition of particular, cognitively accessible, hyperprivileged aspects of culture, such as "saving face" and "avoiding shame" in the case of narratives about Asian Americans. For example, objectivity does not drive the claim that "The avoidance of shame is the principal technique used to control the behavior of family members in Asian families" (Y-O. Kim, 1995, p. 75). The conclusion reflects a presumption about the quality and generalizability of the data upon which that claim is made, decisions about which behaviors constitute control techniques, the conceptual isolation of "avoidance of shame" as a technique, and the privileging of that aspect of culture.

In contrast, the use of hermeneutics and deconstruction could expose the seams in what is taken for granted in the creation and use of the concept of culture to produce a better understanding of the concept and to be in a position to analyze cultural narratives. Take, for example, a postmodern analysis of culture "in terms of a constantly shifting process of signification" (Dickens & Fontana, 1994, p. 7). It shows that the meaning of the concept of, for instance, Asian American culture, is built from its *différance* from other ideas or signs: Much as the meaning of a seven-card stud poker-hand depends on the hole cards, the meaning of concepts is contingent on other texts that do not have immediately apparent and static meaning or relevance. Texts bearing on the meaning of the concept of culture and its significance for Asian Americans include aspects of American culture, which in turn are related to subtexts such as gender, class, geography, race, and historical context; aspects of a particular Asian culture, such as Vietnamese culture, which is itself heterogeneous across generational, gender, class, geographic, and historical lines; the experiences of Asian Americans who are creating their culture; the negotiation of culture by people who differ in their education, generation, economic class, geographical location, gender; and ways in which U.S. culture affects perceptions of Asia, Asian American cultures, and the experiences of Asian Americans.

Concepts of Asia and the United States

Although the conceptualization of any culture could be deconstructed in reference to an endless galaxy of texts, the concept of culture in discussions of Asian American cultures is typically and broadly constructed in relation to only two, hyperprivileged signifying poles, mainstream U.S. and Asian—particularly "traditional" Asian—cultures. In this false opposition, other minority cultures are largely ignored; and U.S. and Asian (American) cultures are cast as mutually exclusive and oppositional. This bifurcation, reinforced by stereotypes, is replicated in popular parlance and it affects the identity of Asian Americans, as in:

> I am Filipino American, but . . . for years . . . sometimes I considered myself either Filipino in a given situation, or American in [another situation]. I felt as if I was living in a dichotomous world where a person must identify with one or the other, but cannot be both.

Inasmuch as the concept of "the culture of Asian Americans" is broadly constructed by its *différance* from U.S. and Asian cultures, understanding its meaning can begin with examining the constructed meanings of those texts. Much as shared experiences at cancer support groups in some ways define what having cancer means for participants, the stories told by and about a culture constitute explicitly or implicitly evoked texts that provide culture's meaning.

Therefore, one way to investigate the meaning of the "culture of Asian Americans" and, more specifically, one related text, U.S. culture, is to analyze stories American culture tells about itself and about Asian cultures. Those stories can be identified by examining texts produced by and about U.S. culture, such as myths, national policies, and other narratives that reveal the United States' self-image and views of other countries (Lowe, 1998). When, for example, the United States characterizes itself in U.S. history textbooks as strong, heroic, kind, relatively young, and holding the promise of equal opportunity, prosperity, and progress, it is painting a cultural self-portrait through which readers are encouraged to view the present (see Loewen, 1995). In effect, the portrayal promotes the idea that, when trying to explain why Asian Americans—including the U.S.-born—do not have incomes commensurate with their education (L. Lee, 1998), institutional inequality is not the place to look, any racist basis will some day be outgrown by our young nation, and the disappearance of racism will be a natural result of the nation's maturation and is, therefore, nothing to be concerned about now. Developing such intertextual analyses helps to clarify narratives about ethnic, racial, gender, or other oppressed groups.

Such an analysis would again highlight the selective application of cultural narratives: Mainstream psychology most often refers to culture in descriptions of the different or "other" (e.g., discussions of gender differences or in cross-cultural psychology); essentialized views of Asian Americans and

Latino/a Americans as Asians and Latino/a respectively, reinforce that tendency. Less honored are narratives emphasizing Asian Americans' identification with the United States, their gender, or age cohort, for example. Much as fortune cookies are commonly viewed as a dessert indigenous to China rather than a confection developed in response to American myths and a marketing niche, Asian Americans' behaviors are too often interpreted solely in terms of an Asian culture, cultural complexity is obscured, and the effects of other pressures are minimized in modernist frameworks that sometimes take the concept of culture for granted.[11]

Fitting within that framework and underpinning many comparisons of ethnic groups is the assumption that ethnicity is a marker for cultural characteristics. Moreover, those characteristics are commonly assumed to be based on the heritage of a centuries-old culture. In public discourse, even those Asian Americans several generations removed from their immigrant ancestors supposedly retain deeply ingrained Asian cultural influences impermeable or only dimly influenced by experiences in the United States. That portrayal has supported interpersonal bias as well as political and economic agendas, as in efforts to rationalize the incarceration of Japanese Americans during World War II with a "Once a 'Jap' always a 'Jap'" mentality. In those situations, the purportedly deeply ingrained values and behavior patterns implicitly reflect unchanging Asian cultures; consequently, how long ago the emigration took place is deemed irrelevant. In fact, however, cultural attitudes, values, and behaviors brought to the United States do not remain unchanged any more than the likelihood of Asian Americans developing particular illnesses is independent of their American diet and other U.S. environmental influences. Although values are created and exist in temporal and social contexts and invoking a value in different situations can transform its meaning, the portrayals imply a stable set of enduring values motivating behaviors across situations (Feldman, Mont-Reynaud, & Rosenthal, 1992).[12]

Orientalizing Narratives

Orientalizing narratives, privileging centuries-old cultural heritage and propped up by perceptions of Asian Americans as "others," are central to many cultural portrayals in which Asian American cultures have been grossly equated and temporally reduced to the presumed values and orientations of some distant Asian past. The behaviors of European Americans today are not customarily explained in terms of Western cognitive influences only 200 to 400 years old, as from John Calvin, because that influence is viewed as far removed from present day, proximal influences. Nevertheless, although few education specialists, psychologists, or social workers specializing in the study of Asian Americans intend to conjure images of Asian American parents quoting Confucius or the *Tao Te Ching* to their children, the behaviors of Asian Americans are commonly explained in terms of the ideas of men 2500 years ago, such as Guatama Buddha and Confucius (e.g., S. Chan, 1992; Ferguson, 1995; Min, 1995a; R. Wong, 1995). As Kenyon Chan (1996) noted, referring to Confucius, Buddhism, and aspects of ancient Asian cultures to explain the behavior of Asian Americans is akin to thinking one understands Chinese Americans by picking up items from a Chinatown curio shop while failing to go behind the store to ask the Chinese shopkeepers about their thoughts and experiences.

Ironically, Orientalizing narratives unprivilege the current and particular values, perceptions, and choices of Asian Americans today who are really of interest. In one study, for instance, while a sample of mostly *sansei* (i.e., third-generation Japanese American) study participants reported that they hesitated to be assertive because they did not want to appear stupid or have others laugh at them, the researchers interpreted that hesitancy as an indication of a cultural imperative to "save face"—even though none of the Asian Americans cited that reason (Fukuyama & Coleman, 1992). If Americans of other ethnic groups responded in ostensibly the same way, an Orientalizing narrative and lexicon is unlikely to have been proffered. Similarly, without evidence that parents mention Confucius or are guided by his ideology, researchers often point to Confucian values passed on from parents to account for high educational achievement among Asian Americans. When Asian American children and parents are asked about educational achievement, however, they instead report that they emphasize education because of racism and economic needs (B. Schneider & Lee, 1990). Nevertheless, a conceptual leap is often made from an assumption that a behavior is culturally rooted to the assumption that the culture is an undifferentiated, Orientalized culture.

For example, the Asian pole used to define Asian American cultures is sometimes described in terms of a vague, atemporal, "traditional" Asian culture somewhere in Asia (e.g., Uba, 1994a).[13] At other times, "traditional" is implicitly equated with "Asian," and "modern" with "American," resulting in a dichotomous caricature. In both cases, Asian (American) cultures are homogenized. However, the assumption that an Asian American group, much less Asian Americans in general, can be defined in terms of a singular culture is brought up short upon weighing the differing Asian cultural backgrounds of even one Asian American group, such as Chinese Americans—with ancestors from Cambodia, Hong Kong, Laos, the People's Republic of China, Taiwan, Thailand, Vietnam, as well as different economic classes and regions in the United States.

Moreover, because their ancestors came from different countries and at different times in history, various Asian American groups are not reconciling the same experiences in America to the same cultural traditions. Post-1965 arrivals to the United States have not shared the historical, political, economic, and social experiences of earlier generations of Asian Americans so most Asian American cultures today are, in some ways, not even continuations of "traditional" Asian *American* cultures of the late nineteenth and early twentieth century. For Japanese Americans, an initially *Meiji*-era culture transformed over the generations, has produced a synthesis of values and experiences different from that of recent Japanese immigrants. Yet little attempt is made to identify which segments of which cultures are being used as a model for the concept of Asian American culture.

Even when a specific Asian culture is invoked as a text, it too is often Orientalized and Asian Americans are made to seem to be essentially Asian or foreigners. For instance, contextualizing suicide rates among Japanese Americans in terms of *hara kiri* (Baker, 1994; Pearson, 1995) egregiously Orientalizes and essentializes them as products of a premodern Japanese culture.

Compounding the emphasis on the stability of Asian cultural characteristics—which encourages the neglect of disequilibriums, doubts, and changes (Meacham, 1999)—popular, mainstream notions about Asian cultural influences are customarily anachronistic and imprecise, if not mythical. The curriculum in primary and secondary education typically offers vague images of everywhere in the world populated predominantly by people of color and that no doubt contributes to prevalent yet hazy, essentialized, popular narratives about people of color as "others."

The creation of homogenizing, decontextualizing, totalizing concepts, narratives, operational definitions, cultural classifications, and characterizations has been among the effects of hyperprivileging Orientalizing narratives and "traditional" Asian culture; innumerable variations, hidden negations, multiple forms, multidimensionality, and complex meanings that give behaviors and values their living meaning have been bypassed; the particular Asian culture underlying Asian Americans' ethnicity has been commonly regarded as irrelevant in public discourse; and concepts, such as culture and immigrant status, have been poorly differentiated bases for explanations. When anachronistic, totalizing narratives about the nature of Asian American cultures are taken as more real than the ways individuals construct their culture for themselves and their collective, the result is a hyperreality in which Orientalized caricatures of Asian Americans are regarded as more real than the ways Asian Americans actually are: Standard modernist fare, media portrayals, and stereotypes of Asian cultures and Asian Americans eclipse the cultures Asian Americans actually create. The resulting caricature and evisceration of diversity can lead to culturally inappropriate public services intended to meet the needs of Asian Americans.

Deconstruction of Orientalizing narratives raises questions about much that has been taken for granted. What bases for differences between Asian Americans and non-Asian Americans are being overlooked by the hyperprivileging of cultural bases for behaviors? Is the disparaging appellation "F.O.B." (for Fresh Off the Boat) a sign of Asian Americans' desire to reject that Orientalized identity? On what basis was the determination ever made that Asian-identified values ascribed to Asian Americans today are actually based on Confucian ideals? Supposing that Confucius and Asian Americans today value honesty does not necessarily mean that Asian Americans value honesty because of Confucianism.[14] Neither the same values nor the same source of those values can be easily inferred from the "same" behaviors. For example, quiet public behaviors of *nisei* (i.e., second-generation Japanese Americans) might have been rooted in socialization by their parents who grew up in thin-walled housing in Japan; their own experiences with porous, concentration-camp walls; other forms of discrimination; or some combination. The facts do not speak for themselves. Behaviors do not have stable referents. Yet attempts to tie behaviors to purported cultural roots sometimes are predicated on tautological assumptions about the cultural meaning of those behaviors.

Even if some values and behaviors of Asian Americans have roots in Eastern philosophy, what is the justification for assuming the survival of only particular values? Why have Confucian rather than, say, Taoist beliefs and Buddhist values predominated in fact and in narratives if, indeed, they do? Why do particular Confucian values still influence behavior, if they do, while the vast array of values Confucius laid down about government structure did not discourage Asians from immigrating to a country whose political structure was different from the one Confucius promoted?

Eschewing taken-for-granted meanings and uses, an examination of privileged and unprivileged intertextual meanings in various local uses can clarify the meaning of cultural explanations of behaviors. Thorough, ongoing hermeneutic examinations of relevant concepts could enhance the grounding of policy recommendations.

Metaphors of Culture

An intertextual analysis of the concept of Asian American culture can entail examination of its *différance* in relation to texts such as the United States, Asia, Oriental, and race; the concept's meaning can also be exposed with a more direct assessment of it as a sign. As postmodernists assert, an analysis of signs, such as references to Asian Americans' "home" countries, can reveal assumptions embedded in rhetorical choices (Bazerman, 1987).

Both in popular and scholarly parlance, metaphoric signs have subtextual meanings. Subtexts, perhaps unconsciously brought to mind by metaphors, orient attention and interpretations in particular directions while obscuring alternatives. Postmodern analyses of the metaphors used in references to Asian Americans' cultural status reveal assumptions, contradictions, and meanings that feed implicit, taken-for-granted ideas about Asian Americans.

One metaphor is that individuals have membership in cultural groups. Membership, in turn, is implicitly defined by "having" particular characteristics privileged as definers of a culture;[15] and criteria for "having" traits signifying membership are taken for granted.

This metaphor homogenizes the presumed cultural characteristics of individual members. The idea that people have or do not have membership in a culture imposes a binary simplicity to the relationships of various individuals to the culture. Even a reading that allows for shades of membership hides differences in the degree to which Asian Americans feel like members in a variety of realms and the significance membership has for them.

Use of the membership metaphor encourages a focus on shared, general characteristics defining membership and diverts attention from other issues, including why some Asian Americans develop particular behavior patterns while others do not; why some cultural values, beliefs, and behavior patterns have been maintained and others have been cast aside or subtly reshaped by different individuals; and which variations are defined as still part of the culture and which are not. It contributes to the treatment of ethnicity as a characteristic standing in for culture, which is problematic because while all members of an ethnic group might be said to share a culture, they have actually partaken and interpreted different aspects of a diverse and multifaceted culture.

At other times, when Asian Americans are said to have cultural characteristics, culture sounds like a possession (Segal & Handler, 1995)—more specifically, a family heirloom given to us—as in, "The cultural values are passed down to succeeding generations." The heirloom metaphor, even more than the membership metaphor or the metaphor of reified cultural influences channeling through conduit humans, implies culture has a static nature. However, a culture's emerging and receding influences transform each generation; each generation and individual, encountering and creating interpretations and responses to different situations, transforms the heterogeneous, multifaceted culture passed on within and across generations. Each breathes life into cultures and makes culture a verb (J. Nagel, 1994). By failing to signify the constant creation of a culture and its heterogeneity, this metaphor downplays the consciousness, agency, and choices behind culture's creation; bypasses ways in which individuals vary in their readings of and propensity to play out cultural scripts; and minimizes ways in which the identity of a cultural group emerges from contingent, particular, and local meanings created in multiple sites (Segal & Handler, 1995).

The heirloom metaphor turns a blind eye to much of what makes culture an interesting and relevant human creation—the flux, the ways in which people continually negotiate and transform culture in ongoing sociohistorical, developmental contexts and in comparison to different texts (Bandlamudi, 1994). It reinforces the Orientalization of present-day Asian Americans as the current holders of the basically same, almost primordial, Asian cultures and fails to address which aspects of which culture are being transmitted in what ways to which people situated in what positions in society. Rather than be distorted as coherent and integrated totalities (Denzin, 1994), ethnic cultures could be viewed in terms of their changing, simultaneous, multiple, and intertextual meanings. Insofar as the concepts we use can limit our perceptions, a shift away from the standard metaphors would suggest new ways of looking at culture—for example, as simultaneously a cause and a result of the behavior of individuals—and perhaps new interpretations of empirical research.

From a postmodern perspective, culture might be viewed as a network of meanings and stories expressed through narratives that bind a group (Polkinghorne, 1988). Rather than be equated with a set of characteristics, culture might be viewed as a historically bound, conceptual invention or tool established to promote and symbolize group cohesion, status relations, values, and behaviors (Hobsbawm, 1983); temporally group people for cognitive ease; or instigate some social action. As a tool or even an epistemological framework, culture becomes a dynamic concept instead of a simple description of English fluency or beliefs.

Such a conceptualization exposes suppressed issues: What meanings are being ascribed to cultures and communities? Given that cultures cannot be viewed from an independent standpoint that is nowhere, what effects does a viewer's standpoint have on how cultures and ethnic groups are perceived? From what quarters, in relation to which other texts and for what reasons do cultural change and resistance to change emerge? In what ways do those holding non-normative attitudes destabilize a cultural group by itching for negotiations over what the culture is and what identification with a culture means (Bandlamudi, 1994)? In what ways are minority communities and cultures being constructed as racial negations or oppositions? What are the specific policy consequences of culturally homogenizing Asian American ethnic groups?

A postmodern frame of reference brings attention to the fact that those cultural metaphors are not used as racial metaphors. For instance, race is not implicitly prized as an heirloom. These days when many people want to avoid racial narratives, little mention is made of passing down over the generations racial behavior patterns which have arisen from experiences with discrimination.

The fact that psychology's cultural narratives have been modernist has meant that rich, intertextual reference, the unending and varied relationships created among signifiers, and the creation of culture's meaning have been ignored. An expansion of textual analyses by psychologists would be a step toward interdisciplinary investigations, an amplification of psychological voices in such discourses, and, perhaps, a discourse more phenomenologically relevant and helpful to study participants.

Culture as Explanation

Despite the inadequate examination of intertextual meanings of culture, explanations of the behaviors of Asian Americans have spun on cultural vortices. The selective use of the concept of culture to explain behaviors suggests bias. For example, similarities in the behaviors of Asian Americans and Asians in Asian countries are assumed to be cultural but similarities between European Americans and Europeans are rarely even noted.[16]

Ethnicity, like race and gender, is an insufficient explanation for behavior.[17] Many cultural explanations are as well. Based on a correspondence between a behavior and an a priori set of characteristics regarded as cultural for Asian Americans, descriptions and explanations of Asian Americans' behaviors frequently have been facile, post hoc, reductionist references to culture as an empirically unassessed formal or final cause (e.g., Ferguson, 1995; Uba, 1994a). Even though most studies are correlational and therefore do not show causality, influential psychologists "have concluded that there is now substantial evidence to document [a] culture-behaviour relationship, [and that] individuals generally act in ways that correspond to cultural influences and expectations" (Berry, 1997, p. 6). Although that conclusion is widely assumed, it has been tautological: A set of characteristics or behaviors is "known" to be due to culture only because it is defined that way. For example, the conclusion that Asian Americans work hard because of their culture reifies culture as an explanation without identifying which aspects of their culture influence the behavior, why hard work by Asian Americans is regarded as cultural, how their hard work is rooted differently from the hard work by others, and at what point in the transition from work to hard work the working becomes assignable to Asian Americans' culture.

Inasmuch as direct relationships seem to require fewer assumptions than indirect ones, Ockham's Razor encourages the assumption of a direct relationship between culture and behavior. The relationship is given additional cognitive force when a modernist order presumably underpins generalizations about that culture-behavior link.

Modernist psychology's use of questionnaires to search for behavioral regularities has contributed to the customary identification of vague, overarching, cross-situational behavioral consistencies or cultural effects in lieu of local, contextualized descriptions of people choosing behaviors based on their values or situational expediency. By not clearly differentiating how people have constructed culture as a network of concepts, categories, implicit theories, perceptual habits, and choices, or how specific aspects of culture influence behavior (Betancourt & López, 1993; Wade & Tavris, 1995), typical cultural explanations are empty. Cultural explanations of differences between Asian Americans and non-Asian Americans have frequently come at the cost of suppressing ambiguity, complexity, within-group difference, and between-group similarities, while pushing potentially meaningful cultural characteristics uncomfortably close to stereotypes (Meyerowitz, Richardson, Hudson, & Leedham, 1998).

Acceptance of facile cultural explanations may be especially broad and easy when the behaviors explained are those of an "other": Insofar as people tend to form more differentiated, precise concepts of in-group than of out-group members (Powlishta, 1995), undifferentiated generalizations about the out-group are probably more likely to be regarded as satisfactory accounts. Further suggesting that Asian Americans are being seen as undifferentiated "others" in cultural narratives, rarely are differences among Asian Americans explained in terms of cultural differences, except when acculturation differences are proposed. Especially when cultural explanations of Asian Americans' behaviors correspond to cultural stereotypes, additional explanations of the behavior are usually halted.

The essentialization of Asian Americans in cultural terms also promotes the tendency to regard cultural explanations as sufficient and culturally rooted behaviors as the near equivalent of natural—as in "Another quite plausible explanation [for the social skills of Asian Americans] is that the Asian culture naturally socializes its young in more compliant, self-controlled behaviors" (Feng & Cartledge, 1996, p. 235). Cultural explanations are made to seem natural or even like a deterministic set of influences (e.g., "Asian Americans don't get into crime much because of their culture"). Why did the Asian Americans behave the way they did? The deterministic and reductionist reply is "Their culture made them do that." Even a chicken crossing the road is assigned more agency than that. Simple cultural explanations only seem natural and sufficient in a void created by removing free will, burying society's disparities, and ignoring other texts.

Viewing culture and dominant narratives about it as contemporary constructions serving contemporary purposes helps to contextualize them. For example, whereas in Kosovo, the culture of an ethnic group can trigger violence, in the United States culture is generally a more benign and less controversial basis for differences than socioeconomic status or race. Here, cultural explanations do not challenge the myths of American acceptance of cultural diversity and equal opportunity. Much as the model minority stereotype is used as a bludgeon against other minorities and as a way of emphasizing what is reportedly brought to situations rather than structural restrictions, the privileging of cultural descriptions and explanations of Asian Americans' behaviors displaces, represses, and negates explanations in terms of other influences, notably socioeconomic status, race, and oppressive practices. Indeed, romanticized versions of Asian cultures—which seem to harken back to a time when minorities were largely silenced and, in Ronald Reagan's words, "Before we [white Americans] knew we had a race problem" (Winter, 1992, p. 789)—are even said to be "admired" as long as they seem empty or do not undermine the status quo.

The public frequently uses the concept of culture as a dismissive, default explanation for behaviors that it cannot or will not try to understand, or euphemistically uses it to describe differences arising from racial experiences, as in claims that racial fights are about cultural differences. For example, casual claims that Asian Americans value education because of their culture can be used to hide desires for easy, nonthreatening portrayals that paint over actual motivations, and circumstances.

Other events support this reading of the purposes behind cultural narratives. For instance, claims of admiration for "traditional" Asian values dissipate as the behaviors supposedly based on those values threaten the distribution of opportunities. Then, the behaviors are no longer seen in nonthreatening, exotic, Orientalizing terms; complaints about a failure to Americanize are leveled; or, in the case of affirmative action dictates, alternative criteria are advocated so that the behavior becomes less advantageous. Cultural explanations, particularly those that are Orientalizing, can become colonialist tools.

When dominant narratives are presented as objective or neutral, they customarily become the presumptively natural and correct frame of reference. However, that framework has biases and attaches unexplored meanings to seemingly simple, straight-forward explanations. When the meanings of the concept of culture are left unanalyzed or unspecified and links between culture and behavior are claimed but not shown, cultural explanations of behaviors can become mere superstition. As popular culture absorbs such narratives, equated with knowledge, a psychologistic hyperreality is created; knowledge is thwarted.

CHAPTER 5

Acculturation and Assimilation

Acculturation has been defined as a process by which an individual's behaviors and a group's cultural knowledge, identity, and behavior styles change in the direction of those of the dominant group (LaFromboise et al., 1993). Whether acculturation is regarded as a form of assimilation (Gordon, 1964), assimilation is thought of as an aspect of acculturation (Berry, 1988; Kitano, 1989), or the two are equated (H. Nguyen, Messé, & Stollak, 1999), degree of acculturation or assimilation is among the principal psychological texts forming the basis for narratives about Asian Americans and other groups of color and is ascribed predictor and explanatory roles (Zane & Sasao, 1992).

Acculturation, however, is not a privileged variable in mainstream psychology where the acculturation of European Americans is unstudied. Instead of being explained in terms of acculturation, their behaviors are accounted for in terms of attitudes and thinking processes. By contrast, degree of acculturation is a ready explanas when accounting for ostensibly similar behavior in Asian Americans.

By hyperprivileging degree of acculturation in descriptions of Asian Americans and Latino/a Americans, researchers run the risk of essentializing the relationship between those minorities and the mainstream U.S. culture. Additional types of relationships to the dominant culture are obscured; relationships to other cultural groups are suppressed; and thornier reasons for exclusion from the mainstream are deemphasized.

From a postmodern perspective, focusing on the acculturation of Asian Americans without reference to other texts is turning a blind eye to the complex, intertextual meanings of being Asian American and the changing, varied intertextual meanings of acculturation in diverse psychosocial locations. By using postmodern analytical methods and beginning with texts hidden in metaphoric references, this chapter exposes intertextual meanings that are unanalyzed and underappreciated in psychological discourse; accesses acculturation's meaning by considering the varying application of acculturation narratives to different racial groups; and shows ways in which acculturation models and tests have been infected with modernist assumptions.

Metaphors of Acculturation and Limits of Race

Given postmodernism's premise that language has a transformative role in the creation and representation of knowledge, an analysis of signification should shed light on the meaning of acculturation. It should also suggest a genealogy of conceptualizations of acculturation.

Teasing out conventional metaphors used to describe acculturation gives us a peephole into its multiple meanings and hidden texts. Perhaps the descriptive metaphor of assimilation and acculturation most often used in U.S. social sciences and in the culture at large has been that assimilation and acculturation are like moving into, or sometimes simply going to, a "host's" home: An Asian country is referred to as the "home country" of immigrants and U.S.-born Asian Americans alike (e.g., Feldman et al., 1992) and the United States is considered to be a "host" culture (e.g., Blanchard, 1991; Lien, 1994). Even extending beyond official restrictions on naturalization, as exemplified by the 1790 Naturalization Act which restricted naturalization to the white, the United States has long been regarded viscerally as a white man's country; the United States and white Americans are still viewed as the "hosts" not only to the foreign-born but to all people of color except Aboriginal Americans. Therefore, the social meaning of acculturation and its privileging as a text have long been linked with race: Even when people of color have become very acculturated, they have still been considered to be outsiders.

The implication of this metaphor is that, for the most part, the foreign-born and people of color have the status of guests, which implies a not-fully and never-fully integrated status. Those regarded as guests must be on their best behavior, earn their rights, and fit into the standards established by the owners of the home without becoming overly familiar—or they are not welcome.

Thus, notwithstanding myths about America's embrace of diversity, the onus of accommodation is on the "other" rather than shared by the dominant group.[1] Indeed, claims that the United States is becoming increasingly "multicultural" more accurately refer to demographic changes in the ethnic populations than to changes in core U.S. culture.[2] Although demographic changes bring about a de facto broadening of U.S. culture, the core U.S. culture has not incorporated many of those changes. That recalcitrance is subversive: Like translating the refusal to accommodate to the feelings of others as a failure to be politically correct, expecting others to do all the accommodating diverts attention from the issue of why and how a society that ostensibly embraces diversity closes off cultural options.

An implicit meaning in the guest-host metaphor is that the guests, the "other," should not try to dominate but should instead know "their place." If people cast as guests want extensive changes in society, they are thought to ask for too much and to be out of line; if they persist, they are asked to leave. So a common rejoinder to any protest by people of color is, "Go back where you came from." That is not an order normally hurled at white protestors. Accordingly, the guest metaphor reinforces attitudes toward people of color as interlopers: As guests, their status is perpetually tenuous. It is the host's prerogative to make accommodations or not.

Just as no one narrative provides complete and final knowledge, neither does deconstructing one metaphor. Consider too, then, the metaphor of acculturation as becoming a team member—as in being "a member of that culture." Again, this metaphor speaks to the necessity of entrants learning the ways of the dominant and seeking roughly the same goals, without trying to disrupt the existing distribution of power and status, much as an animal must demonstrate to the dominant alpha male a willingness to fit into the existing order.

Criticisms of minorities for not acculturating or assimilating to a devalued role are sometimes façades for fears about the consequences of pluralism. So Asian Americans speaking an Asian language in a mall occasionally encounter disdainful glares for not speaking English while the high school requirement for learning a "foreign" language is not met with a lot of opposition because it is not read as a sign of a push for pluralism.

Language is frequently treated as a salient indicator of a willingness to fit in; consequently, not speaking English is often perceived as an especially irksome refusal or failure to acculturate in prescribed ways and suggests a rejection of established hierarchies and relationships. Accordingly, more criticism is probably directed against Vietnamese Americans speaking Vietnamese in a shopping mall than to Swedish immigrants speaking Swedish because of this braiding of otherness, race, and acculturation. This perhaps unconscious orientation toward the status quo may be one basis for mainstream interest in acculturation as a defining variable of Asian Americans. Acculturation is not used to classify third-generation European Americans but is used as a barometer for classifying third-generation Asian Americans (e.g., Kitano, 1970) and Latino/a Americans because white immigrants seem to have a one-lifespan identity as the "other" whereas people of color are often considered to be "others" as long as endogamous generations are racially identifiable as nonwhite.

Today the social meaning of acculturation is still tied to race and basic social acceptance is still largely contingent on signals of a willingness to join the team, albeit in a subaltern role. Indeed, acculturation generally seems to be sine qua non, though insufficient, for the acceptance of racial minorities, perhaps because signs of a willingness to assimilate to the existing social order makes racial otherness seem less threatening.

A link between acculturation and race is also illustrated by a Filipina American:

> Because of racism, I decided to become as American as possible. I would learn their ways, associate with Euro-Americans, engage in American recreation, and most importantly, I would learn to understand their sense of humor and wit. I remember staying up late every night to watch the "Tonight Show" because I thought if I could understand the humor, then I'll be just as smart and witty as any Euro-American. I wanted so badly to be accepted. It came to a point where I disassociated myself from my own race. When I did come across any Filipinos, I would pretend not to know the language and culture.

As in this immigrant's statement, when many foreign-born Asian Americans and white Americans refer to "Americans," they mean white Americans; they refer to minorities as, for example, "Asian" or "Latino." The foreign-born are demonstrating a sense of alienation from the concept of "American."

That way of thinking is reinforced when the terms "acculturation" and "Americanization" are used as codes for being indistinguishable from white Americans. It is manifested in conversation when "all-American good looks" almost always refer to someone white. Insofar as acculturation is the product of teaching thinking habits, values, and versions of knowledge that define a culture, acculturated schoolchildren learn a limited meaning of being American. They are socialized into thinking that the history of white Americans is American history, for example; and overlooking the history of minorities sends the old message, "If you're not white, you're not right," — or, "you don't matter."

A consequence of conflating "American" with "white American" is the presumption, alluded to in the previous chapter, that white Americans are entitled to define and dominate. Therefore, when a racial (or homosexual) minority population reaches a size that is phenomenologically regarded as too big, various segments of the established population admit to an uncomfortable feeling that the minority is "taking over" the community. Similarly, intraethnic interdependence is perceived as cliquishness, which is also considered threatening and maladaptive to those segments of society. Their view of how social life should be is being challenged and they balk at the task of adjusting; they want the minority to fit in (or, in the case of homosexuals, become invisible) and become superficially "like I am."

Thus, the meaning of acculturation is contingent on texts defining who is American. The prevalent racial paradigm describing Americans as white or black, albeit hyperprivileging the former, creates doubt that members of groups that are neither white nor black are Americans and is an unseen scaffolding beneath the perpetual depiction of Asian Americans and Latino/a Americans as foreigners. Even in the research, references to the "loyalty" of Asian Americans presumably lying with Asia (e.g., Feldman et al., 1992; Lien, 1994) coupled with contrasting reference to non-Asian Americans as simply "Americans" (e.g., Jeong & Schumm, 1990) imply that Asian Americans are not really Americans. In popular conversation, when immigrants or people of color do not become sufficiently like the dominant group in ways it sanctions, their identity, loyalty to the United States, and good citizenship are questioned. Acculturation and assimilation become equated with "good" citizenship, as in a rationalization for the World War II internment of Japanese Americans on the grounds that they were unassimilable. (That rationale overlooked the fact that they were prevented by racism from structurally assimilating.)

In contrast, even though African Americans have ethnic cultures that do not coincide with the mainstream culture and acculturation issues arise for black immigrants from the Caribbean and Africa, their nationality or acculturation are usually not considered issues by the mainstream.[3] The difference in attention given to the acculturation of African Americans and Asian Americans probably reflects differences in the proportion of foreign-born and the former being perennially defined by race and the latter being ostensibly viewed more often as a cultural group.

Why does race trump acculturation in narratives about African Americans but not Asian Americans? Why is race a typically unprivileged text in descriptions of the acculturation of Asian Americans? Perhaps the timing of the 1965 Immigration Act is relevant. Before that Hart-Cellar Immigration Act and particularly before World War II, media portrayals of Asian Americans were usually either racialized or prototypically Orientalizing. However, the initial post-1965 influx of foreign-born Asians occurred when civil rights issues were temporarily at the forefront of the general U.S. consciousness, spurring deracialized narratives about Asian Americans. A difference in acculturation may thus have become a more socially acceptable basis for social distance than race.

Translating racially-based criticisms of Asian Americans into attacks for purportedly being "un–American" and using acculturation narratives to mask race-based social distance prop up the fiction that exclusion from the mainstream is rooted in cultural differences.[4] The implicit promise behind this hedge is that the acculturation "problem" or "deficit" will disappear in a few generations and free minorities of their marginalized status.[5] Ostensibly downplaying race and otherness as texts informing acculturation helps U.S. society to maintain the myth that equality is just around the acculturation corner. However, the acceptance that acculturation promises is a mirage because racial biases remain.

Privileged Intertextual Meanings

In both scholarly and popular discourse, two other texts are commonly taken to be part of the meaning of acculturation: the concepts that acculturation constitutes development and is adaptive. As metonyms, those privileged texts, like psychological models and measures which will be discussed subsequently, illustrate postmodernism's point about concepts and knowledge being constructed rather than a simple reflection of reality.

Assimilation and Acculturation as Development

The idea that acculturation signals development can be traced at least to the colonialist age when European colonialists assumed that white people were not only militarily advanced, but also morally and intellectually more developed than those being colonized. Dichotomous thinking contributed to characterizations of colonized people of color as immature and childlike (e.g., Werner, 1948). (Kagiticbasi [1989] describes a parallel premise used to explain the curtailed political power and socioeconomic status of non-Anglo Saxon, white immigrants.)

A dominant narrative, holding that assimilation to the ways of the dominating group signaled progress and maturation, seems to have sprung from the misplaced American optimism Alexis de Tocqueville (1848/1945) described and contrasted with older African, Asian, and European countries and incorrect ideas about the theory of evolution—notably the idea that evolution necessarily is toward higher, more mature, adaptive, and complex states. Acceptance by the dominant group has long been predicated on the perception that Aboriginal Americans and immigrant groups, particularly those of color, have "raised" themselves up, "washed off" vestiges of any other culture, and embraced the dominant society's cultural rules, normative behaviors, beliefs, values, and attitudes.

Development is commonly assumed to occur in stages or linearly progressive, continuous levels (Manicas, 1987; Osajima, 1995b), which speak to an implicit, essentialized, underlying, modernist orderliness. A universal, often mechanistic determinism presumably dictates that everyone saunters down the same or analogous developmental acculturation trails. Similar responses to an acculturation test are assumed to have the same meaning as though the same point in a trail indicates that the same territory has been traversed. The point a traveler reaches can be quantified and compared because, as rampant references to "degree," "level," or "amount" of acculturation show, acculturation is thought to be a quantifiable process.[6]

Instead of being viewed as preexisting points along a developmental path, acculturation differences might instead be viewed as personal creations of cultures. That creation is not defined by a mere collection of cultural characteristics akin to a collection of rocks in which a few are added here and a few are thrown out there. Rather, the very combining and balancing of values, behavior styles, and ways of interpreting within different personal and social contexts could be viewed as a dynamic, integrated process: Individuals uniquely create their acculturative status based on their synthesis of different texts and interpretations of experiences arising from, for example, the region of the United States or neighborhood in which they reside, their socioeconomic status, point in history, racial experiences, gender, intelligence, or gang affiliation. In those terms, acculturation is not as stable as modernist outlooks assume.

Perhaps due to the modernist scientific tendency to look for mechanistic principles at the expense of interpretive consciousness, the same research and narratives that imply that acculturation marks a developmental progression give little attention to reasons some people resist such "progress" or choose to acculturate in some ways, but not in others. With almost mechanistic efficiency, people changing their acculturation status supposedly unlearn "aspects of [their] previous [cultural] repertoire that are no longer appropriate" (Berry, 1997, p. 13), as though particular behaviors are completely dropped across all situations, habit has no role, and behaviors are forgotten once they have no anticipated usefulness.

Also downplayed in such characterizations of acculturation are whose norms and power interests are favored in judgments of progress. In many instances, the alienated, who might push for changes so that society will not continue to marginalize them, are implicitly regarded as less mature or well-adjusted and, therefore, less credible than the sanguine who are unlikely to press for change.

Assimilation and Acculturation as Adaptation

Dominant narratives deem acculturation to be good and adaptive (e.g., Berry, 1988; Shah, 1991), as in references to Asian Americans "achieving" assimilation (e.g., Min, 1995c), the maintenance of connections with an Asian culture as a "failure" to assimilate, and the "need" to change some aspects of ethnic culture that do not easily coexist or complement the dominant culture (e.g., Zhou, 1998). Conforming to existing ways, which reflect the interests and ideologies of the dominant, is made to seem natural. In contrast to the plurality associated with ethnicity, generation-based cultural plurality, as in cultural differences between baby boomers and the echo generation, seems to be more tolerated by society, perhaps because it seems, to some, like a natural evolution of U.S. culture.

In addition, acculturation is thought to be adaptive insofar as it presumably leads to assimilation which is also considered adaptive. That premise is itself grounded in multiple subtexts, notably which group is assimilating and to which culture they are assimilating.

Who is Assimilating?   Several sociological assimilation models have been based on immigration models (Sumida, 1998). Perhaps because most acculturation models have been based primarily on earlier generations of white, European, Protestant immigrants to the United States, many sociological as well as psychological assimilation models have assumed that immigrants traverse the same essentialized stages: Each postimmigrant generation moves up economically, increasingly melds into the dominant culture, eventually forsakes all identification with the ancestral culture, and becomes indistinguishable from the dominant group (LaFromboise et al., 1993).

Those immigration models suggest that like assimilation, acculturation is adaptive because it promises equal access to opportunities.[7] However, assimilation does not necessarily have the same meaning for various groups and individuals. The assumption that present-day immigrants and refugees assimilate in the fashion that early European immigrants did skirts the effects of stereotypes, racism, premigration experiences, societies/classes whence immigrants came, relationships between the United States and those countries, changing U.S. political and economic structures, and times in U.S. history when immigrants arrived (e.g., affecting whether they could be easily absorbed into the economy, as during the Industrial Revolution, or not, as during the Depression). The U.S. myth that complete assimilation is possible for all who want it to the extent they want it implies that assimilation merely reflects choice and effort. Again, the ring of modernist beliefs about universal regularities reverberate.

A consequence of ignoring those varied texts and basing models of acculturation on the experiences of European immigrants has been that the interplay between assimilation and race has been overlooked or cast aside as irrelevant. The limited assimilation of the highly acculturated African American population, though, speaks to the lack of automatic linkage between acculturation and assimilation. Historically, only selective assimilation has been available to people of color. In many circumstances, Asian Americans, like other racial minority groups, have been similar to the Aboriginal American guides in the Donner party: Assimilating to key but socially marginalized roles as subordinated, useful technicians or laborers, they are used but are the first to be targeted when difficult times are at hand. Thus, the adaptiveness of acculturation is largely contingent on the potential for assimilation.

As a result of this contingency and the relevance of race, various groups are likely to see the adaptiveness of acculturation differently. For example, many *nisei* decided to raise their children to be very Americanized to minimize the chances that their children would be put into concentration camps (Nagata, 1991) whereas other second-generation Asian Americans, not having had the same pressure to assimilate, look at acculturation differently.

Assumptions about the adaptiveness of acculturation have also diverted attention away from other repressed or negated texts that give meaning to acculturation. For example, to what can or are minorities of color assimilating, if not the racially and economically dominant group?

Assimilating to Which Culture? The aspect of U.S. culture to which people are assimilating and acculturating is another subtext defining the meaning of acculturation and bearing on whether acculturating is adaptive. Assumptions about the adaptiveness of becoming like the dominant group imply a singularity to the dominant culture. However, much is obscured when a study treats people in a binary fashion, as either acculturated and integrated or unacculturated and marginalized from the mainstream because the mainstreams are multiple.

Inasmuch as the United States is composed of multiple cultural or social groups, "U.S. culture" has multiple meanings. Because the U.S. culture is changing, fragmented, and heterogeneous across economic, racial, ethnic, gender, and age groups, acculturation is not simply to *the* American way, modernist biases toward assumptions about orderly regularity notwithstanding. At times, the mainstream is defined by the white, college-educated, middle class or by the upper class (in some circumstances, pretending to be middle class to have the social currency of being similarly situated as others and, again, a self-concept as just normal), with disproportionate political power and control over the narratives propagated by the principal news magazines, newspapers, and networks. At other times and in other domains, the mainstream is defined by what some consider a socioeconomic or educational fringe, ranging from sometimes insipid internet discussion groups to Americans who get their "news" from talk radio or the openly racist elements of society. So when reference is made to the acculturation of a group, to which parts of the culture are they supposedly acculturating or are psychological tests measuring?

Adding to those multiple, fluidly crisscrossing societal mainstreams is the mainstream defined by an individual's peers. A minority group is not necessarily assimilating only to the racially and economically dominant group.

Some people are assimilating to their own ethnic group or hyperreal media images. Groups create and constantly transform cultures in multiple niches, resulting in a vast multiplicity of changing acculturative states, strategies, target groups, and goals.

In particular domains, such as "acceptable" academic grades or ways of stating wishes, Asian American children might be acculturating toward one or several locally defined cultures, such as that of whichever ethnic or racial group dominates in their school, their own ethnic group, representatives of hip hop culture, or middle-class America as depicted on television. For example, in my elementary school, populated predominantly by African Americans and Japanese Americans (and to a lesser extent, Chinese Americans), the non-Japanese Americans were taught the few Japanese words the *sanseis* used, thereby contributing to their acculturation toward the latter's styles of interacting; in junior high school, Asian Americans adopted some of the behavior styles of the more numerous African Americans. Such experiences suggest that, rather than being composed of established stages, acculturation could more aptly be viewed in relation to different, changing, social situations; self-perceptions; desires to fit in; and willingness to change.

Many west-coast Japanese American children reside in areas with a relatively small population of their ethnicity. One reason some join Japanese American basketball leagues is that their parents want to help them develop or maintain a behavioral repertoire that enables them to behave biculturally. In such ways, Asian Americans become acculturated to their ethnic communities and not simply to the U.S. mainstream. Further suggesting that the orientation is toward a Japanese *American* culture is the absence of a parallel flocking to Japanese tea ceremonies or flower arranging, which are more Japanese than Japanese American.

Besides suppressing the U.S. culture's diversity, psychological discourse also represses its contradictions, which have been present from its inception. The United States has been, for example, simultaneously based on egalitarian principles, such as the ideal of equal opportunity and justice, and unfair ones, such as the initial restriction of enfranchisement to white males and the present glass-ceiling limitations on equal opportunity, which impede advancement on gender, racial, and, in some cases, religious grounds. Therefore, instead of being an unambiguous indication that one has adopted mundane mainstream views about the nature of society or social differences, acculturation could be to the adoption of U.S. ideals. If that is what acculturation signifies, then instead of mimicking dominant narratives, acculturation might take the form of countering the status quo to create equal opportunity.

Given those contradictions, adopting the ways of the dominant group does not have the same valence for various groups and the adaptiveness of assimilation and acculturation is ambiguous. For example, would not the adoption of racist and xenophobic views be a sign of assimilation and acculturation to a racist society? Do unbridgeable gaps between socially approved goals and available means to achieving those goals make rebellion adaptive (Merton, 1938)?

Much as the meaning of shared cards in a "Texas hold 'em" poker game differ for various players, the meaning ascribed to assimilating and acculturating, what is to be gained by identifying with an American mainstream, and the benefits of becoming acculturated differ for various people. The meanings are multiple.

Therefore, researchers will not find one meaning of acculturation except as a conceptual fiction and, because acculturation can take various forms, the adaptiveness or unadaptiveness of acculturation cannot be assumed. They also will not find, once and for all, *the* relationship of Asian Americans to one identified culture because relationships and cultures are multifaceted, constantly changing, and contested. The multiplicity of cultures to which people are acculturating is nevertheless a repressed text.

Uncovering those buried texts might take the form of asking about which behaviors have been adaptive for which people in which circumstances. What multiple and simultaneous rather than simply mutually exclusive forms of acculturation do individuals create (Espiritu, 1994)? Failure to analyze privileged narratives that link acculturation to adaptation covers up different meanings of assimilation, marginalization, and adaptation.

Modernist Research Texts

Ironically, when psychological treatments overlook texts that contribute to acculturation's meaning, scholarly conceptualizations, models, and measures are themselves among those overlooked privileged texts. However, hermeneutics—which contextualizes conceptualizations, models, and measures to produce understanding of them as texts bearing on other texts—and deconstruction expose the constructed nature of what have become normalized assumptions and narratives, reveal other modernist assumptions, and open dialectic discursive opportunities.

Those methods show that, along with the assumption that acculturation takes the form of linear development, models of acculturation have often been saddled with other simplifying modernist assumptions. The acculturation of Asian Americans, for example, is still often viewed in terms of placement along a line anchored by vaguely defined Asian and U.S. cultural poles or at a point of intersection in terms of U.S. and Asian axes. (See Tables 5.1 and 5.2.) Although some models recognize bicultural options, others have treated acculturation and assimilation as zero-sum processes

(LaFromboise et al., 1993; Padilla, 1980a; Porter & Washington, 1993): Becoming like one group is necessarily matched by a loss of ties to another group so that the possibility of synthesis or simultaneously acculturating to multiple cultures is denied.

Even bicultural models see Asian Americans in terms of their acculturation to American culture or an Asian American culture. They do not start from the point of view that Asian Americans are already part of America (West, 2001).

The concept of biculturalism points to other biases in modernist acculturation models as well. The oversimplified, dichotomous portrayals of two opposing cultures, one Asian and one American, are reductionist and overlook the multiple aspects of each. Biculturalism is more complex than an additive combination of dichotomous "American" and "Asian" influences. As a Thai American pointed out, it is also emergent:

> I'm only part Thai. I have some Chinese in me and the rest of me is American. I don't think I can ever be fully Thai as my

TABLE 5.1   Acculturation in the Form of Types

Traditionalists	These Asian Americans adhere to traditional Asian values and identify with an Asian culture to the exclusion of the dominant U.S. society; including many of the more recent immigrants, traditionalists strongly identify with the ethnic group but are not very assimilated.
Assimilationists	These highly assimilated individuals adopt European American values and behavioral norms and identify themselves as Americans to the exclusion of their Asian American ethnicity, which is acknowledged only superficially, as in eating ethnic food and occasionally participating in ethnic holiday celebrations. Most of their friends are white.
Marginalized	They reject and feel alienated from both American and Asian cultures.
Bicultural	Maintaining ties and comfortable with both Asian and American cultures, these Asian Americans tend to identify strongly with their ethnic group while being simultaneously assimilated to the dominant, American culture.

Note. The conceptual and methodological treatment of acculturation and ethnic identity overlap considerably. Based on "Chinese American personality and mental health," by S. Sue and D. W. Sue, 1971, Amerasia Journal, 1, 36–49.

TABLE 5.2 Acculturation as the Sum of Dichotomies

Low assimilation; high ethnic identity

Low assimilation; low ethnic identity

High assimilation; low ethnic identity

High assimilation; high ethnic identity

Note. Combining simple, dichotomous characteristics, such as low- or high-assimilation and ethnic identity, has resulted in jejune portrayals of forms of acculturation. Based on *Asian Americans: Emerging Minorities* (2nd ed.), by H. Kitano & R. Daniels, 1996.

parents would like, because almost everything I do I do using some parts of each culture. I eat some American food with chopsticks and a spoon. When I pray to the Buddha, I speak to him in English. When I speak to my sisters or Thai friends, I blend the two languages together (but they can still understand me). I mix both cultures so much, sometimes, I think I've started my own new culture.

In such ways, individuals' cultural choices—which behaviors, attitudes, values, world views, and ways of expressing and interpreting events and behaviors they choose to change—modify their behavioral repertoire and signify the continual creation and alteration of ethnic cultures and identity.

Disassembling the construction of the concept of biculturalism reveals other modernist assumptions. Doing so shows, for example, that when researchers list some traits thought to characterize bicultural competence and state that "... we do not know whether these are the only skills of biculturalism, or whether a person needs to be equally competent in all or a particular subset, in order to be biculturally competent" (LaFromboise et al., 1993, p. 408), they imply that bicultural competence exists apart from our construction of the concept, it is characterized by a single set of transcendent, decontextualized skills, and psychologists are just discovering its nature. Those modernist conceptualizations misdirect psychology toward a modernist metaphysic and hyperreal portrayals. They detract from consideration of ways in which biculturalism is a process reformulated in everyday life by specifically situated individuals and is personally, situationally, and qualitatively variable. Little attention is given, for instance, to how the bicultural foreign-born might switch between parallel neural networks (Hong, Morris, Chiu, & Benet-Martínez, 2000) whereas the bicultural U.S.-born might more often develop blended cognitive frameworks. Likewise, researchers seemingly seldom step back and ask how treating pluralism as antithetical to acculturation affects researchers' narratives.

The impression of order created by acculturation models is achieved by selecting some aspects of acculturation as normal and relevant and others as statistical error or deviant, irrelevant residue (Cantell & Pedersen, 1992). Ambiguity is delegitimated and the instability of acculturation is obscured: The ways in which people constantly make subtle shifts in their behaviors and attitudes as they encounter new situations are deemphasized. Acculturation models have given few hints about criteria to be used in determining whether incorporating some "American" cultural beliefs and behaviors without forsaking, for instance, their Korean counterparts, is a sign of adaptation (e.g., Hurh & Kim, 1984) or cultural confusion (e.g., Shrake, 1998).

Perhaps the most well-known acculturation/adaptation model in psychology, John Berry's, is classically modernist. That model defines possible types of acculturation in terms of the intersection of two variables: whether individuals essentially (1) value holding on to ethnic cultural identity, customs, and other characteristics and (2) value maintaining vaguely defined, positive relationships with the dominant group and other "cultural" groups (Berry, 1988). The model dictates dichotomous, all-or-nothing categorizations, forming the reductive basis for identifying four totalizing types of adaptation reflecting different forms of acculturation. (See Table 5.3.)

In his characterization of possible adaptive strategies, Berry leaves room only for three strategies: People can (1) adjust by reducing conflict and increasing congruence between themselves and their environment; (2) "retaliate" against or change the environment to avoid making cultural or

TABLE 5.3   Acculturative Forms Defining Types of Adaptation

Relationships with other groups	Ethnic identity or characteristics	
	Value maintaining	Do not value maintaining
Value maintaining	Integration	Assimilation
Do not value maintaining	Separation	Marginalization

Note. Berry thinks of adaptation as psychological acculturation and, as with other models, regards the cells' labels as neutral signifiers. However, clockwise from the upper left, the cells defining the four types of adaptation could have been labeled: multicultural, uncritically accepting, or sociable; Anglo-conformist or ethnically isolated; antisocial, thinking beyond the boundaries, or individualists; and rejected, alienated and segregated by others, or racist and ethnocentric. Based on "Acculturation and psychological adaptation: A conceptual overview," by J. W. Berry, 1988, in *Ethnic Psychology: research and practice with immigrants, refugees, native peoples, ethnic groups and sojourners,* edited by J. W. Berry and R. C Annis, and "Imagination, acculturation, and adaptation," J. W. Berry, 1997, *Applied Psychology: An International Review, 46*(1), 5–68.

behavioral adjustments; or (3) withdraw from the environment to reduce environmental pressure to change. The first strategy of "adjustment" is implicitly preferred: Certainly "retaliate" does not imply that the second strategy is mature or reasoned and "withdrawal" (Berry, 1988, p. 43) does not suggest satisfactory adaptation in our socially oriented species. This portrayal indirectly negates efforts to transform the status quo and valorizes trying to fit in.

Models like this one mediate how scholars describe and think about acculturation. Like metaphors, they constrain attributed meanings.

By classifying individuals in dichotomous, totalizing ways, acculturation models like Berry's (e.g., Moy, 1992; Wong-Rieger & Quintana, 1987) promote a static world view, treat adaptation as a state, and imply stability, simplicity, and foundational orderliness to the acculturation and adaptation of individuals. Factors influencing acculturative orientations and decisions are not identified (Leong & Chou, 1994). Local variations are downplayed.

As the basis for narratives, the false oppositions in those models foreclose on questions such as, "How might any general, albeit contingent and transitory, acculturation patterns be understood from multiple perspectives?" Explanations of emergent regularities are impeded by the concentration on explanatory laws (Bertalanffy, 1969; Polkinghorne, 1983, 1988).

Acculturation measures, too, have become privileged psychological texts and warrant particular scrutiny. A look at the measures reveals metaphysical assumptions that are often at odds with stated conceptualizations. For example, while acculturation models are moving away from linear assumptions, questionnaire response options are often linear and analyzed using statistics with linear assumptions.

The measures are also based on modernist epistemology. Some behaviors or aspects of American culture are privileged in conceptualizations and measurements of acculturation to the point of seemingly being indispensable to acculturation whereas others are silenced (Tropp, Erkut, García Coll, Alarcón, & Vázquez García, 1999). That prime, preordained set of attitudes, behaviors, and characteristics regarded as indicators of acculturation, include English proficiency, values, friendship patterns, attitudes toward exogamy, preferred foods, preferences for television programs in English (Anderson et al., 1993; Min & Choi, 1993), adoption of American customs (Celano & Tyler, 1991), and birth in the United States or age at emigration. The assumption that multiple, quantifiable aspects of acculturation can be bundled into a neatly packaged measure or level of acculturation (e.g., Oetting & Beauvais, 1990–1991) obscures the variability that is part and parcel of life in order to incarnate modernist, universal, laws and regularities. Despite what acculturation measures might indicate, my acculturation did not change the one year I lived in Nashville even though I did not eat in Japanese restaurants or go to *obon* festivals (because there were none) and I did not associate with any Asian Americans (I never even saw another Asian American).

Nevertheless, closely basing the widely used Suinn-Lew Asian Self-Identity Acculturation Scale (SL-ASIA) on an acculturation test developed for Mexican Americans (Cuellar, Harris, & Jasso, 1980)[8] implies that the same dimensions[9] define acculturation for different minority groups and for different Asian American groups. Undermining the expectation that psychological tests reveal universal structural components, however, researchers have found that the SI-ASIA produces less consistent and, in modernist terms, less valid results for noncollege samples than for the college student samples upon which Asian American norms for the test were developed (Iwamasa, Pai, Hilliard, & Lin, 1998).

Instead of assuming that acculturation is one, testable entity composed of the same central characteristics for all people and that a single test will be equally valid for them, suppose acculturation were thought of as a cocktail and an acculturation measure as a teaspoon extracting samples of different cocktails. Just as quantitatively comparing the alcohol content of a Manhattan and a highball would not tell us much about what makes the cocktails different from each other, how different people metabolize alcohol, which cocktail they prefer, why they drink it, and why they behave the way they do afterward, focusing on quantitative aspects of acculturation narrows researchers' visual field. Using a modernist, quantitative measure of acculturation occludes much of what is interesting about acculturation for the lives of Asian Americans and why, as a concept, it is useful.

Acculturation is not just a variable mediating how Asian Americans behave. Although researchers typically define acculturation in demographic terms or based on their interpretations of responses to a questionnaire, acculturation is sometimes phenomenologically and interpersonally the degree and ways in which individuals are more broadly perceived to be acculturated. That perception is also intertextually defined. Like Las Vegas chips that have phenomenologically lost their monetary identity and their grounding in the customary intertextual meaning of money and now have a situationally attenuated identity, responses to questionnaires are now privileged conversions that have lost their phenomenological recognizability. Their meanings are limited to modernist arenas and categorical classifications and nonoverlapping stages are privileged over phenomenological experiences.

Another consequence of this concentration on acculturation as an independent variable and the reliance on modernist acculturation scales and investigative orientations has been that acculturation processes have frequently been overlooked. Ignorance of the processes of acculturation—such as how individuals are socialized in an ethnic minority culture, integrate a new culture with an existing one, or uniquely mold (if not meld) varied cultural influences in specific contexts—leaves little understanding of its relevance to people's lives or experiences.

The addiction to modernist scientific methods alone has also obscured differences in the way people acculturate and which acculturative domains are influential in which situations. Adoption of cultural characteristics can vary across domains and situations: People adopt some values, behaviors, and attitudes, but not others; apply what they know with varying frequency and in different situations (Feldman et al., 1992); and acculturate at different speeds in different domains (Celano & Tyler, 1991). Nevertheless, the ways in which acculturation is an uneven process are usually ignored.[10] Also typically ignored in measures of acculturation are questions about qualitative differences in relationships to various cultures (LaFromboise et al., 1993); reasons people have mixed feelings about different cultures; attitudes various people have toward assimilating and how those attitudes change; diverse forms of acculturation various individuals want; ways in which decisions about acculturating might depend on definitions of success in life; and relationships between acculturation and structural limitations on mobility. Complex, emergent, and temporal forms of acculturation are forgotten or never conceived.

An examination of both the assumptions models or measures make about humans and the consequences of focusing on particular texts reveals that the complexity of personal consciousness, agency, ascribed meanings, and particular experiences are silenced in the acculturation research in favor of a decontextualized and modernist narrative. Responses are so circumscribed by the methods, the thoughts and experiences of the respondents are hardly tapped, much less their degree and forms of acculturation, reasons for their acculturation choices, their attitudes toward acculturation in particular circumstances, and reasons their behaviors might not reflect their attitudes.

By building within the walls of modernist empiricism's quantifiable and testable foundations, psychology's construction of acculturation has not only been biased but also conceptually stunted. The nexus between mainstream modernist psychology and social history and cultural studies, for instance, has been weak.

As Foucault anticipated, dominant narratives have hidden how conceptualizations of acculturation have served the interests of the powerful. For example, many psychological models overlook the contradictions between the myth that the United States is generally willing to accommodate the "other" and actual oppressive pressures to assimilate. Claims that the bicultural are somehow free to objectively pick the culturally best of both worlds mask the ways in which society forces certain types of behavior and insists on acculturation to the dominant group. Another related, unstudied issue that would be put back on the radar screen by the disassemblage of constructed concepts is the way in which Asian Americans are disempowered when the concept of acculturation, like the model minority stereotype, is defined from the perspective of fitting in or coinciding with the mainstream. Psychology gives too little attention to how to improve social conditions.

Acculturation has multiple, simultaneous identities: as a process and as a characteristic; as a group-level and as individual-level phenomenon; as a cause that can produce varying effects and as a result of various pressures; and as an empirical relationship and as a narrative. These alternative meanings suggest that different methods might be fruitfully used to study them (Williams & Berry, 1991; Palinkas & Pickwell, 1995).

In conclusion, the acculturation research has not been very informative about acculturative processes, the impact of social structures on psychological functioning, the meanings of acculturation, or experiences. Its primary usefulness has been in identifying test responses as predictors of, for example, usage of mental health services or educational achievement; but research findings do not show how acculturation accounts for educational achievement and, accordingly, are not particularly efficient bases for policy planning. The oversimplified models also inadvertently encourage therapists unfamiliar with an ethnic group to form stereotypes.

In the end, do modernist psychological studies of acculturation really provide more knowledge than psychologists would have found if they discursively asked many people about their lives and attitudes, listened to the complexity and idiosyncracies of their answers as well as commonalities, and deconstructed or hermeneutically analyzed what they heard? Hermeneutic analysis of topics, such as acculturation, and contrast with other texts expose knowledge claims as constructions. Hermeneutics, like deconstruction, opens up more in-depth and engaging issues.

In the next chapter, I take up the concepts of ethnicity and ethnic identity, which are often poorly distinguished from culture and acculturation (Roberts & Phinney, 1999).[11] Although reference to acculturation usually emphasizes relationships to the dominant culture whereas reference to ethnic identity concentrates on relationships to the ethnic group (D. Sue, Mak, & Sue, 1998), redundancies abound. For instance, acculturation is sometimes defined as "changes in the . . . subjective domains of ethnicity" (Tanaka et al., 1998 p. 55) while changes in a sense of peoplehood are regarded as changes in ethnic identity. Nevertheless, examining the concept of ethnicity can broaden understanding of scholarly and popular portrayals of Asian Americans in a way that thinking about acculturation does not.

CHAPTER 6

Ethnicity and Identity

Giving themselves a congratulatory pat on the back, some people proclaim, "I don't see an Asian American, I see a human being," as though the latter is a superior narrative to the former and even though the contrast implies an almost dichotomous classification. The statement is soaking in implications about the speakers' supposed egalitarianism while simultaneously wringing any relevance from ethnic or minority experiences. It is also clearly disingenuous: Failing to notice a minority member's ethnicity or race is almost as rare as failing to notice someone's sex. Ascriptions of ethnicity (or inquiries about it) are probably most frequently directed to a member of a racial minority outside the black-white racial paradigm or, more broadly, apparently an "other," such as a European immigrant with an accent.

Accordingly, in both popular conversation and research, ethnicity and ethnic identity are privileged characteristics in descriptions of Asian Americans. In this chapter, uses of those concepts are treated as discursive moves which can be dissected to reveal hidden meaning. I begin by deconstructing the concepts to show how modernist assumptions hide their complexity, instability, and multiple meanings; expose ways in which ethnic identity scales are reductive and self-referential; and illustrate the emphasis on modernist orderliness and linearity underlying essentializing identity models.

Demographic Versus Emergent Ethnicity

Ethnicity's meaning is a construction which has generally been equated with membership in a group that behaves and interprets in ways that reflect shared ancestral background, history, cultural values, notions of acceptable behaviors, and options (Sorenson, 1996; Zane & Sasao, 1992). Insofar as cultural groupings constitute ethnic groups, definitions of culture as a shared consciousness or an imagined, abstract equivalence among members of a collective also define ethnicity (Bandlamudi, 1994; Lowe, 1998).

Although ethnicity has been used as a metonym for relatively stable, shared, and presumed psychological characteristics, such as a sense of peoplehood, reified values, behaviors, and interpretive habits arising from a culture, ancestry has outweighed culture or a sense of peoplehood as an indicator of ethnicity both in casual conversations and in operational definitions. The synecdochic use of ethnicity as a categorical stand-in for complex, diverse cultural propensities is matched by social science's operational treatment of ethnicity as an objective, demographic characteristic, grossly assessed by self-reports in terms of conventional ethnic–group classifications. Reduced to Asian ancestry, ethnicity has been treated as a categorical predictor or independent variable.[1]

Both the aforementioned conceptual definitions and their operational counterparts overlook much, and that has had typically unstudied consequences. For example, the treatment of ethnicity or shared ancestry as a synonym for historical, cultural experiences or a historical, sociocultural sense of peoplehood (Torres & Ngin, 1995; Zane & Sasao, 1992) seems to imply that ancestry has a deterministic effect on a sense of peoplehood and hides the ways in which a sense of peoplehood is constructed rather than automatic and isomorphic with ancestry.

The disparate groups said to constitute the Asian American population are also presumed to have enough in common (Gim Chung, 1995) and important, shared experiences or characteristics to warrant their treatment as a group. However, empirical and rational justification for that presumption is typically vague, if noted at all, even though science identifies itself in terms of its self-ascribed bedrock foundations in empiricism and rationality. Left unanswered are questions such as, which shared characteristics justify regarding Asian Americans as a group of a kind? How much or what kind of commonalities constitute privileged definers of Asian Americans? How does a sense of peoplehood purportedly based on ancestry affect behaviors and attitudes in a way that cannot be explained by more proximal factors?

Privileged Ethnic Groups

The idea that Asian Americans have a common ancestry has taken for granted and privileged particular ways of dividing the world. The presumption that a particular set of countries unambiguously constitutes Asia glides over the fact that any way of conceptually dividing the world is a construction without universal, timeless parameters. Current constructions of the Asian Pacific region of the world usually do not include Kazakhstan, so Kazakhstani

Americans are not considered to be Asian Americans; people disagree over whether Bharatiya Americans are Asian Americans in part because they differ on whether they think various regions of India are part of the "Asia" defining the common origins of Asian Americans (Hune & Chan, 1997); and Pacific Islanders are often grouped with Asian Americans when particular geographic characteristics are privileged.

While Asian American groups whose ancestors came from East Asia are chronically hyperprivileged, more generally, the Asian (Pacific) Americans studied by psychologists have primarily included those of Cambodian, Chinese, Filipino/a, Hmong, Japanese, Korean, Lao, and Vietnamese ancestry. Groups such as Guamanians, Indonesians, and Thais are rarely studied. Emphasis on Confucianism and Buddhism as the shared grounding of Asian American cultures has further marginalized Pacific Islanders and Filipinos whose ancestors were not as influenced by those ideas (Min, 1995a) and has minimized the effects of colonialism.

This emphasis on particular groups is replicated by Americans generally. If asked, "Who are Asian Americans?" most U.S. residents would probably name Chinese Americans, Japanese Americans, and Korean Americans. Rather than simply a natural, obvious, or objective selection, though, the privileging of those three groups is a construction, demonstrated by the contrasting narrative in Great Britain where South Asians are the conceptually privileged Asian British group (Kibria, 1998).

While physical appearance might account for the privileging of the American trio and the unprivileging of Filipino/a Americans and Bharatiya Americans, appearance alone probably does not account for the privileging; if it did, more physically similar groups would be more privileged. The privileging in part reflects population sizes; yet numerical dominance alone does not account for privileging the trio. The comparative sizes of early twentieth-century Korean-, Filipino/a-, and Asian Indian-Americans does not support the contention that the privileging is based on historical predominance either.

Whatever the probably shifting combination of bases for privileging the trio, classifications of Asian Americans in terms of these three groups marginalize other Asian American groups, much as black-white racial paradigms marginalize everyone else. Spotlighting the three groups raises questions about how some groups, such as Bharatiya Americans, have been treated as "others" in Asian American communities (Nguyen & Chen, 2000). What are possible consequences for panethnic identity as "Asian American" when one's ethnic group has centered or decentered status? What are the implications for relationships among Asian American communities when some have more power than others (e.g., heterosexuals for their predominance; Chinese- and Filipino/a-Americans for their number, or Japanese Americans for their average level of acculturation)? What does the comparative marginalization of some groups mean for interpersonal relationships and public policy?[2]

Meanings from Uses of Ethnicity

One way to begin to address those questions is to examine the constructed meanings of ethnicity. In particular, consideration might be given to how the uses of ethnicity become created meanings and affect characterizations of ethnic groups. Meanings are contingent on the narratives of which they are a part, the situations in which they are used, who has contributed to their meaning, and how they have been contested. Therefore, examinations of the contexts in which ethnicity is used, by whom, and for what purposes clarify the social brewing of the significance of ethnicity.

Ethnicity used as a basis for institutional pluralism, which Torres and Ngin (1995) called ethnicity-in-itself, is especially evident among immigrant groups. That use is often unwelcome by those members of the dominant group who, failing to see that institutional expressions of peoplehood are often responses to exclusion, interpret them as simply potential sources of civil Balkanization. Consequently, ethnicity-in-itself has long been a basis for characterizations of immigrants or otherwise marginalized groups as cliquish. The charge was made against Southern Europeans and Irish immigrants, for example.

Ethnicity-for-itself, the conscious use of ethnicity for entitlement and empowerment with possibly pluralistic goals (Torres & Ngin, 1995), is a text that speaks to ethnicity's transformative power. It can include instances in which, as Bauman (1992) argued, groups assign relevance to certain types of conduct which become seductive and desired. A behavior like giving money to mourning Filipino/a families might begin as ethnicity-in-itself but become ethnicity-for-itself.[3] Such a use of ethnicity, often unnoticed by those outside the ethnic group, can become a symbolic way of reinforcing the formation of ethnic identity.

A sense of ethnicity is at times manifested and promoted by some type of commitment to the ethnic culture, such as participation in ethnic festivals or the display of Korean art in a Korean American's home. That symbolic ethnicity (Gans, 1979), a means by which people locate themselves in relation to others, has multiple meanings and is expressed in varied ways by different individuals so that the same behavior, such as attending an ethnic festival, does not have the same significance for dissimilar individuals. Across groups too, differences in the meaning of expressions of symbolic ethnicity are likely. For U.S.-born white Americans, ethnicity is often restricted to this symbolic form, which is itself restricted to leisure activities and without social cost (Waters, 2001); it is not used to fill a void created by historical exclusion from mainstream U.S. culture. On the other hand, minorities are marginalized from a U.S. cultural pot showing little evidence of having melted in components from minority cultures. Consequently, symbolic ethnicity is expressed in different cultural contexts for dominant and subordinated groups, and groups are likely to differ in the meanings they assign to ethnicity.

Not all symbolic uses of ethnicity have the same meaning. While symbolic expressions of Irish ethnicity, such as St. Patrick's Day, have been treated as innocent spectacles to the non-Irish, symbolic expressions of ethnicity by African Americans, such as Kwanzaa, have been disparaged. The uses and meanings of ethnicity have varied across racial groups at least partly because the significance of ethnicity has long been connected to and usually trumped by race. Implicit racial narratives affect how expressions of ethnicity are perceived. Whereas ethnic identity could be a temporary way station that was largely abandoned by the descendants of white immigrants as they became accepted as full-fledged members of mainstream U.S. society (Perlmutter, 1999), it has less frequently been regarded that way by people of color whose acculturation has not meant full assimilation or comparable status.

Analysis of the uses and, therefore, the meanings of ethnicity might also focus on panethnicity. When is panethnicity adhibited or resisted and in what ways is it fluid? In one studied high school, many Korean American students thought that other Asian Americans carried social baggage (e.g., a lower socioeconomic status) that interfered with the former's assimilation and acceptance by white Americans (S. Lee, 1996). Light is shed on the created meaning of ethnicity by examination of that type of local ascription of meaning to ethnicity; motivation to construct or resist panethnic boundaries; interpretation of panethnic identification; and creation of ethnic boundaries that simultaneously divide, unify, shift, vary in salience, and marginalize (particularly the numerically, culturally, or geographically different).

Local Creation of Ethnicity

Linking an undifferentiated sense of peoplehood with common origin in Asia is, for many U.S.-born Asian Americans, phenomenologically a fiction akin to feeling a common origin with Adam and Eve. Therefore, rather than assume ethnicity reflects a global sense of peoplehood born directly of common ancestral origins, ethnicity and ethnic identity might be viewed as constructed senses of connection. Doing so shifts focus away from distal ancestral origins and toward proximal links establishing situationally variant bases for and fluctuating, permeable boundaries of a sense of peoplehood—behaviors, roles, interpersonal styles, educational and economic statuses, or ways of interpreting events and behaviors.[4] In that context, the heavy involvement in Japanese American basketball leagues—evidenced by willingness to transport children all over town, weekend after weekend, for basketball practices and games—exemplifies a commitment not only to the children but again also a proximal link to the ethnic group.

Local, concrete interpersonal relationships based on and contributing to the construction of a sense of shared values, behavior patterns, and ways of interpreting behaviors probably form the grounding for the construction of an abstract sense of common ancestry, cultural background, and peoplehood. An ethnic sense of peoplehood, therefore, might develop much as we develop a sense of peoplehood with friends.

The ongoing cognitive and social construction and disassembly of ethnic boundaries provide changing, local intertextual meaning to ethnicity. Therefore, ethnicity is not a static, demographic characteristic; it is a continual, creative process "which incorporates, adapts, and amplifies . . . communal solidarities, cultural attributes, and historical memories" in particular, contemporary real-life situations (Conzen, Gerber, Morawska, Pozzetta, & Vecoli, 1992, pp. 4–5). Its construction in the present means that for Asian Americans ethnicity is "not a way of looking back at the [country from which ancestors came but] rather a way of being American, a way of defining yourself [in a somewhat] pluralistic culture" (Greeley, 1976, p. 32). A Thai American recounted the way she is creating her ethnicity:

> If I were at school . . . with all my friends, I would speak English and use the American side of me. I think if I spoke Thai and behaved in a Thai manner at school, most likely people would not see me as an American, but probably as a "FOB." In contrast, if I were at home with my family and relatives [I] would speak Thai and use my Asian side. If I don't my family would feel that I am losing my ethnicity as a Thai person and would feel that I do not have respect.

She and her family are creating and negotiating her ethnicity, whose meaning and salience can change in different contexts. In such ways, ethnicity's content and form reflect choices made by individuals and groups. As members of an ethnic group create their culture in concrete actions, "ethnicity becomes a means by which culture is transmitted" (Betancourt & López, 1993, p. 631).

The local creation of the significance of ethnicity means that its groundings and meanings are likely to vary. For example, ethnicity, as a sense of peoplehood, probably has different meanings for multiracial, homosexual, or deaf Asian Americans because their ethnicity has a different significance in various communities. Likewise, some Asian Americans have a more transnational or multinational ethnic identity than others.

For some individuals, concrete racial experiences, including awareness of racist trauma experienced by parents (Renteln, 1995) or racial stereotypes, are texts brought to bear in the construction of ethnicity (see Dower, 1986). During the "Vietnam" War, for example, Asian Americans were treated as the enemy in real fights with other U.S. soldiers and in medical treatment; blamed for ambushes based on stereotypes of Asians as untrustworthy; and witness to cultural racism against Vietnamese. Despite attempts to deny links with the Vietnamese and their own identity as Asians so that their loyalty would be clear and they would not be mistaken for the enemy, many found feelings of connection to the Vietnamese hard to avoid (Kiang, 1991; Loo, 1994). As was explained by a Chinese American, whose family originated in southern China,

> If my grandparents had not migrated to Hawaii, I'd be on the other side of the war . . . carrying an AK-47 . . . speaking Chinese. . . . I could [dehumanize]. But after a person is dispatched, dead, wounded . . . the human part becomes evident . . . and they looked just like my uncle [or] cousin. (Loo, 1994, p. 650)

Constructions of ethnicity are also based on shared experiences. One source of those shared experiences is today's hyperreal society in which ethnicity is constructed. Postmodernism characterizes that hyperreal society as archly self-referential (Winter, 1992); composed of images, simulations, and artificiality that supplant the actual and individual (Dowd, 1991); populated by commodified mass consumers; and ordered by the arbitrary authority of consumerism. Among the texts relevant to the formation of a sense of ethnicity for minorities living in such a society are instances in which ethnicity is co-opted or presented in hyperreal ways; polysemic identities are created in relation to commodified signs, such as cultural images, Asian American television game-show contestants, media and textbook representations, or simulations and images of sexuality, race, status, and ability; and manipulated consumer preferences, beliefs, and academic knowledge (Gubrium & Holstein, 1994).

Some of the instability in ethnicity's created meaning is, accordingly, probably due to the drawing of texts from fluctuating hyperreal portrayals. When depictions of Asian Americans as exotic, secretive, or foreign strike a chord with an audience, however inappropriately (see Hamamoto, 1994), ignorance and voracious capitalism usually supersede ethical considerations. For instance, the still rerunning television series "MASH" presents the vast majority of white Americans as skilled and compassionate, but most Koreans as intellectually, morally, or socially incompetent. Those types of portrayals produce ideologies and even syndication-perpetuated versions of knowledge bearing on ascribed ethnic identity (see Everett, 1994). An immigrant Korean college student reported, for instance, that the hyperreal image of assertive, confident, and glib Americans as portrayed on television "left a lasting image in my head [that] I could never become an American." Images, including racial stereotypes, are part of the local, intertextual meaning of ethnicity.

Stereotypes, from the decades-old standbys about inscrutability to the model minority and more recent and local ones, are texts bearing on the created meanings of ethnicity. Some Asian Americans believe the stereotypes and some even try to match them (S. Lee, 1996; Mayeda, 1998; Tan, 1994). Still others, saying the equivalent of "I'm not an Asian American; I'm Terry," create a negated, submerged ethnicity because of their fear that stereotypes about their ethnic group deny their own merits as individuals. Spurred by their own stereotyping narratives about Asian Americans, they reject an identity as an Asian American (or avoid Asian American Studies) because they do not identify with the narrow range of behavior patterns, interests, or outlooks they associate with Asian Americans: They create a meaning of their ethnicity that denies the complexity and multiple meanings of being Asian Americans.

The creation of meanings of ethnicity, however, is not only a cognitive process; it is also a social process. Ethnicity is a sign created, used, and manipulated by people to define themselves and others; consequently, portrayals of Asian Americans sometimes reflect and serve the interests of those who characterize. Depicting Asian Americans as foreigners, for instance, might reinforce a non-Asian American's sense of belonging or even superiority. Some individuals try to stop the negotiation of competing meanings of ethnicity: They try to define for other Asian Americans what being Asian American means. For example, just as some African Americans might perpetuate oppression within the African American community by denouncing opposing community members as racially inauthentic or not black enough (West, 1992), some Asian Americans complain that an Asian American female who protests sexism in Asian American communities is not acting "Asian" (S. Lee, 1996).

Indeed, ethnicity is sometimes more of an externally ascribed characteristic than a personally felt one. The constructed meaning of one's ethnicity might not even match one's own sense of peoplehood, as when a Filipino American is mistaken for a Chicano. Similarly, when people ask, "Are you Chinese or Japanese?" and then (if the response is, for example, "Chinese") go on to say "I love Akira Kurosawa [sic] movies and I was really impressed when I saw the Great Wall a couple of years ago," their insipid definitions

of Chinese are not embraced as one's own. Nevertheless, their conceptualizations—full of implications about their views of the individual,
Asian ethnicity, and the sociopolitical status of Asian Americans—have a
social weight.

Viewing ethnicity as a sign sheds light on perceptions of ethnic groups,
meanings of ethnicity, and always shifting and differing senses of belonging.[5]
As a sign, ethnicity will have different meanings for disparate audiences and
the concept will vacillate in its usefulness across settings (J. Nagel, 1994). It
has a fluidity that "can be called upon, hidden, or imbued with [differing
degrees of] importance in line with . . . specific social situations" (Hayano
1981, p. 158).

Thus, ethnicity's meaning is diverse and complex. As a personal and
collective social construction, it is tied to various texts, such as the experiences individuals associate with ethnicity; uses by Asian Americans and non-
Asian Americans alike; and political, economic, and social processes, including
ethnic conflict, mobilization, and change (J. Nagel, 1994). The constant
choosing, molding, creating, and applying of meanings to ethnicity contrast
with the narrowness and lifelessness of categorical conceptualizations of
ethnicity. To treat ethnicity as a demographic variable with unambiguous
meaning simply reflecting ancestry shortchanges much of its multiple, contested, complex, emergent meaning and significance.

Breaking away from a framework depicting ethnicity as a demographic
characteristic provides the freedom to look at it anew and perceive different
issues. In the context of heterogeneity among Asian Americans, when is
significance assigned to their ethnicity? How do people try to hide, trivialize,
or ignore the relevance of social, historical, and economic issues to the
meaning of being part of a minority (San Juan, 1992)? When does perceived
ethnicity affect perceptions of people's work? Whence comes a desire for
ethnic identification in a hyperreal society that removes many of the experiences that support a sense of connection to others and produces
marginalizing feelings of insignificance?

Privileged Modernist Assumptions About Ethnic Identity

The treatment of ethnicity as an objective, demographic classification pervades
psychological discussions of ethnic identity. The same pale cast over the
complexity of ethnicity does likewise to ethnic identity, which in popular
parlance might be described as "knowing what your ethnic background is"
and which researchers have defined as a strong, secure, positive sense of
belonging; a sense of commitment to and knowledge of a culture; engagement

in the customs and traditions of one's ethnic group; or a sense that one's ethnic culture is salient in everyday life (Meyerowitz et al., 1998; Roberts & Phinney, 1999; Rosenthal & Feldman, 1992). Even aside from the muddy distinction between ethnicity and ethnic identity when both are defined as a sense of peoplehood, regarding ethnic identity only as a characteristic of an individual throws shadows over the ways in which identity is defined by others, constantly transformed and reinterpreted, and perpetually uncertain because of those reinterpretations. Just as ethnicity cannot be assessed objectively, neither can ethnic identity; and much as ethnicity has unstable meanings, so must ethnic identity.

Many of the problems with researchers' treatment of ethnic identity can be tied to modernist metaphysics. Deconstruction of conventional characterizations helps to expose taken-for-granted meanings that form a conceptual prison preventing free consideration of other aspects of ethnic identity.

Reductionist Measures

Modernist ontology and methods have been bases for the psychological fiction that ethnic identity, defined by characteristics such as sense of peoplehood, cultural values, and commitment to culture, can be assessed by looking at objective, quantifiable, continuous or categorical traits and behaviors (see Vaihinger, 1924). That "as if" fiction has been perpetrated by psychological tests that obscure the multiple, emergent and changing meanings of ethnicity and privilege particular behaviors as manifestations of ethnic identity. It has also been boosted by the pretense that the meaning of questionnaire responses is as unequivocal as the rhetoric of modernist methods and traditions implies.

Here, again, the recrudescence of a familiar interpretive pattern is illustrated: Assumptions of rationality lead to overlooking irrationalities and contradictions in the ways people construct social identities; impartial researchers are purportedly simply looking for evidence of types of ethnic identity that exist "out there," apart from their constructions; and a set of questionnaire responses is assumed to have a constant, objective meaning, assigned—particularly when a theory is being tested—before the responses are made. However, the use of the same questionnaire items to assess acculturation and ethnic identity demonstrate that the meaning of the responses is not objectively inherent in the signifying tests. Because of the constructed relationship between signifiers and signified, ethnic identity tests do not directly reveal ethnic identity. They refer to other signifiers. Psychological tests are like researcher-created languages. In a move akin to providing only the words for brown, red, blue, green, and gold, and then asking people to use their new vocabulary to describe their motivations or what they had for

dinner last night, study participants are given severely limited response options and researchers try to describe behavior patterns from that circumscribed data.

Individuals interpret texts, such as psychological questionnaires, in terms
of a multitude of unspoken texts which are not constant in meaning or
cognitive accessibility; so researchers cannot objectively know the meaning
of those responses. For example, rather than indicate a strong ethnic identity,
a respondent's ability to speak an Asian language might simply reflect a
practical need to be able to communicate with parents who are not fluent
in English. Why regard a preference for ethnic food as evidence of ethnic
identity rather than a reflection of developed tastes and recipes learned from
family and friends? Americans usually do not think of Labor Day as an
occasion to feel kinship with other laborers, yet ethnic identity scales assume
that celebrating ethnic holidays reflects ethnic identity and the official, transcendent meaning of the holiday. Instead, the get-together could indicate a
commitment to family and friends—and it would not have the same meaning for a mere guest as it would for the person going through the sacrifice
and hard work of hosting the holiday. The basis for assuming that such
transient, symbolic behaviors restricted to leisure time are a noteworthy indication of ethnic identity is usually not provided; and reductive, simplifying
methods simultaneously reflect and become metaphysical assumptions about
which aspects of ethnic identity are relevant to people's lives and what various behaviors mean.

Contrast reductionist measures with how the following Japanese student sees her ethnicity in terms of other people's constructed notions of her
nationality and race:

> Everybody teaches me a lesson that I am Japanese, not an Ameri-
> can even I do not want to think about it. For example, sometimes
> in class at university, I feel like I do not belong there at all. I feel
> so alone.
>
> [In one class] while an American student was giving a pre-
> sentation, other American students listened to it quietly and gave
> some advice and comments. On the other hand, when I was doing
> my presentation, some American students started chattering, and
> they seemed not to care about my presentation at all. I thought
> that they did not listen to my presentation because I am a Japa-
> nese. They might think that my project will not be good because
> I am not an American, and not good at English skills. Things like
> this did not happen just once; it happened a lot in my life in this
> country. I thought [this reflected] racism. I felt so angry and dis-
> appointed. However, I knew I could not do anything about it.

Her ethnicity is apparently being viewed through a social status filter by an audience unwilling to make the slightest of accommodations; but measures of ethnicity do not come close to examining those relationships that her simple description exposes. The meaning of behaviors and the creation of identities arise in social interactions, not in abstensia; so understanding must be in terms of context to guard against mistaking the perceptual isolation of behaviors, meanings, and texts for actual independence (Bruns, 1987). Nevertheless, commitment to reductionist measures has meant that the dynamics and phenomenological complexity of ethnicity and its melding with other identities are barely glimpsed.

Notwithstanding the prevalence of modernist frameworks today, ethnic identity cannot be understood through logical inference about data gathered under faulty metaphysical and epistemological assumptions. Yet the use of psychological tests and the meanings ascribed to tests and models have emerged as normal, natural, correct, and privileged. This rhetorical effect is helped along by modernist psychology's hegemony which hides study participants' consciousness and construction of ethnic identity. It is compounded when only research questions that can be contorted to fit the confines of the empirical method are permitted.

Researchers do not need to either severely limit respondents' voices or simply accept all statements as truth. As facilitators of psychological discourse, postmodern psychologists could engage respondents as creators of their ethnic identity, learn how they define and contest definitions of their identity, and analyze the contextualized meanings they develop. Doing so may well mean abandoning extant models.

Models

Models are narrowly focused theories and like theories, they are isolated, closed, constructed systems that cannot be compared to a theory-neutral reality (Gergen, 1988; Manicas, 1987). Ethnic identity models, commonly extensions of modernist myths of ontological order in psychological realms, create order by simplifying: They conceptually force heterogeneous experiences and ethnic consciousness into one of several logically possible types or stages. For example, ethnic identity is sometimes viewed in terms of an artificial dualism, reflecting Western rather than, for example, Taoist orientations (Woollett, Marshall, Nicolson, & Dosanjh, 1994). (Table 6.1 summarizes a sample model.) Typologies generally have been de-emphasized in favor of stage models, perhaps partly due to the suspicion that some typologies developed during the civil rights movement of the 1950s and 1960s reflected characteristics and experiences of that time rather than universal regularities (L. Myers et al., 1991).

TABLE 6.1 A Psychological Model of Ethnic Identity

Stage

1 Individuals have neither explored nor committed to an identity.

2 Individuals have committed to an identity but have done so by adopting parental values without independently exploring their own identities.

3 Due to a significant experience that forced them to become aware of their ethnicity, individuals are in the process of exploring their own identities but have not yet settled on or committed themselves to an identity.

4 Individuals have explored their identities and have firmly committed themselves to an ethnic identity.

Note. This summary of a general identity-development process is based on J. Marcia's model in "Identity in Adolescence," 1980, in *The Handbook of Adolescent Psychology*, edited by J. Adelson.

Like typologies, though, stage models are replete with modernist assumptions. Although psychologists concede that they do not know whether ethnic identity development is (best understood as) linear (e.g., D. Sue et al., 1998) and some researchers have argued that it is not (e.g., Marsella, Johnson, Johnson, & Brennan, 1998), stage models are based on reductive, linear stages built around a handful of essentialized characteristics that presumably determine or summarize a person's identity orientation.

To illustrate, the Minority (Cultural/Racial) Identity Development Model (Atkinson, Morten & Sue, 1989; D. Sue et al., 1998), like most ethnic identity models, reduces the development of a well-balanced sense of self-worth and individuality to basically one path, reached by the same, simple, almost Manichean cognitive processing.[6] (See Table 6.2.) Its claim that at the last stage individuals can view ethnic groups objectively exemplifies its embrace of the modernist belief that people can step outside of their consciousness to make objective appraisals. The last, most autonomous stage is implicitly treated as the most developed and ideal, which is a value judgment resurrecting modernist beliefs in progress as well as a Western cherishing of individuality. Models of identity development that treat minorities as only orbiting around and defined primarily in relation to white Americans are not only reductionist but also, in some ways, colonialist.

Treating a behavioral or attitudinal syndrome characterizing a type or stage as though it has the same meaning for different individuals pushes perceptions of ethnic identity into a model's narrow categories and washes out heterogeneity. Marginalization, for example, is situationally specific for some people whereas it is pervasive and transforming for others, such as the following fourth-generation Japanese American:

TABLE 6.2   Minority (Cultural/Racial) Identity Development Model

Stage

1 Minority members at this stage want to completely adopt the cultural values and lifestyles of European Americans and consciously and unconsciously denigrate the physical and cultural characteristics of their minority group.

2 Exposure to new information and experiences motivates questioning of prior attitudes and triggers ambivalent feelings about both the dominant and minority group.

3 At this point, individuals totally reject the dominant group; they strongly identify with and completely and unquestioningly embrace their minority culture. A growing understanding of the effects of societal forces on minorities motivates the formation of tentative alignments with similarly oppressed groups but conflict with other minorities can undermine the alliances.

4 Feeling sufficiently secure about their identity to question their previously held, dogmatic beliefs, individuals at this stage question their total and unthinking allegiance to the minority group at the cost of personal identity and resist blanket disparagement of the dominant group.

5 Having a sense of self-worth and individuality and recognizing that accepting and valuing one's own ethnic group does not preclude positive attributes in other groups, members of minorities accept or reject the cultural values of the dominant and minority groups on an objective basis.

Note. Based on D. Atkinson, G. Morten, & D. W. Sue's (1989) Minority Identity Development Model (later renamed a Cultural/Racial Identity Development Model) in "A minority identity development model," in *Counseling American minorities*, edited by D. Atkinson, G. Morten, & D. W. Sue.

between the ages of thirteen [and] eighteen . . . I realized [for] the first time people looked at me as being Asian. I realized the stereotypes of being Asian and didn't want to fit in to it. Part of me trying to deny my culture was to join a gang of predominantly Mexicans. With them I felt protected from that stereotype. . . . Hiding my culture was more important to me than staying out of all the trouble I knew I was going to get into. With the initiation in the gang came a lot of negative peer pressure. I strayed away from my good friends and enforced my violent lifestyles [and] carelessness. My best friend sold drugs in school. . . . He persuaded me to sell martial arts weapons that I bought through the mail [and sold] to all the students. We both made more money than we needed but got even greedier. Later that year a group of us got arrested for breaking into someone's home.

By the time I entered high school I almost made a complete turn around. . . . even though our relationship was short, [my girlfriend] introduced me to a whole new set of friends [who] were all Asian for a change. With my new group of friends came the stereotype of being smart, quiet, and obedient. . . . I was never good at being any of these. My family background was not the same as any of my friends that lived sheltered lives. It was very difficult to be around people who are smarter than me. Having a 2.7 GPA was considered failing to many of my friends' parents. Even though I have improved so much from Junior High, I was still looked at with disappointment. I always had a problem accepting my identity and wanted to avoid being Asian. I understood the restrictions of being Asian while traveling outside of LA every summer [on family vacations]. . . . I feel like everyone is watching us. It seems so unfair . . . how unwelcome we are even in our own country.

In contrast to narratives such as his, modernist models are orderly fictions that obscure phenomenologically recognizable ethnic identities and the effects of varying choices, agency, and perceptions of discordance between one's behaviors and those of other members of the ethnic group.

Homogeneous stages and meanings are part of a broader presumption of a modernist coherence, order, and rationality trumping diversity, fragmentation, and irrationality; separation displacing imbrication; determinacy overtaking contingency; synthesis and unity vanquishing difference; stability superseding change; and simplicity and reductionism ironing out complexity (Ritzer, 1997). Varying forms of ethnic identity created by, for example, middle-class Filipino/a Americans in Los Angeles and Chinese Americans in New York City's Chinatown are silenced in modernist metaphysics that clothe ethnic identity in one-size-fits-all transcendent stages.

Hermeneutic analysis of those models could reveal how modernist portrayals emphasizing diachronic, mutually exclusive, markedly differentiated, crystallized stages brush over the ways in which identity is constantly unraveling and becoming (Zoreda, 1997). It could show how the downplaying of the synchronic obscures the murky, changing, simultaneous contortions and contrasting faces of individuals' ethnic identity.

These types of issues are typically overlooked, however, in part because of the rhetorical power of modernist science. The enthroning of scientific narratives in U.S. culture has produced a hyperreality so that modernist psychology's simulations of reality are equated with reality. Self-knowledge is measured by its conformity to a simulation (Denzin, 1994): The hyperreal ethnic identity models are regarded as mirrors of reality so test-takers look at identity models or their scores on an ethnic identity test to "learn" about their identity. Alternative descriptions of ethnic identity are suppressed and a communal knowledge built from an open, dialectic discourse with study participants does not develop. Instead, the model becomes a reigning rhetorical device.

Posing new frameworks, on the other hand, can expose the constructed nature of ethnic identity models and make them look less natural and convincing. A postmodern psychology would not only reanalyze modernist research and models of ethnic identity; it would offer alternative portrayals with different premises as discursive moves. For example, ways in which individuals develop diverse, complex, category-defying identities might be appreciated if ethnic identity were likened to beams of light refracting through different particles or combinations of refracted light producing different colors or images. Alternatively, ethnic identity might be characterized as being like the stock market—with lots of pauses, corrections, surges, and retreats; simultaneous, conflicting indicators; and individual differences in vulnerability to a crash, defined in different ways.

Another option might be to think of ethnic identity as a river with variations in shoreline, water patterns, and obstacles, like the vicissitudes of consciousness; identity might be linked to point of view, much as the river's perceived nature depends on whether it is viewed in terms of microbiology, aesthetics, thirst-quenching qualities, or prime fishing spots. Although a particular angle seems to show the river's orderly "state," focusing on the regularities shifts attention from random influences, such as air pressure changes, and random litter; in a parallel way, focusing on similarities and orderliness in ethnic identity occludes its richness and local variation. Like a modernist psychological measure of behavior, measuring the river by extracting a handful of water misses its dynamism and relationship to other phenomena as well as the ways in which the river not only transforms itself, but transforms its environment; similarly, concentration on isolated, quantified aspects of ethnic identity diverts attention from the qualitative and dynamic or ways ethnic identity might influence how situations are interpreted. A postmodern investigation would look at the local meaning of ethnic identity in specific, nonclinical contexts and freely relayed narratives.

Postmodern Intertextual Meanings

Alternative frameworks open new vistas to what has been excluded, the quality of the existing data, and links between standpoints and modernist rhetoric. Stepping away from the emphasis on modernist order, foundational meaning "out there," and people as mere actors in a play about deterministic relationships between variables allows consideration of individuals as constantly reconstituting their identity by their choices and reorganization of themselves in different periods of life, in interaction with changing people, in relation to new ideas, and in new situations. It provides a view of the construction of Asian Americans' identities, whether by Asian Americans or non-Asian Americans, within unstable, multidimensional, interpreted cultural and racialized contexts.

Like a speck of paint in a pointillist painting, identity needs to be examined in relation to a polysemic slew of defining texts and interpretations, semiotic traces of what it is not, and *différance*. Among those texts are power/knowledge relations; whether different individuals consider ethnic identity to be a cardinal, central, or secondary Allportian (1961) trait type; society's purportedly realistic self-representations; the dominant culture's ways of justifying its denial or marginalization of alternative readings of reality (Lennert, 1997); interpretations of racial hostilities; varying degrees of emotional linkage to an Asian country; Orientalist views; material conditions; intergroup competition; forces pushing toward assimilation and those pushing toward cultural pluralism; portrayals of Asian countries as military threats, exploitable sources of cheap labor, economic and political allies, or competitors; different types of statuses; capitalist tendencies to promote class divisions; immigration and naturalization policies; social and legal narratives; and changing social conditions, needs, and interpretations. Insofar as a sense of self is also configured by weaving personal events, multiple pasts, and possible futures (Polkinghorne, 1988; Segal & Handler, 1995) into an integrated, meaningful narrative, even photographs we have seen of ourselves and our families are potentially relevant texts. Analysis of ethnic identity in relation to economic, historical, or photographic texts need not be conceded to the province of other disciplines; without needing to become experts in other fields, psychologists would bring psychological orientations to the discourse.

The relevance of such a multitude of texts speaks to the different texts individuals invoke and interpret in the creation of their ethnic identity, which is always under construction and without a blueprint. Some people might treat the "Asian" in "Asian American" as an integral text, for example; others will emphasize a duality in the term "Asian American"; biracial Asian Americans might also construct identities in relation to their physical appearance, surname, or shifting closeness to one parent over the other (Pinderhughes, 1995).[7] A community's ethnic composition or shared feelings of alienation can be texts bearing on ethnic identity, as illustrated by a Korean immigrant: After her family moved from a white, middle-class neighborhood to Los Angeles' Koreatown, she felt "non-American" and her acculturation slowed; but she "started to get the sense of belonging. [At school, she] did not feel strange any more because everybody was an immigrant also."

Individuals also use varied normative standards as texts in the construction of their ethnic identity. When Asian Americans expect another person of the same ethnicity to be aware of ethnic behavior norms, for example, and that person fails to do as expected (e.g., appropriately reciprocate a kindness), she or he might be judged more harshly than similarly behaving non-Asian Americans would be. The feeling that the Asian American has breached ethnic cultural expectations or undermined a sense of peoplehood may be a manifestation of ethnic identity and hint at the meanings ethnicity has too.[8]

An intertextual postmodern analysis of ethnic identity could entail inspection of texts that have been implicitly excluded in popular conceptions of the ethnic community, as in the case of some Asian Americans who have voiced surprise at the existence of homosexual Asian Americans. It might lead to examinations of how the juxtaposition of excluded texts and ethnicity can complicate social marginalization, as in the case of an unwed, pregnant Korean American who felt, "Whether I tried to be American or Korean, I didn't fit in anywhere because I was a pregnant teenager. I wanted to somehow blend in with the rest of the crowd of unmarried girls who became pregnant but I couldn't because I was Asian." In such ways, identity is created in a constantly reciprocal, reformulating, interplaying system of social relationships and concepts; yet the identity created at one point can linger and affect the creation of subsequent identities.

Interrelated Identities

Some of the complexities of ethnic identity are due to the fact that, although phenomenologically singular, identities are conceptually and socially multiple, interconnected, and in flux. A Filipina American's description of her identity as simultaneously Filipina, female, and American provides an example:

> [I] cultivated two faces: . . . I was going to do what I had to do to be independent, even if it meant letting [my parents] see exclusively one face—the face that they only wanted to see which was the respectful and abiding Filipina. [They] said that it would be different if I was a boy. A boy can go out and take care of himself, but what can a girl do? My gender played an important role in this part of my personality development. Meanwhile, my friends were telling me to wear makeup, to dress "hip", to flirt with boys, and go out and have fun with them. My parents on the other hand were telling me to stay home, clean the house, cook rice, do my homework, and just do what I am told.

Although this book has discussed Asian Americans in terms of race, culture, acculturation, ethnicity, and identity, I do not mean to imply that the latter are independent influences on Asian Americans. While modernist models encourage portrayals of ethnic identity apart from gender, Orientalizing narratives, race, and class, in the meaning realm ethnic identity is not so independent. For example, the meaning of being a member of a minority can, when coupled with gender and, for many Asian American women, petite size, compound perceptions of Asian American women as powerless or weak. The gender messages a Japanese American woman was taught affected how she interpreted her own identity, the choices she made in her life, and her experiences:

> There were two main cultural beliefs that were given to me by my parents, and they both have to do with gender. The first is the role model my mother displayed as submissive, catering to the husband, and that women took care of the children and the house.... The second gender message I received was that women should be nice, quiet, petite, and pretty. I was overweight at about age 7, and then grew tall while I was in elementary school. I developed a negative attitude about my body [and] a false sense of sort of "belonging" to the "other" group. I felt disapproval from my family, which later grew to disapproval from all Japanese.
>
> I definitely know that these two messages led me to marry outside of my race and accept an abusive relationship. With feelings of unacceptance from Japanese men, I began radiating toward other races....
>
> Today, I know I have anger, but being a "good girl," I was finding socially appropriate ways to express this—aerobics, writing. I was still telling myself, on some level, that feeling anger was wrong.

For a male, too, his ethnic identity as a Korean American is not isolated from other identities:

> Being an Asian American male I must be tough mentally because if I show emotions I can be seen as being not tough ... when a problem comes up then it is the part of the male to solve that particular problem.... If I go to [my] parents they often say try to figure it yourself or try to handle it ... because they feel that I, as a male, should be able to either handle it or figure it out.

Notwithstanding implications of modernist structuralism, gender does not necessarily have the same meaning or play the same role in the behavior of people of the same sex. Therefore, postmodern discourse on ethnic identity would neither treat gender as a factor inserted into some formula of identity nor regard it as one discrete variable intersecting with another discrete variable, ethnicity: Neither gender nor ethnicity has a singular, categorical meaning.

Starting with different premises and metaphors—instead of regarding identity as an independent, additive, categorical classification—opens the way to the contemplation of different issues and new ways to address them. Suppose, for example, identity were thought of as a malleable ball of yarn composed of multiple, colored, interwoven threads, each representing an aspect of a person's identity, such as being a Korean American, middle class, or divorced. Those with a proclivity toward seeing particular colors may perceive those colors predominating, especially when a snapshot view is taken. A more dynamic perspective, however, reveals that inverting parts of the sphere in different situations causes different surfaces to seemingly dominate. Because threads are intertwined in unexpected and unique ways, pulling on any thread has reverberating effects elsewhere even if they are not obvious. Moving a thread changes the spin of the ball, which makes the effects of environmental stimuli on particular threads unpredictable. Even if this model opens perspectives, it too would be a deconstructed discursive move; deconstruction of it would highlight that, despite what this model implies, ethnicity, race, class, minority status, religion, occupation, and gender do not simply contextualize each other but also have confluent meanings. This alternative also does not show how those interlocking bases of meaning are used to legitimate particular social practices, affect who has access to power, determine social conditions and experiences, and contribute to the meaning of identity. However, it can be a basis for contesting narratives.

Even short of proposing new models, a postmodern framework raises issues that are ignored by modernist frameworks. For example, given that the meaning of being Asian American is constructed from competing discourses (Handler, 1992), how might race, gender, class and sexuality inform and transform the ethnic identity of Asian Americans and bear on the perceived relevance of ethnicity? What different meanings does ethnicity have for homosexual and heterosexual Asian Americans? In a cognitive manipulation akin to the defense mechanism insulation, in what ways might some people confine race and ethnicity to narrow areas of identity? How do people synthesize texts to form an identity? How do Asian American gang members' views of Asian American-ness differ from those of Asian American professionals? If ethnic identity were viewed as opposition to the hegemony of the cultural mainstream, what would that framework tell us about the United States and the meaning of ethnicity in the United States? Addressing many of those issues would be difficult, if not impossible, by using solely empirical methods; hermeneutics, deconstruction, and postmodern qualitative approaches constitute alternative investigative methods.

The Social Negotiation of Identity

Because the meaning and importance of the multiple texts defining ethnicity are equivocal, ethnic identity is not best viewed as a static, reified entity; it is more usefully viewed as an ongoing process of social negotiation in multiple arenas—in social relationships, research, business, government, and through discourse and political struggle—with age, generation, education, nativity, gender, and sexual orientation commonly bearing on how and with whom the ethnic identity is negotiated. Instead of being akin to a board game in which options are very restricted and contestants are judged in terms of reaching the a priori winning position, the forms of an ethnic identity might be compared to a game of go with its different textual interpretations of the significance of placed stones and multiple, messy, and simultaneously negotiations.

Some innovative studies have suggested ways to explore the social negotiation of ethnic identity. For example, by using a questionnaire to prime study participants to think about ethnic identity issues and then conducting focus groups addressing related issues, Mayeda (1998) illustrated how Hawaiian Filipino/a- and Samoan-Americans chose to deal with stereotypes about them. By reporting on his analysis of their responses and extensively quoting respondents, he opened discourse over the meanings of those responses: He gave readers a chance to evaluate how responses were categorized and interpret the responses for themselves.

The social negotiation of identity can also be recontextualized. Psychology has explored identities within the framework of the United States and dominant psychological ideologies. But how would minorities' identity be viewed in the context of a worldwide population in which white people are minorities (Moore, 1988)? In which cases might interpretations of the behaviors or experiences of minorities be reinterpreted if the United States were viewed as part of the Americas defined by the colonization of Aboriginal Americans, Inuit, and Central and Southern Americans, as well as Hawaiians (V. T. Nguyen & Chen, 2000)?

Decentered, diasporic viewpoints might focus on the identity of the world and the place of Asian Americans in it. A description of a Cambodian boy's experiences hint at the impact of events in Asia and the world's reaction to them on his ethnic identity. Without the rest of the family, he and his father were forced out of Phnom Penh by the Khmer Rouge. During the pogrom, he heard whispers of the starvation deaths of his relatives, saw the Khmer Rouge kill people for no apparent reason, and realized that no one dared ask why they had been killed. As a three-year-old put into a children's work detail to keep the Khmer Rouge's buffalo comfortable, he surreptitiously tracked his father's nearby work gang so that when the gang was moved, the toddler would ask to go to the forest to urinate and, once in the forest, sneak into his father's moving work group, as his father had instructed. He recalled watching his father beg the Khmer Rouge to let the toddler stay with him, his own frequent experiences with starvation, the Khmer Rouge threats to kill him, and the sights and smells of artillery and machine gun fire and death until, at the age of 6, he and his family escaped to a Thai refugee camp. After describing his experiences, as a young man he concludes:

> There are many things I do not understand. The whole world knew that there was a killing field [taking] place inside Cambodia and yet the world just . . . decided not to do anything. We lived day by day without hope for the future. I was hungry, sick [with malaria] for years, and physically working hard. Each and every step, death was waiting. . . . A kid for my age, supposed to be love[d] . . . by neighbor, relative, [and family]. I did not have any of those. The Khmer Rouge turned us human to robotics. Age did not matter. . . . I was told to spy [on] my own father. What was father? Khmer Rouge took away word such as father, and son. Friend was the word used to call each other. Each . . . individual was belong to Central government, Angkar Lou. Love, affection was forbidden. My father could not showed the love he had for me and I [could not show the respect] a son [is] supposed to [show] his father. Family value was completely a 180 degree turned up-side down. The normal kid in my age supposed to go to school and learned while I was [in the] jungle under the pouring rain with no clothes on, taking care of the buffaloes. Worst, I was walking across the killing field that buried hundreds and hundreds of human bodies. Some of the body were old, some freshly new. The smell of death was terribly unbelievable. The rain washed away the body parts, the juice of the death body was carried by the raining water. Did not [matter] how much I was sick, I had to go to work, as long as I could stand on my both foot. Disease left untreated. . . . Kid needed appropriate food and cared, for the brain is developing. It was sad while American kid worried about gaining weigh while I had no

food to eat. . . . I had to worked so hard. I wasted my life for
nothing. Who had the right to put me and millions of Cambodian in a position that nobody dare to imagine? Where was the
compassion of humanity? Why we as an Cambodian [experi-
enced this] suffering and life?

It is hubris for those who have not had such experiences to think that their
extensive formal education provides them the best conceptual framework, in
the form of clinical theories, psychological tests, or research models to help
him understand his identity as a Cambodian American, much less suppose
that a model of minority identity has the same applicability to him as it
might to a tenth-generation black American. Hearing his narrative can stir
social action and understanding that statistical analysis cannot.

CHAPTER 7

Conclusion

At its birth, psychology was pulled by divorcing parents, humanism and scientific realism, and custody was given to the latter. Now past its youth, it can step out on its own.

Psychology need not completely abandon its roots: Some of the current research, such as that done in neuropsychology, would withstand being stripped of problematic modernist metaphysics and remain provocative and informative; and correlational studies of social characteristics and health status or knowledge about particular diseases would still serve public policy purposes. Nevertheless, largely because modernist science's assumptions and quantitative methods are too infrequently appropriate for addressing relevant psychological concerns, the usefulness of modernist psychological research has not equaled the effort put into it or the successes of some other fields.

Sociology is split into modernist and postmodernist camps; but psychology need not choose, a priori, one approach or the other. The all-or-nothing thinking that gave rise to the previous century's nature-nurture debate would be just as misguided now. While retaining modernist science's skepticism and reliance on evidence and reason rather than faith or authoritarian declarations, the orientation chosen should depend on the ontological and epistemological assumptions deemed appropriate for the particular psychological issue at hand—and that is why I have not argued for a particular set of postmodern assumptions and methods.

Scientism casts science as the sole epistemological foundation underlying any legitimate, rational claims of knowledge and the prime basis for judging "real" knowledge and meanings (Bauman, 1978; Bernstein, 1983). However, other epistemic frameworks and investigative tools are available and they can be carefully used to address the unique characteristics distinguishing humans from physical objects.

Compared to modernist frameworks, postmodern orientations lend themselves to the study of a wider variety of human behaviors and psychological issues, some of which have been suggested in earlier chapters. The broadening of philosophies and methods beyond modernist boundaries enhances opportunities to address psychological issues by creating closer phenomenon-method and premise-method fit (Slife & Gantt, 1999). This final chapter points to the expanded realm of psychological inquiry opened by postmodern perspectives, the implications of postmodernism for public policy and social change, and the new roles postmodernism creates for psychologists.

New Issues and Alternative Methods

As exemplified by postmodern feminist psychology, postmodernism's emphasis on analysis moves psychologists away from mechanistically churned, cookie-cutter empirical studies that, while multiplying, provide quite limited knowledge. That analysis offers a way to think anew about psychological issues and concepts, such as exposing ways operational definitions do not do justice to concepts.

A postmodern psychology does not treat people as interchangeable, modernist specimen; instead, it treats study participants as unique individuals who are meaning creators and choice makers. Knowledge is to be gained through careful, in-depth studies of individuals and their experiences in hundreds and thousands of samples. Those in-depth studies include analyses of the intertextual meanings created by study participants; the ways in which locally ascribed meanings affect behaviors, perceptions, and constructs; the ways meanings are communicated and negotiated; and the significance of the genealogy of meanings. For example, how can study participants' responses that reflect thoroughly considered interpretations be distinguished from those that merely reflect the uncritical reiteration of what they have heard others express and what significance does the genealogy have on behaviors? A postmodern framework might also lead to an examination of ways in which personal and public systems of meanings anticipate, challenge, direct, or conflict with each other (Denzin, 1994).

New questions about facts arise from this orientation. For example, what criteria are or should be used in declaring facts? If the Enlightenment view of knowledge as the accumulation of new facts were discounted, in what ways might new organizations of "facts" define knowledge?

Abandoning scientific objectivism and the concomitant view of values as subjective contaminants of a value-neutral science, postmodernism concedes that value judgments underlie epistemological norms and theories of knowledge (Watson, 1992). What are regarded as neutral, objective interpretations are often simply those that correspond to tacit values. Therefore, rather than turn a blind eye to values, postmodernism examines them; and rather than accept one of psychology's classic goals, learning how to control behaviors, a postmodern psychology specifically and explicitly examines values and ideologies behind quests for control and subjects them to contestation. In addition to scrutinizing the ideology and power moves behind goals, it illuminates ways in which study participants and researchers submit to or exercise power (Racevskis, 1993): It sheds light on researchers' role as narrative shapers, arising from their definition of what is to be learned from study participants and their choices of research methods, language, and emphases. A decentered, postmodern psychology explores connections between psychology and ideology (Hollinger, 1994); which and how social interests are served by modernist premises and interpretations; and how knowledge is used.

Thus, postmodernism fights proclivities toward disguising social influences on the construction and uses of knowledge (Hoshmand & Polkinghorne, 1992). It sees that ideology is used to legitimate the distribution and use of power and recognizes that truth claims and power distributions are expressions of society's moral premises (Fowers & Richardson, 1996). Accordingly, postmodern psychologists subvert the habit of privileging particular perspectives, decenter portrayals, showcase buried efforts to dispose people toward particular interpretations (Parker, 1997), deconstruct explanatory concepts and narratives, and uncover hidden meanings and ideologies and their oppressive consequences.

Moving beyond the empirical and quantitative, postmodernism's methods also broaden the psychological issues that can be studied. Although qualitative methods can present problems (see Buchowski, 1994), specific, qualitative postmodern research methods have been successfully used and discussed elsewhere (e.g., Ellis & Flaherty, 1992) and are seen in feminist journals as well as ethnic studies journals, such as *Amerasia Journal* and the *Journal of the Association of Asian American Studies*. Postmodern scholars engage in deconstructive, hermeneutic, naturalistic, and phenomenological analyses of interview or observational data, descriptions of commonplace, problematic moments, and other texts (Denzin & Lincoln, 1998).[1] Theories, methods, research findings, and interpretations can be constantly deconstructed.

Hermeneutics can be used to compare meanings produced from assorted standpoints or to analyze bases of validity, such as grounds for accepting propositions. Hermeneutic psychological inquiries more broadly might examine the social conditions that make understanding possible (Fowers & Richardson, 1996). Or more specifically, they might examine communicative conditions, such as the presence of authoritarian discussants, that can create temporary, albeit distorted, consensus about knowledge (Bauman, 1978).

Reliability in postmodern research refers to trustworthy methods of data gathering (Polkinghorne, 1988). Validity is no longer circumscribed by the definitions of modernist science; instead, it is defined by the strength of an analysis of data—the explication's ability to reveal coherent links to other statements, themes, or values.

Knowledge, therefore, is not equated with the "discovery" of universal covering laws or judged only in terms of the ability to predict and control; instead, it might take the form of described meanings. Rejecting a role as finders of objective facts, postmodern psychologists are behavior analysts and explorers of multiple layers of experience and meanings. Investigative methods are judged by their usefulness in producing meaningful understanding of human experience and quotidian life and not by their adherence to positivist rules (Polkinghorne, 1988).

Hermeneutics' premise that human behaviors and expressions of thoughts and feelings are "incomplete, partial, and often characterized by concealments and distortions" (Fowers & Richardson, 1996, p. 616) dovetails with another method. That method, narrative analysis, involves the collection and deconstruction of narratives. It can take a form paralleling therapeutic attempts to understand interpretive habits, everyday logic, and metaphoric links. Or it can involve the inspection of myths as not simply repeated tales but as ways of organizing and classifying reality. How are people retrospectively selecting, revising, and organizing their experiences to produce coherent, meaningful, self-satisfying self-narratives? What organizing themes are underlying the assignment of meaning to events and the contextualization of particular experiences (Polkinghorne, 1988, 1991)? A methodological shift to narrative analysis would be consistent with revamped cognitive perspectives and a decentered psychology of individuals. In a challenge to traditional narratives used to explain behaviors or statements, psychologists might analyze the ways in which cultural texts give meaning to lived experience (Denzin, 1993).

The incompleteness of human expressions, such as explanations for one's own behavior, also opens the door to psychological narrative analysis of what is elided. Psychologists entering that domain might scrutinize what study participants do not say; about what they are evasive, inarticulate, or uncomfortable; and what gaps and confusion are left in their narratives. Why do they choose to express ideas or feelings "through the explicit negation of [their] opposite" (Rogers et al., 1999, p. 88), as in "*un*acculturated"? Is it related to the Western tradition that postmodernism maintains has favored presence over absence, as in Freudian attributions of male superiority to the presence of the male penis and female inferiority to its absence—even if that privileging results in convoluted references to the nonwhite being without the absence of certain skin pigmentation? Which aspects of study participants' narratives seem not to fit or sound rhetorically pat, ambiguous, contradictory, or untrustworthy (Nielsen, 1999)? When do people hesitate or revise their own statements? When do they misdirect attention so that they seem to emphasize the trivial and avoid the obvious or relevant? Examination of unexpressed nuances, connotations, or purposes would enable research psychologists to construct more meaningful and coherent interpretation than is customary now (Fowers & Richardson, 1996).

Studies with a postmodern orientation could also address a problem that has vexed psychologists. Over the last few decades, psychologists have expressed concern that study participants are exploited by researchers. The reward most participants receive for being in a study is fulfillment of a requirement for an introductory psychology class or a modest monetary sum. However, respondents can be repaid in other ways when they are not treated as objects to be observed and the point of research does not, in practice, just center around the researcher's interests.

Instead of simply gathering data from a group or allowing the goals of modernist science to supersede what people want to know or what would empower their communities, researchers could help study participants make sense of what is happening in their lives and in the lives of members of their diverse communities: They can advance the latter's efforts to understand the sociohistorical, economic, and cultural influences on their behaviors, ways of thinking, values, goals, and experiences. Postmodern psychological research could engage in discourse that enables study participants, "who have never known what it is to be either an author in modernist terms (in control) or a post-modern reader (active, creative, and inventive)" (Rosenau, 1992, p. 173), to articulate and make sense of inchoate feelings and experiences never discussed with family, at school, or at work. That discourse could help validate their feelings and experiences, give them a new power to direct their experiences, and enable them to make sense of their multiple locations in U.S. society (S. Chan, 1989).

Research might raise provocative issues that eventually become part of public discourse (Gergen, 1997). In such ways, a reconstructed, postmodern psychology encompasses a larger domain and takes a more encompassing and relevant place in the life of our society than does modernist psychology. The expansion of psychology's realm of inquiry, in turn, could widen psychology's impact on public policy: A postmodern psychology is potentially relevant to all policies having to do with what people express, how they behave, and the meanings they ascribe to events and situations, and, therefore, would have a noticeable presence in a range of policy arenas—such as economics, urban planning, and political science—where it is now often in the shadows.

Public Policy and Discourse

Compared to modernist psychology's premises, postmodernism's premises offer a framework that is, in many ways, more suited to policy analysis. For example, ideologies are critical to policy decisions and postmodernism's quest to uncover ideologies is better suited to examining the values underlying public policy.

In contrast, by wrapping themselves in the pretense of neutrality, modernist psychologists undermine their social worth as scholars and leave leadership to politicians, some of whom advocate oppressive policies and transform carefully crafted and limited research conclusions into overblown "facts" to prop up their prejudices. Thorough analysis in terms of multiple texts would broaden policy makers' perspectives while potentially making the manipulation of research more difficult.

Politicians, bureaucrats, political appointees, and other policy makers frequently seek not only information from but also refuge in studies: They seek protection against criticism from others by claiming that their representations simply reflect facts speaking for themselves. Providing thoroughly argued, reasoned interpretations from multiple standpoints, highlighting a range of considerations, making sense of and historically contextualizing competing claims, and identifying oppressive constructions can help policy makers feel even less vulnerable for accepting those interpretations than they do with modernist psychological research.

Ignorance about the minutiae of a particular form of postmodernism will not necessarily diminish the likelihood that policy makers will accept a researcher's analyses. Psychologists will not need to explain the metaphysical premises of postmodernism to every policy maker any more than they have to explain multivariate analyses. For those policy makers who are not mathematically inclined, a reasoned argument based on data from a variety of sources may have more credibility than a conclusion whose mathematical underpinning is taken on faith. Even those elected officials who are mathematically inclined are hard pressed to explain their positions to voters in terms of studies' multiple regressions.

Undoubtedly, some policy makers will feel uncomfortable with postmodern uncertainty and messiness and want to gravitate back to neater conclusions based on traditional views. On that basis, some might argue that the development of a postmodern psychology should be resisted. However, to the extent that existing modernist research is not well founded, should psychology be clinging to undeserved power to sway? In addition, the argument that a move toward postmodernism should be avoided because of a potential loss of influence on policy makers presumes that the net effect of offering a different type of knowledge would be a loss of a critical mass of policy makers who now find psychological research compelling. Like introductory psychology students who turn away from psychology because it differs from what they expected, naive policy makers may already be turned off by modernist psychology. They may find that postmodern psychological approaches are in some ways more accessible and credible than positivist psychology is.

Indeed, psychology's voice in public policy discourse can be amplified by the wider range of methods postmodernism uses, which increases the chances of issue-method matches. Instead of trying to sell policy makers on the idea that modernist assumptions are appropriate for every psychological issue, thereby leaving those unsold only with the option of disregarding psychological perspectives, psychologists could outline for them instances in which modernist assumptions might be appropriate (e.g., in searches for a mathematical relationship between types of mental health insurance coverage and unmet needs for mental health services) and instances in which postmodern premises and analytical approaches might be superior (e.g., narrative analysis of signs of psychological distress). Explaining those premise-issue matches and transmitting those postmodern forms of knowledge will require the self-conscious use of rhetoric.

Rhetoric

Practically speaking, in policy contexts and popular psychological discourse, psychology already is, at least partly, a rhetorical exercise. It should be, especially in a democratic society.

After all, what is the point of psychological research? The academy is not a playground in which the intelligentsia simply entertains itself musing over arcane topics. Don't psychologists hope that their efforts will enable people to have greater understanding of their own behaviors and the behaviors of others? Don't they seek to show policy makers credible, compassionate ways to help those with psychological problems and to better society? Those goals require dissemination of psychological concepts and research beyond journal readers. That communication, in the service of those goals, requires effective rhetoric.

Despite claims that scientific knowledge defrocks rhetoric, even the scientific method is a rhetorical move shaping researchers' assumptions, interpretations, conclusions, and ways of presenting psychological research. In textbooks and news reports, the premises of psychological research are downplayed because the studies are supposedly objective and research findings are presented as facts. In an act emblematic of the hyperreal, publishers advise textbook writers that a convincingly authoritative tone must be assumed for the book to be broadly adopted.

Psychology needs some credibility if the public is to gain any benefit from psychological concepts and research or support public mental health services. Yet, intellectually serious psychology is largely missing from public discourse. It is generally confined to the scholarly community. The news media commonly equate psychology with snippets of studies finding the obvious or inconsequential. The airways frequently feature some psycho-babbling clinician (or imitator) who characterizes a stranger's behavior in simple yet unabashedly self-assured ways and, no doubt encouraged by time-conscious broadcast media, pronounces authoritative bromides. Knowledge is distorted in textbooks in the name of being made understandable, keeping to page limitations, and seeking a large audience. To increase the chances that the public hears statements based on clear thinking and to increase the credibility of psychology in public policy debates, critically thinking psychologists need to be publicly willing to undercut the pablum.

Take, for example, the extension of clinical narratives about "rape survivors," a term many clinicians use to try to assuage a victim's misdirected sense of responsibility and to emphasize that the person survived. The credibility of psychology would be enhanced if psychologists were willing to counter the extension of the term to "divorce survivors" on the grounds that the hyperbole makes death sound like a common outcome in divorces. Psychology's credibility would likewise be improved if psychologists defied APA instructions that, in a misdirected attempt to avoid sounding pejorative, urge psychologists not to use terms like stroke "victim" or stroke "sufferer." Those instructions encourage psychologists to downplay difficulties most people have following a stroke and can sound like attempts by representatives of the establishment to minimize the existence of suffering. Postmodern psychologists might deconstruct such psychological portrayals as simulations or as consumed commodities.

A postmodern psychology would neither pretend nor seek to be nonrhetorical. Yet psychologists would not be turned into barkers. Their rhetoric would serve social purposes, which would likely be consistent with critical theory; their research's rhetorical validity might be defined by its ability to exert power over the reader (Denzin, 1995) and by its effect on policy.

Critical Theory

In contrast to modernist science's faith in allegedly morally neutral knowledge leading to progress, if not utopian social relationships and conditions, postmodernism rejects the presumption of a necessary link between knowledge and progress. Kindred critical theory argues that mainstream research usually, albeit unwittingly, contributes to the continuation of class, race, and gender oppression (Kincheloe & McLaren, 1998). It laments the emphasis on scientific technique and supposed objectivity over moral concerns (Richardson & Fowers, 1998). Social constructionists, for example, urge careful consideration of the pragmatic implications of scholarship and the relevance of moral criteria (Richardson & Fowers, 1998).

Postmodernism's subversiveness and rhetoric could undercut the use of knowledge to promote primarily traditional, dominant social interests and mediate the relationship between powerful and dominated populations (Racevskis, 1993). Eschewing the traditional exoticizing of the "other" and suppression of race, class, and gender differences as politically disabling, for example, postmodern critical theorists argue that "a good text exposes how race, class, and gender work their ways into concrete lives of interacting individuals" and interplay in a specific event or experience (Guba & Lincoln, 1998; Lincoln & Denzin, 1998, p. 415). They anticipate that critical social science could "eventually lead to a more egalitarian and democratic social order" and more social justice (Kincheloe & McLaren, 1998, p. 262); identify the specious underpinnings of oppressive social practices; expose the ways in which power dynamics are disguised as natural forces to deflect attention and impede the regulation of power (Silbey, 1997); and challenge historically and culturally situated, popular understandings and power relationships. Notwithstanding modernist orientations that often criticize practical reasoning—combining theories, research, clinical and nonclinical experiences, and moral judgments—for being unsystematic, unscientific, and inferior to formal logic and scientific reasoning, a counterhegemonic, postmodern analysis might use practical reasoning to address "not only . . . what is, but also . . . what ought to be" (Hamilton, 1998, p. 118). Thus, a postmodern, critical psychology points to different epistemic values, such as the critique and transformation of social, cultural, ethnic, and gender structures that restrict and exploit; highlights hidden connections between power and knowledge; and opens possibilities for social change by exposing assumptions and practices that impede social justice, by uncovering socially supported, false representations of individuals, groups, and social conditions, and by replacing ideologies.

Inasmuch as it is on the alert for the ways institutions co-opt and then dissipate much of the potential force behind calls for change, a postmodern critical psychology would not be surprised by efforts to label it biased. Indeed, some psychologists will protest a postmodern reformulation of psychology because in objectivist psychology, reference to values often raises charges of bias. Bias, however, is a component of most dialogues; whether it is problematic depends on the degree of bias and the context, purpose, and kind of dialogue (Walton, 1992). Bias is problematic when the lack of neutrality is inappropriate for the kind of dialogue, as in logical arguments. However, psychology is concerned with human behavior that does not occur in those terms and, therefore, does not need to be analyzed from that framework. Its advocacy arguments are not necessarily inappropriate on that count.

Nevertheless, the postmodern, critical study of minorities is likely to elicit charges of bias and politicization, especially when it runs counter to mainstream values. So be it. Scholars have the potential to alter representations of reality that, as Foucault argued, already are used to dominate people and affect their behaviors, values, ethnic identities, and perceived options. They can sometimes debunk hegemonic representations or ideologies operating within, for example, popular culture and educational institutions (Gottdiener, 1993; Richardson & Fowers, 1998).

To continue to use the lexicon of American psychology implies that the limited texts institutionally considered relevant to psychology are adequate for studying minorities. They are not. If, as standpoint theory argues, some locations are more conducive than others to understanding oppression (Mann & Kelley, 1997), it is especially incumbent on those who are in such key locations to uncover hidden, multiple truths in the corners of minority communities that are invisible to those outside them and make their voices heard. Psychologists studying minorities could take up the challenge "to develop a new critical ontology of ourselves" (Racevskis, 1993, p. 67): Studying the interpretive epistemologies of people of color, they could analyze the narratives and texts minorities invoke to describe their perspectives and experiences (Denzin, 1993). In addition to concentrating on identifying ways in which Asian Americans differ from non-Asian Americans or why Asian Americans have more or less of a certain characteristic than other Americans, psychologists might explore the meanings Asian Americans create (cf. Mickelson, Okazaki, National Research Center on Asian American Mental Health, Zheng, & Asian Youth Center, 1993). Rather than use the need for more research as a sop signaling the end of their engagement, researchers can instigate social action; at some point short of complete knowledge, action is already taken by policy makers and others anyway.

Scholars interested in issues regarding minorities could take the lead in decentering psychology's conventional framework, a de facto focus on white America and Western philosophy, and disrupting the resulting knowledge base. While some psychological research on minorities moves toward scholarship that energizes people to resolve the injustices and inequalities in U.S. society (Hune, 1997b) and challenges whose depictions of reality are heard, more studies could. That research can have an impact on racial relationships by giving voice to a wide range of minorities; valuing narratives minority and majority groups tell about themselves, their experiences, and events in their lives; countering hegemonic media monologues from media-defined community leaders; and analyzing racist narratives by and about Asian Americans.

Studies might ask about the ways in which Asian Americans are simul-taneously marginalized and not marginalized: Which Asian Americans are marginalized in relation to which groups and which mainstreams, and to what effects? For example, just as Asian Americans are not marginalized in some professions but are marginalized in the upper–management tiers of corporations, they might not be marginalized in friendships as much as they are in interracial dating. How do such experiences create tensions that con-tribute to perceived behavior options, preferences, interpretations, and choices? Under which conditions do Asian Americans make which decisions about how to behave? In what types of situations or circumstances is being Asian American likely to be noticed or judged? If psychologists were not hand-cuffed by modernist methods, what could be learned about Asian Americans?

While resisting the enticements of falling into old intellectual habits, postmodern psychologists also have the chance to be influential in the prac-tice of postmodern inquiry itself. Presently, those postmodernists studying Asian Americans are said to be

> more likely to APPLY the terms associated with postmodernist discourse to an Asian American experience than . . . to invoke Asian America to discuss the context in which debates about postmodernism might be further considered, developed, changed, or even forsworn . . . we *borrow from* rather than *invest in* debates about the postmodern. (Takagi, 1995, p. 40)

Psychologists can simultaneously create ways of modifying postmodernism and socially useful forms of research that affect policy.

Changing psychology and developing postmodernism will require more than calls for open attitudes: They will require changes in graduate curricula and criteria for judging scholarship. To the extent that the production of knowledge is a fight for adherents (Fuller, 1992), the direction psychology takes will depend on which strategy accrues the most funding and recruits the most productive and influential psychologists of the following genera-tions (Ward, 1995). (See Appendix B for a description of one protocol for teaching deconstruction.)

New Roles for Psychologists

As Foucault argued, freedom is in the capacity to change established practices rather than simply follow a script (Racevskis, 1993). Resistance to the
temptations of modernist science still leaves psychologists a role—perhaps a
more activist social role than modernist psychology does. Psychologists have
a role in showing the inadequacy of truth claims, producing new forms of
knowledge, and improving society.

Some people are more insightful and careful than others; some readings of texts are more comprehensive or internally consistent than others. To
the extent that psychologists—because of personal disposition, extended practice, or education—are able to think and provide useful interpretations,
postmodernism does not necessarily mute their voices in a relativistic cacophony. Indeed, a postmodern critical psychology would reject relativism
because it leads nowhere, renders critique implausible, and undermines
activism (Racevskis, 1993). If readings of knowledge claims were rigorously
judged on their qualities rather than on the social position or presumed
experience of their creators, what would distinguish psychologists might be
not so much their mastery of scientific techniques as what their rationality,
perceptiveness, and extended experience engaging in attentive, inquiring
discourse about psychological issues contribute to the quality of their interpretations, deconstruction, and discourse.

Without necessarily or always being at the center, seeding discourse,
alone identifying the overlooked or marginalized points or oppressive forces
(Bauman, 1987, 1992; Rosenau, 1992), producing or directing all the questions and issues, or being given an elevated status, social scientists could be
participants in postmodern discursive creations of knowledge. That discursive conversation would blur disciplinary boundaries which currently cause
sociologists, anthropologists, and psychologists to barely notice much less
contest work in each other's disciplines. If the purpose of research on Asian
Americans is to understand Asian Americans' behaviors, experiences, needs,
and outlooks, then academic boundaries should not circumscribe analyses
or dictate which texts are taken into consideration. More attention to other
disciplines would widen the breadth of intertextual analyses.[2] Even poetry,
drama, proverbs, autobiographies, and philosophical dialogues could be
treated as psychological texts with cognitive meaning and social implications (Hernadi, 1987).

Given disciplinary differences in aims and orientations, psychologists
need not compete with literary critics or historians in interdisciplinary con-
testations of truth claims. They might interpret texts with an eye toward
public policy or psychotherapy, for example, rather than toward a more
literary or artistic creation of multiple interpretations.

At this point, most psychologists have not adopted postmodern perspectives so taking such an approach carries practical risks. A department promotion committee, for instance, might not value interdisciplinary research as an advancement in its specific academic domain. In the face of mainstream academia's historic marginalization of ethnic research, systemic biases against publications of research on minorities (S. Sue, 1999), and devaluation of publications in ethnic journals, psychologists studying minorities already frequently face particular pressure to continue to conduct modernist research because a failure to publish much will decrease their chances of becoming tenured. Since postmodern psychological articles might meet with resistance from hidebound or unswayed journal reviewers who dismiss that switch in orientation as unscientific and, therefore, worthless, psychologists have much to risk by trying to change psychology. Those risks are to be weighed against the potential for increasing the influence of psychology in policy and public discourse, creating new ways of looking at what constitutes knowledge, and producing research that leads to a broader base of decentered social change and improvement of social relationships than psychology typically seeks or produces.

The choice to have an impact on both postmodernism and psychology is at hand. The opportunity to transform the academy, psychology, pedagogy, and society through critical postmodern psychological analyses is presenting itself now.

Traditional Types of Psychological Studies

Modernist psychology uses four types of studies: experiments, field studies, case studies, and surveys although the first two types are relatively rare in studies of Asian Americans. Experiments most closely follow the guidelines defining the scientific method: Typically, psychologists either compare how people with different defining characteristics behave in the "same" situation or compare the behaviors of the same or similar people in different situations. In contrast to the often obviously artificial settings of experiments, field studies are observations of naturally occurring behaviors; however, obtaining permission to study people in everyday situations can be difficult and discerning which of several naturally-occurring events caused a behavior is fraught with ambiguity.

To suggest bases for psychological disorders or illustrate treatment methods, psychotherapists frequently rely on case studies, focused examinations of a person's past and present experiences, behaviors, memories, feelings, and thoughts. Most case studies concern unusual, anonymous clients receiving psychotherapy.

Much of the research on Asian Americans is based on psychological tests or surveys in the form of questionnaires or, less often, interviews. Researchers try to control for extraneous, confounding variables by the way they design studies and analyze data. However, they face many obstacles.

Finding what psychologists would regard as representative Asian American samples is difficult. Some biases arise from respondent self-selection: Among those unlikely to be willing to participate in a study are Asian

Americans who are culturally unfamiliar with surveys or leery about divulging personal information, such as income, or in the case of a telephone survey about AIDS risks (e.g., Prohaska, Albrecht, Levy, Sugrue, & Kim, 1990), describing their sex lives to a stranger over the phone. Even when respondents are given an informed-consent form stating that they can, without penalty, withdraw at any time from any study that makes them feel uncomfortable, some people are more willing than others to disrupt proceedings, inconvenience others, and deal with the anxiety of not knowing whether they will be questioned about their withdrawal from the study; and college students in a sample would worry that they might be assigned a harder, substitute project.

Seeking samples by randomly selecting possibly Asian last names in the telephone directory is problematic: Non-Asian Americans are accidentally contacted, adding to the expense of the study; Filipinos with Hispanic-sounding last names, those with unusual Asian surnames, women who have changed their name to that of their non-Asian American husband, and some biracial Asian Americans are systematically overlooked; and those without a telephone and those with unlisted numbers (e.g., more than 60% of Los Angeles residents) are consistently omitted, which introduces a class bias. The use of convenience samples, unsystematically drawn from any source (e.g., Matsuoka, 1993), or snowball samples, based on word of mouth (e.g., Munet-Vilaró & Egan, 1990) also undermines any claim of sample representativeness.

In addition, interpretations of questionnaire responses can be problematic. People vary in their response biases, their tendency to respond to statements in particular ways. Most psychological questionnaires are worded in ways designed to account for response biases such as the intentional or unintentional tendency to answer in ways respondents think will make them look good or ways the interviewer desires. However, they are customarily constructed using the response biases of European American samples even though what is considered socially desirable varies across groups. For instance, some Asian Americans think that admitting to feeling happy and enjoying life indicates immodesty or frivolousness (Okazaki & Sue, 1995; Ying, 1989); they might be especially likely to balk at the former self-characterization. Complicating the interpretation of responses, negatively worded questions, sometimes used to counter response biases, can be confusing to translate for foreign-speaking Asian respondents.

Response biases also arise from inaccurate memories, variations in the care taken in responding, and differences in the accessibility of concepts used in reporting one's behaviors and experiences. That accessibility is often affected by extraneous factors, such as mood, recently encountered situations, the nature of a question, the manner in which it is posed, or the time of year. For example, if I were asked as a child whether I was often quiet, my answer would have differed depending on whether I was asked during summer vacation when I played a lot (and usually loudly) or during the school year when my contrasting classroom behavior might have been more accessible. Downplaying the effects of temporary cognitive accessibility in an effort to "find" transcendent patterns flies in the face of classic psychological research demonstrating that people show biases toward remembering what fits their interpretive schema and more recent research suggesting that in some situations, merely self-reporting one's race can heighten the accessibility of some concepts and alter subsequent behaviors (Steele & Aronson, 1995).

The order in which survey questions are asked can also unintentionally affect responses and, therefore, determine whether statistically significant relationships between variables are found (e.g., Echabe & Gonzalez Castro, 1999). For example, when a network news organization posted the Kenneth Starr independent counsel report on its website and, at the end of the report, conducted a public opinion poll asking what should happen to President Clinton for his egregious personal behavior, almost 50% of the polled passed judgment; but if respondents had first been asked whether they think they should hear balanced accounts before passing judgment, no doubt a larger percentage would have replied, "I don't know yet." Frames of references can be highlighted or obscured by the order or omission of questions.

Most research psychologists are well aware of these problems but, holding their collective nose, continue to conduct such studies and dutifully note the shortcomings at the end of their studies. In fact, a laudable acknowledgment of sample and procedural limitations is a standard, institutionalized section of a psychological journal article although the value of a string of publications with such limitations is usually taken for granted.

Deconstructing in the Classroom

Postmodernism may sound too abstract for most undergraduates but a trip to the Internet shows that many professors have incorporated it into their courses. Since about 1995, I have been discussing postmodernism in my undergraduate Asian American Studies psychology class, using my research-summarizing book, *Asian Americans: Personality patterns, identity, and mental health* (Uba, 1994a), as a fodder for deconstruction.

After discussing the modernist metaphysics underlying most psychological research, I lecture on postmodern premises and deconstruction, with many examples. Presenting deconstruction as a form of critical thinking, I try to teach students to deconstruct. Students are so accustomed to writing journals in which they simply give their opinions or going to the library and writing reports on what other people think, they often do not know how to think; when merely instructed to "critically analyze," many simply give opinions supported by anecdotes. Therefore, I must begin at basic levels.

My current approach, based on prior false starts and modifications recommended by students, involves several steps to assuage anxiety over a task that seems daunting to them. After I lecture on postmodernism, the class divides into groups, and each group orally deconstructs a different issue. To prevent students from falling back into old cognitive habits, I provide a deconstruction summary that identifies many of the analytical issues in this second chapter's deconstruction list, along with multiple, written examples of deconstructed concepts or explanations. After the groups deconstruct their topics and describe their deconstructive results to the rest of the class (a task to which the latter can contribute), the class again divides into new groups to repeat the protocol with new topics. Meanwhile, students are assigned a topic to deconstruct for their homework so that they spend concerted effort on understanding outside of class rather than just continue to wait for an epiphany in class.

For their term papers, students can either critically analyze a topic or form groups that discursively deconstruct a topic. Term papers are normally worth 20 points but group deconstructive term papers can be worth as much as 40 points with any points over 20 as extra credit. Groups deconstruct topics of their own choosing, such as parental reasoning they have heard, Asian American gender stereotypes, or portrayals of research findings. To prevent procrastination and ensure that students keep trying to learn how to deconstruct without me, I formalize the steps in writing a term paper: Students turn in a list of their possible term paper topics and later a summary of the ideas they intend to include on their selected topic, both of which we discuss as a class.

Over several weeks, any time a group feels stuck, someone from the group can write the group's topic on the blackboard and the class orally helps to deconstruct the topics while I restrict my involvement to asking questions. Doing this as a class helps the inquiring students learn to deconstruct; gives students experience teaching others how to deconstruct, which develops their own deconstructing skills; lets students know they are not the only ones having difficulty with this way of thinking so that they do not become too discouraged; and tells students that other groups are not procrastinating on their term papers so they should not procrastinate either. (Students know that grading for the class is not on a curve. To further encourage the practice of deconstructive skills, I sometimes tell students that those who provide help to other groups in the class discussion will have their lower midterm thrown out and their higher midterm score doubled.)

After the term papers are turned in, the students are given another homework assignment: They deconstruct the same topic they tried to deconstruct on the earlier homework assignment. Although by the end of the semester about 10% of the class still does not know how to begin to deconstruct, most of the class has made significant strides and some "complain" that they now cannot stop deconstructing—in other classes and outside the classroom. A more thorough report with three assessment measures, including quotations from student papers, is available at the following website: http://www.csun.edu/~hcaas001/bookappendix/pedagogy.html

Notes

Preface

1. I use the term "Asian American" rather than "Asian Pacific Islander American" because the psychological research on Asian Americans vastly outnumbers that on Pacific Islanders. I think that pretending that Pacific Islanders are included in the research marginalizes Pacific Islanders as mere appendages to Asian Americans and minimizes their historical, demographic, and cultural differences. Psychological research conducted at the University of Hawai'i has not slighted Pacific Islanders as much, but many of those publications are marginalized in psychological discourse because prior to publication on the Internet, they have often been difficult to obtain through university libraries.

2. I generally use the term "European American" when I want to emphasize culture and "white American" to emphasize race.

3. In this book, references to modernist psychology or postmodernism "doing" something are meant as metaphors and not as reifications of modernism, psychology, or postmodernism.

Chapter 1. Modernist Epistemology

1. I do not emphasize Asian philosophy or any non-Western research methods in Asian countries because they are not the basis for psychological research on Asian Americans, I am not arguing that they should be, and I do not want to implicitly reduce Asian Americans to Asians. I just want to contextualize present-day assumptions, albeit without trying to establish what Robinson (1976) notes is an unprovable, linear development of ideas from early science to present research.

2. I refer to "reality," "nature," and the "world" interchangeably.

3. The original reference, of course, was only to "man."

4. Another root of strident defenses of psychology as a science may be the sexual metaphor of science in which seeking knowledge is viewed as a form of sexual consummation—generated by desire; embodying yet transcending the carnal; and obtained by laying nature bare, stripping it of its mystery, arousing and subduing it. Just as erections have been linked with power and females have been associated with the soft, emotional, irrational, and uncontrollable, sciences that produce hard, potent, fertile facts are hard sciences whereas others, such as psychology, are regarded as subjective, inexact, poorly controlled, emotionally tinged, soft sciences. Although relevant in discussions of human behavior, the irrational, emotional, desirous, indecisive, and ambivalent—traits that used to be associated with females—have been downplayed (Bauman, 1996).

5. Although Epicureans questioned the assumption that nature is structurally unchanging (Toulmin, 1972), their view was not given much credence because they were tagged as atheists.

6. Scholars such as Galileo and Newton thought that even if psychological laws existed, they would still not be comparable to physical laws whereas French materialists held they would be versions of the same principles (Robinson, 1976).

7. One purported "law" of psychology, that rewarding behavior increases the likelihood of the behavior recurring, is actually a well-known tautology: Reward is defined as whatever increases the probability of a behavior recurring.

8. One contradiction of modernist research is the way researchers selectively take consciousness into consideration: Their single-blind experiments acknowledge study participants' consciousness; but they then downplay the researchers' consciousness by often not having double-blind experiments and by treating the researchers' interpretations as simply logical conclusions.

9. An operational definition is the specification of a particular study's method of measuring a variable or a concept.

10. The higher the level of statistical significance, the stronger the evidence is thought to be. Statistical significance does not mean, however, that findings have ontological or conceptual significance, differences between groups are large, or a conceptual or methodological error is unlikely. Nevertheless, it is customarily assumed to be meaningful, as evidenced by the conclusions drawn from statistically significant findings and by the publication of such results.

Psychologists usually select from 15 to 25 statistical tests based on their underlying assumptions. For example, some tests assume classifications that are independent (e.g., discriminant analysis); dichotomous (e.g., t-tests); normally distributed (e.g., parametric tests); linear (e.g., most multiple regressions); or additive (e.g., discriminant analysis; most multiple regression analyses). These assumptions can be problematic. For example, absent any way of establishing that causes are additive, statistics with additive assumptions are metaphysically and phenomenologically almost totally meaningless (Manicas, 1987).

11. This restriction does not cause much protest from typical study partici-pants, students unaccustomed to being able to reword test questions or choose other than given response options.

12. Aristotle distinguished among four types of causes of a behavior, event, creation, or other activity. Final cause is the goal or purpose behind the latter. Formal cause is the reason the latter has its essence or form. Material cause refers to the substances used to bring an object, event, behavior, or activity into existence. Efficient cause is the applied activity that brings about the latter. Modernist psychologists have focused on material and efficient causes and given little attention to the distinction between proximate and final cause or the role of chance and impulse.

13. Much of the public, too, judges psychological research intuitively. It seems that in whichever city the American Psychological Association annual convention is held, a local newspaper has a column on the silliness or obviousness of some of the psychological studies presented. Granted, sometimes the journalists are simply com-bining arrogance with ignorance (e.g., about the value of basic research) to pander to the antiintellectual sentiments of readers. Still, the contrast to the regard for medical and physical science research is stark, perhaps because psychological research seems so accessible or indistinguishable from psychobabble.

14. Ritzer (1997) discusses whether postmodernism is a continuation of modernism, the counter-Enlightenment, or radically different from that which has come before.

Chapter 2. Postmodernism

1. Indeed, although scientific discoveries can produce new facts, premier scientific landmarks have been provided by the creation of new meanings accounting for events, triggering paradigmatic reconceptualizations of the plausible (Kuhn, 1970; Polanyi, 1946/1964; Toulmin, 1951, 1961). For example, Einstein's insights arose not so much from conduct of experimental observations of phenomena, but from exami-nations of pervasive yet unacknowledged assumptions (Slife & Gantt, 1999).

2. Reference to "members of a dominant group" is not a code for "white people." The Japanese government, for example, exercises such power over narrative when it sanctions the teaching of fallacious versions of Japanese history and imposes its reading of reality on schoolchildren in Japan. Similarly, when historians writing for the World Book Encyclopedia describe various countries in a way that gives the impression that nothing happened in those countries until white people arrived, their narratives become reality for generations of readers.

3. Sometimes behaviors, such as empathy in women, are considered bio-logically "natural" when they stem from social characteristics, such as a lack of power, when they are interpreted from the perspective of those who want to downplay power differences, or when alternative tellings are ignored. Similarly, hyperreal,

computer-generated simulations of crime scenes can be convincing because they so favor one version of events and obscure ambiguities.

4. Reasoning that particular ways of thinking and perceiving are embedded in languages, Leibniz sought a universal language so discourse could be undistorted by linguistic conventions and discussants would be free to reason together without concern about misinterpretation (Toulmin, 1990). However, a universal language would not free us of the linguistic mediation of meaning. We would just share the same bias which would, in fact, make recognizing the biases all the more difficult.

5. Postmodernism shares many of the orientations of critical theory which developed in reaction to the conflict between U.S. egalitarian rhetoric and racism and classism. Concurring that traditional science is not neutral, postmodernism and critical theory alike hold that social constructions of experiences and reality reflect the social, historical discourses and power relations in which they are produced; facts are not independent of values and ideology; language plays a central role in the formation of conscious and unconscious awareness and knowledge; and the relationship between signifier (concept) and signified (behaviors) is always unstable (Kincheloe & McLaren, 1998).

6. Alternatives to modernist validity include ironic validity, the promotion of multiple interpretations and the exposure of the strengths and limitations of each; neopragmatic validity, the examination of heterogeneity and multiplicity that destabilize authoritative claims; and reflexive validity, the ability to promote the constant questioning of interpretations of texts (Denzin, 1995).

7. Postmodernists disagree over whether deconstruction has an ultimate destination (Faulconer, 1990).

8. At the beginning of experiments, study participants are dichotomized into control and experimental groups. Such a move is useful in some areas of research, but its usefulness in psychology is sometimes questionable because it implies that people either do or do not have an experience rather than that experiences are determined by how events are interpreted.

9. Early, modern hermeneutic reasoning focused on Biblical exegesis as the Protestant rejoinder to the Council of Trent's ruling that the Bible could not be directly understood by individuals without the intervention of the Catholic Church. Psychoanalysis was a foray into psychological hermeneutics, albeit with much refutable baggage.

10. Although some overlap between Mahayana Buddhism and postmodernism has been described (e.g., Peacock & Berry, 1992), Buddhism and Taoism, while not modernist, are not postmodern either.

11. Many psychologists already seem to deny that claim: When they have personal problems and seek to know as much as they can before making a decision, they are much more likely to talk with friends than to try to make impartial observations of events or review psychological research. The reason they do so is not

simply that research concerns groups rather than individuals; if it were, therapists would not be encouraged to extend their familiarity with existing research to individual clients or link their practice with individuals to research on groups.

12. Postmodernism's acknowledgment of the constructive nature of psychological findings encourages an interpretive activism from readers whose role is not simply to check the rigors of the scientific method and remember findings and conclusions. Newbrough (1992) and Polkinghorne (1983) discuss alternatives to modernist psychology.

13. Radical postmodernism views society as more hyperreal than real whereas strategic postmodernism does not (Lennert, 1997).

Chapter 3. Privileged Methodological Texts and Narratives

1. Roughly 64% of the psychological research on Asian Americans has been in four areas: social processes and social issues; health or mental health treatment and prevention; educational psychology; and psychological and physical disorders (Leong, 1995).

2. The shift from a reference to "subjects" to the term study "participants" is more widespread than the adoption of an epistemological basis for the terminology change.

3. From a postmodern perspective, the emergence of postindustrial societies and multinational capitalism, the cultural dominance of media image, and the ability of information technologies to define reality have contributed to a postmodern, hyperreal society in which the distinction between real and unreal is blurred; the apparently real is considered real; the continual proliferation of signs (Dickens & Fontana, 1994) produces illusions; and people are judged in terms of media images and simulation models (Denzin, 1994).

4. Sometimes size is equated with importance, as when a book about Asian Americans, a relatively small proportion of the population, might face pressure to encompass minorities generally whereas a similar book about African Americans would not. (Such was not the case with SUNY Press.)

5. Often, a sample composed of people from a variety of Asian American groups is simply called "Asian American" for statistical analysis and differences are glossed over.

6. Although psychological research is not the servant of some vast conspiracy to oppress, some narratives and ready-to-use "tests" seem to reflect the interests of an establishment that is often oriented toward maintaining existing hierarchies and institutional biases. Psychology typically ignores the ways in which society needs and forces the production of particular facts (Racevskis, 1993).

7. Perhaps in part reflecting interest in the "other," much of the nonclinical research has focused on Asian Americans who are most culturally different from the

mainstream while little has recently concentrated on, for example, third- and fourth-generation Chinese Americans and Japanese Americans.

8. As an alternative to regarding families in Asia at some unspecified time in history as the prototype for traditional Asian American families, "traditional" Asian American families could refer to families that historically developed in the United States. Then the comparative texts might be first-generation Japanese American families, the most common, early twentieth-century Asian *American* families, or the pre-World War II Chinese bachelor *families*.

9. At the 1990 census, the number and percentage of Asian Americans marrying Asian Americans of another Asian American ethnic group equaled or surpassed those marrying members of other races (Shinagawa & Pang, 1996). Of the foreign-born children adopted in the United States in 1996, a plurality of 29.3% have come from China; Korean and Russian children were the next most commonly adopted children at 14.0% (King & Hamilton, 1997).

10. Assumptions of metaphysical orderliness and efforts to maintain the status quo may be bases for the term psychological "disorders": To have a dis–order is to be out of synchrony with the ordered and orderly reality.

11. Inadequate attention is paid to the reasons some responses are not provided and the effects of the missing data. They are usually dealt with statistically but not conceptually.

12. Other questions could expand understanding. For example, when white Americans who associate primarily with Asian Americans are kidded about their cross-racial associations, are the meanings and consequences comparable to being called a banana? If black Americans who prefer Asian foods and use Asian medical techniques face questions about their cultural identity, what does that tell us about race relations and identity in the United States? If they do not, what does that tell us about Asian Americans?

Chapter 4. Constructions of Race and Culture

1. Early in U.S. history, federal and state governments identified three races: white, Negro [sic], and Indian [sic]. In California, Mexicans were classified as white and Asians as Indians (Kincheloe, 1999).

2. A racial identity is manifested, for example, when Japanese Americans say that the increasing outmarriage of succeeding generations will lead to the disappearance of the Japanese American community more than they say that about cultural changes. However, physicality is not regarded as a simple indicator of Japanese American–ness.

3. The term *minority* has historically been reserved for those groups whose minority status adversely affects experiences and available opportunities (S. Sue, 1991). Thus, English-French American males, for example, are not considered a minority group.

4. The colonialist belief in a divinely created social hierarchy was used to justify racism and discrimination against the colonized, who were frequently people of color, and the lower economic classes. Racial dynamics were both creators and products of colonialism and, more broadly, the international division of labor. The power-related meaning of race is still linked to capitalism, as when employers think of cheap labor in racial terms (Omi & Winant, 1994).

5. The optimistic belief that "racism will decline [as it becomes evident that race and ethnicity are constructions and, therefore,] that our previously held notions of race and ethnicity are false and unfounded" (K. S. Wong, 1995, p. 310) is itself unfounded. Most people will not be cognitively able or psychologically willing to adopt such an abstract position. Moreover, racism, often a proxy for efforts to keep an economic or social edge over others, for example, is not predicated solely on notions of race.

6. Old-fashioned racism, based on claims of biological inferiority, is a different text than modern (i.e., contemporary) racism. Denying that discrimination still exists and defending the traditional roles that promote the unequal distribution of wealth and power across racial groups, modern racists claim that the disparity is due to the subordinated's absence of character or lack of competence in American culture. They imply that any inferior position held by minorities (or females, in the case of modern sexists) must be due to their abilities rather than characteristics of society or the behavior of those with power.

7. When blaming the media for stereotypes, many Americans quickly assign the members of the media to the role of "them" and conveniently overlook the media's reflection of America generally.

8. McIntosh (2001) lists other privileges associated with being white.

9. For an exception, see Cianni & Romberger (1995).

10. The idea that racism's omnipresence belies its seriousness implies that what is widely dispersed (e.g., AIDS) is not serious. The position also implies that the United States should be compared to other countries formed on the basis of ethnic ancestral homeland rather than to its unique, founding ideals. The implication that racism is simply human nature and, therefore, unchangeable would suggest — contrary to the intention of those making this argument — that ostensible U.S. standards, such as equal justice and opportunity, are impossible.

11. Perhaps the emphasis on ancestral culture has also contributed to misperceptions of research on Asian Americans and its significance. Even a candidate for the board of the Association for Asian American Studies described the role he thought he could play this way: "I offer the mediating and consensus-building influence of a colleague whose connection to this Association stems from the passion of scholarly interest rather than ancestral ties to one of its constituent groups" (Candidates' Biographies and Statements, 1999).

12. Significantly, references to Asian American values in terms of ancient, mythical cultural values are rarely combined with actual studies of current values

because in a modernist social science concerned with objective facts, values are usually considered subjective (Richardson & Fowers, 1998). Consequently, explaining behaviors in terms of values might arouse charges of being unscientific although, ironically, not even the claim that values are subjective is objective.

13. Many social scientists and clinical psychologists have attempted to characterize prototypical, traditional Asian American (Uba, 1994a), Chinese American (E. Lee, 1997); Filipino/a (Agbayani-Siewart, 1994); Korean (Min, 1995c; Park & Cho, 1995); Vietnamese (Cimmarusti, 1996; Matsuoka, 1990), or "very Asian" individuals or families.

14. A parallel argument might be made regarding the underpinning of psychology in modernist science except that psychology explicitly traces its identity as a science to its use of modernist scientific methods whereas psychological research is not demonstrating a specific link between the behaviors of Asian Americans and their familiarity with Confucian thought.

15. According to psychology's critical features model of concept formation, an object, event, person, quality, or idea must have particular characteristics to be included in a concept; if it possesses the critical features, it must be a member of that conceptual category. A contrasting prototype model states that each concept is based on an exemplar that is most typical, has most of the characteristics of members of the concept, or is the most memorable entrant of the category. Although culture has not been analyzed in terms of those models, the critical features model suggests that a person must have certain cultural characteristics (such as roots in an ancestral country or appearance) to be a member of a culture whereas a prototype model suggests that a person in a culture will have a general family resemblance to the prototypical members of the culture but none of the cultural characteristics is essential.

16. Generally, discussions of cultural groups concentrate on ethnic or national groups while other collectives, such as gender, socioeconomic or age groups, are much less likely to be called cultural groups.

17. Explanations in terms of cultural values are also often vague. For example, the fact that Bharatiya have the lowest divorce rate among Asian Americans has been vaguely explained in terms of Asian Indian values (Sheth, 1995); however, a parallel reference to values would be invoked if another Asian American group had the lowest rate.

Chapter 5. Acculturation and Assimilation

1. In perhaps another indication of cultural recalcitrance, some Americans have claimed that "if we change our lives because of terrorists, the terrorists win" as though the goals of terrorists is to change our way of life rather than, more immediately, to kill Americans. When applied to a multicultural nation, the attitude becomes, "If I have to change because of the growing diversity in the United States, I lose." That attitude probably even has some bearing on America asking the election-

year question, "Am I better off now than I was four years ago?" rather than "Is the country better off than it was four years ago?"

2. The claim that "the popularity of the movie *The Joy Luck Club* . . . reflects the [high] magnitude of Asian *Americans'* [italics added] impact on American art, music, and movies during recent years" (Min, 1995b, p. 273) is an overstatement: Any impact has been unusual, fleeting, and narrowly influential. In the face of societal pressures to lose a sense of ethnicity, a dispensation is granted when an (heirloom) culture is brought out for special occasions, such as Chinese New Year, or other ways that do not seem threatening. Meanwhile, the mainstream culture can pat itself on the back for "tolerating" diversity—within very circumscribed boundaries.

3. Unlike studies of Asian Americans' personalities that have concentrated on characteristics earlier and predominantly studied among European Americans, studies of African Americans' personalities have integrated Afrocentric personality theories, effects of racial status, and the mixing of cultural influences from Africa, the Caribbean, and the U.S. mainstream.

4. Some criticisms imply an overriding rationality while burying other bases for attitudes, such as convenience, modeling, chance, and irrational interpretations.

5. Implicitly holding the promise of an unspecified yet new relationship to U.S. society, many studies compare disparate degrees of acculturation across Asian American generations (e.g., Rosenthal & Feldman, 1992), between Asian Americans and Asians in Asia (e.g., Feldman et al., 1992; Suinn, Khoo, & Ahuna, 1995), and among Asian Americans residing in the United States for a varying number of years (Kim & Rew, 1994).

6. Level or form of acculturation, operationally defined by a set of behaviors and attitudes, is frequently used as an independent variable in portrayals of the relationship between acculturation and behaviors. It is used to account for behavior differences among Asian Americans, such as differences in educational achievement (Padilla, 1980b) or willingness to seek counseling (Atkinson, Lowe, & Matthews, 1995), and as predictor of psychological problems, well-being, chronic disease (Palinkas & Pickwell, 1995), and stressors (Williams & Berry, 1991). However, processes are seldom scrutinized.

7. By emphasizing meanings, postmodernism goes beyond organic views of reactive, transforming organisms trying to thrive in an environment or evolutionary models of different species adapting to varied environments in unique and innovative ways.

8. Paralleling the development of the SL-ASIA acculturation scale, the Minority Identity Development model just plugged the words "Asian American" into earlier models developed for African Americans (D. Sue et al., 1998), suggesting an expectation of ultimate orderliness and a questionable application of Ockham's Razor. The fact that the responses of Asian Americans do not cluster as they did for African Americans (Liu, Sue, & Dinnel, 1992) undermines such expectations.

9. Scales offering the same, limited response options imply that the same dimensions constantly underlie acculturation and have the same meaning. The SL-ASIA asks about an individual's commitment to Western values but people who think that Western values have included oppression of people of color will have different "Western values" in mind than do those who are unaware of the history of oppression or do not think about Western values in those terms.

10. Simplicity is often imposed by psychological tests. For instance, a test might require respondents to characterize their friends and peers from age 6 to 18 in terms of one ethnicity, as though respondents did not change schools or move during those years, their friends and peers were of the same ethnicity, and influences after the age of 18 have had little impact.

11. Both acculturation and ethnic identity have been viewed in terms of an a priori set of shared affective, cognitive, and behavioral dimensions, including attitudes; identity; knowledge about, positive evaluation of, involvement in, and commitment to an ethnic group or target culture; and competence in associated behaviors. The overlap between measures of both concepts illustrates the lack of direct correspondence between the behaviors supposedly measured and interpretations of them: Both types of measures ask about the respondents' English proficiency; ethnic friendships; adoption of U.S. customs (Celano & Tyler, 1991); preferred types of food; and preferred language of reading material, music, and television programs (Anderson et al., 1993; Min & Choi, 1993). The SL-ASIA, used as a measure of both, asks about the words respondents use to refer to their ethnicity; degree of ethnic pride; participation in Asian festivals; self-rating from "very Asian" to "very Westernized" (although "very Asian American" is not an option); self-rated belief in "Asian" values and "American" values; and self-rated "fit" with non-Asian Americans and other Asian Americans of the same ethnicity (Suinn, 1998). So much emphasis has been placed on acculturative stress that psychological measures of acculturation sometimes poorly distinguish between acculturation and acculturative stress (Betancourt & López, 1993).

Chapter 6. Ethnicity and Identity

1. Reducing ethnicity to common ancestry implies that a monoracial Asian American is more ethnic than a multiracial one; defines ethnicity by a quantitative difference in "bloodline" reminiscent of historical, racist criteria; and raises questions about what defines the implicit continuum of Asian American–ness.

2. Public opinion surveys about racial or economic issues hyperprivilege white and black Americans and rarely include Asian Americans. If Filipino/a Americans, for example, were not included as Asian Americans, their voices would probably be even more ignored than they are now.

3. One way many Japanese Americans in Orange County, California, express and promote their ethnicity is by belonging to Japanese American churches, which are often important ethnic institutions among Japanese Americans (Fugita &

Fernandez, 1999). Because Orange County does not have a large, Protestant Japanese American church and seemingly because supporting their sense of ethnic peoplehood outweighs their emphasis on religious orientation, many Christian Japanese Americans support Orange County Buddhist church (Ellies Hihara Watanabe, personal communication).

4. Pointing to the local meanings of ethnicity, a sense of peoplehood varies depending on the issue at hand. A Vietnamese refugee might feel a bond with some people in Vietnam but feel little in the way of a political sense of peoplehood with the Vietnamese government. Such global conceptualizations and attributions of deterministic links between ancestry and identification with a group were historical bases for the prejudice that Japanese Americans during World War II identified with Japan and that Chinese Americans during the McCarthy Era were loyal to the People's Republic of China rather than the United States.

5. Across Asian American ethnic groups, a sense of peoplehood with those in Asia will be unstable in degree and form because of differences in experiences, country of birth, and so on.

6. In this model, however, the boundaries between the stages are fluid; not all stages need be traversed; and reversion to "lower" stages may occur.

7. I have heard some cross-racially adopted Korean Americans express confusion about the meaning of being Korean American when their white parents tell them how hard the children's life would have been in Korea had they not been adopted and regard their identity as Americans as sufficient. Although the parents' rejection of their children's ethnic identity may reflect parental insecurity over the potential distancing that identity could create, it may also recapitulate colonialist efforts to distance the children from what the parents perceive to be groups of a lower social rank.

8. Many Asian American women's preference for men without extremely hairy chests (Liu, 1994) might signal a transformation of ethnic identification with (their fathers or more generally with) Asian American men into sexual preference.

Chapter 7. Conclusion

1. In one methodological variation that could be used for postmodern purposes, focus groups were asked to respond to hypothetical situations or videotaped behaviors (Yau & Smetana, 1993).

2. Besides the scientific method, psychology's borrowing from other disciplines seems to have primarily taken the form of adopting metaphors (e.g., economic exchange theories of interpersonal attraction and physics' concept of forces).

References

Agbayani-Siewart, Pauline. (1994). Filipino American culture and family: Guidelines for practitioners. *Families in Society: The Journal of Contemporary Human Services, 75*, 429–438.

Allport, Gordon. (1961). *Patterns and growth in personality*. New York: Holt, Rinehart & Winston.

Anchor, Robert. (1967). *The enlightenment tradition*. Berkeley, CA: University of California Press.

Anderson, J., Moeschberger, M., Chen, M. S., Jr., Kunn, P., Wewers, M. E., & Guthrie, R. (1993). An acculturation scale for Southeast Asians. *Social Psychiatry and Psychiatric Epidemiology, 28*, 134–141.

Atkinson, Donald R., Lowe, Susana, & Matthews, Linda. (1995). Asian-American acculturation, gender, and willingness to seek counseling. *Journal of Multicultural Counseling and Development, 23*, 130–138.

Atkinson, Donald, Morten, George, & Sue, Derald W. (1989). A minority identity development model. In Donald R. Atkinson, George Morten, & Derald W. Sue (Eds.), *Counseling American minorities* (pp. 35–52). Dubuque, IA: William C. Brown.

Baker, F. M. (1994). Suicide among ethnic minority elderly: A statistical and psychosocial perspective. *Journal of Geriatric Psychiatry, 27*(2), 241–264.

Bandlamudi, Lakshmi. (1994). Dialogics of understanding self/culture. *Ethos, 22*(4), 460–493.

Barbiero, Daniel. (1999). Defense of science. *Issues in Science and Technology, 16*(4), 76–79.

Barrett, William. (1967). *The illusion of technique: A search for meaning in a technological civilization*. Garden City, NY: Anchor Press/Doubleday.

Baudrillard, Jean. (1983). *Simulations*. (Paul Foss, Paul Patton, & Phillip Beitchman, trans.) New York: Semiotext(e).

Bauman, Zygmunt. (1978). *Hermeneutics and social science.* New York: Columbia University Press.

Bauman, Zygmunt. (1987). *Legislators and interpreters: On modernity, post-modernity and intellectuals.* Ithaca, NY: Cornell University Press.

Bauman, Zygmunt. (1992). *Intimations of postmodernity.* London: Routledge.

Bauman, Zygmunt. (1996). A space of one's own: The self and the construction of the other-she. *International Review of Sociology, 6*(3), 443–452.

Bazerman, Charles. (1987). Codifying the social scientific style: The APA Publication Manual as a behaviorist rhetoric. In John Nelson, Allan Megill, & Donald McCloskey (Eds.), *The rhetoric of the human sciences* (pp. 125–144) Madison, WI: University of Wisconsin Press.

Becerra, Rosina & Chi, Iris. (1992). Child care preferences among low-income minority families. *International Social Work, 35,* 35–47.

Bem, Daryl. (1996). Exotic becomes erotic: A developmental theory of sexual orientation. *Developmental Psychological Review, 103,* 320–335.

Berger, Peter, & Luckmann, Thomas. (1967). *The social construction of reality.* Garden City, NY: Doubleday.

Bernstein, Richard J. (1983). *Beyond objectivism and relativism.* Philadelphia: University of Pennsylvania Press.

Berry, John W. (1988). Acculturation and psychological adaptation: A conceptual overview. In J. W. Berry & R. C. Annis (Eds.), *Ethnic psychology: Research and practice with immigrants, refugees, native peoples, ethnic groups and sojourners.* (pp. 41–52). Berwyn, PA: Swets North America.

Berry, John W. (1997). Imagination, acculturation, and adaptation. *Applied Psychology: An International Review, 46*(1), 5–68.

Bertalanffy, Ludwig Von. (1969). Chance or law. In Arthur Koestler & J.R. Smythies (Eds.), *Beyond reductionism: New perspectives in the life sciences* (pp. 56–84). Boston: Beacon Press.

Betancourt, Hector & López, Steven. (1993). The study of culture, ethnicity, and race in American psychology. *American Psychologist, 48*(6), 629–637.

Bevan, William. (1991). Contemporary psychology: A tour inside the onion. *American Psychologist, 46*(5), 475–483.

Biever, Joan, Bobele, Monte, & North, Mary-Wales. (1998). Therapy with intercultural couples: A postmodern approach. *Counseling Psychology Quarterly, 11*(2), 181–189.

Blanchard, Kendall. (1991). Sport, leisure, and identity: Reinventing Lao culture in middle Tennessee. *Play & Culture, 4,* 169–184.

Botella, Luis. (1998). Clinical psychology, psychotherapy and mental health: Contemporary issues and future dilemmas. Retrieved [April 27, 2000] from the World Wide Web: http://www.massey.ac.nz/~ALock/virtual/Clinical.htm

Botella, Luis. (1995). Personal construct psychology, constructivism, and postmodern thought. In Robert A. Neimeyer & Greg J. Neimeyer (Eds). *Advances in personal construct psychology* (Vol. 3, pp. 3–36). Greenwich, CT: JAI Press.

Bower, Bruce. (2000). Cultures of reason. *Science News, 157*(4) 56–59.

Bruns, Gerald. (1987). On the weakness of language in the human sciences. In John Nelson, Allan Megill, & Donald McCloskey (Eds.), *The rhetoric of the human sciences* (pp. 239–262) Madison, WI: University of Wisconsin Press.

Buchowski, Michael. (1994). Enchanted scholar or sober man? *Philosophy of the Social Sciences, 24*(3), 362–377.

Bütz, Michael. (1995). Chaos theory, philosophically old, scientifically new. *Counseling and Values, 39*(2), 84–98.

Cahill, Thomas. (1998). The gift of the Jews. *Commonweal, 125*(9), 22.

Candidates' Biographies and Statements. (1999, January). Unpublished candidate statement accompanying ballot for the Association of Asian American Studies board.

Cantell, Timo & Pedersen, Paul Poder. (1992). Modernity, postmodernity and ethnics—an interview with Zygmunt Bauman. *Telos, 93,* 133–145.

Carlston, Donal. (1987). Turning psychology on itself: The rhetoric of psychology and the psychology of rhetoric. In John Nelson, Allan Megill, & Donald McCloskey (Eds.), *The rhetoric of the human sciences* (pp. 145–162). Madison, WI: University of Wisconsin Press.

Cassirer, Ernst. (1951). *The philosophy of the enlightenment.* Princeton, NJ: Princeton University Press.

Celano, Marianne & Tyler, Forrest. (1991). Behavioral acculturation among Vietnamese refugees in the United States. *Journal of Social Psychology, 131*(3), 373–385.

Chan, Kenyon. (1996, June). Interrogating educational research on Asian and Pacific Americans. Paper presented at the annual meeting of the Association for Asian American Studies, Washington, DC.

Chan, Kenyon. (2000). Rethinking the Asian American Studies project: Bridging the divide between 'campus' and 'community.' *Journal of Asian American Studies, 3*(1), 17–36.

Chan, Sam. (1992). Families with Asian roots. In Eleanor Lynch & Marci Hanson (Eds.), *Developing cross-cultural competence* (pp. 181–257). Baltimore: Brookes.

Chan, Sucheng. (1989). On the ethnic studies requirement: Part I: Pedagogical implications. *Amerasia, 15*(1), 267–280.

Chung, Rita Chi-Ying, & Kagawa Singer, Marjorie. (1995). Interpretation of symptom presentation and distress: A southeast Asian refugee example. *Journal of Nervous and Mental Disease, 183*(1), 639–648.

Cianni, Mary & Romberger, Beverly. (1995). Interactions with senior managers: Perceived differences by race/ethnicity and by gender. *Sex Roles, 32*(5/6), 353–374.

Cimmarusti, Rocco. (1996). Exploring aspects of Filipino-American families. *Journal of Marital and Family Therapy, 22*(2), 205–217.

Connor, John. (1975). Value changes in third-generation Japanese Americans. *Journal of Personality Assessment, 39,* 597–600.

Conzen, Kathleen, Gerber, David, Morawska, Ewa, Pozzetta, George, & Vecoli, Rudolph. (1992). The invention of ethnicity: A perspective from the U.S.A. *Journal of American Ethnic History, 1,* 3–41.

Cuellar, Israel, Harris, Lorwen C., & Jasso, Ricardo. (1980). An acculturation scale for Mexican American normal and clinical populations. *Hispanic Journal of Behavioral Sciences, 2,* 199–217.

Delucchi, Michael & Do, Hien Duc. (1996). The model minority myth and perceptions of Asian Americans as victims of racial harassment. *College Student Journal, 30*(3), 411–414.

Dembart, Lee. (1994). Not-so-popular science. *Reason, 26*(1), 59–61.

Denzin, Norman. (1993). The postmodern sensibility. *Studies in Symbolic Interaction, 15,* 179–188.

Denzin, Norman. (1994). Postmodernism and deconstructionism. In David R. Dickens & Andrea Fontana (Eds.), *Postmodernism and social inquiry* (pp. 182–202). New York: Guilford.

Denzin, Norman. (1995). The poststructuralist crisis in the social sciences: Learning from James Joyce. In Richard Harvey Brown (Ed.), *Postmodern representations: Truth, power, and mimesis in the human public culture* (pp. 38–59). Champaign, IL: University of Illinois Press.

Denzin, Norman & Lincoln, Yvonna. (1998). Introduction: Entering the field of qualitative research. *The landscape of qualitative research: Theories and issues* (pp. 1–34). Thousand Oaks, CA: Sage.

de Tocqueville, Alexis. (1848/1945). *Democracy in America.* New York: Vintage.

Dickens, David & Fontana, Andrea. (1994). Postmodernism in the social sciences. In David R. Dickens & Andrea Fontana (Eds.), *Postmodernism and social inquiry* (pp. 1–21). New York: Guilford.

Dowd, James. (1991). Social psychology in a postmodern age: A discipline without a subject. *American Sociologist, 22*(3/4), 188–210.

Dower, John. (1986). *War without mercy: Race and power in the Pacific war.* New York: Pantheon.

Echabe, Agustin E. & Gonzalez Castro, Jose L. (1999). The impact of context on gender social identities. *European Journal of Social Psychology, 29,* 287–304.

Edmondson, Ricca. (1995). Rhetoric and truthfulness: Reporting in the social sciences. In Richard Harvey Brown (Ed.), *Postmodern representations: Truth, power, and mimesis in the human sciences and public culture* (pp. 20–37). Champaign, IL: University of Illinois Press.

Ellis, Carolyn & Flaherty, Michael. (1992). *Investigating subjectivity: Research on lived experienced.* Newbury Park, CA: Sage.

Espiritu, Yen Le. (1994). The intersection of race, ethnicity, and class: The multiple identities of second-generation Filipinos. *Identities, 1*(2–3), 249–273.

Everett, Shu-Ling. (1994). The endangered post–modern childhood—growing up with unicultural TV in a multicultural society. *Intermedia, 22,* 30–33.

Fabrega, Horacio Jr., & Nguyen, Han. (1992). Culture, social structure, and quandaries of psychiatric diagnosis: A Vietnamese case study. *Psychiatry, 55,* 230–249.

Faulconer, James. (1990). Heidegger and psychological explanation: Taking account of Derrida. In James Fulconer & Richard N. Williams (Eds.), *Reconsidering psychology: Perspectives from continental philosophy* (pp. 116–136). Pittsburgh, PA: Duquesne University Press.

Faulconer, James & Williams, Richard N. (1990a). Introduction. In James Faulconer & Richard N. Williams (Eds.), *Reconsidering psychology: Perspectives from continental philosophy* (pp. 1–8). Pittsburgh, PA: Duquesne University Press.

Faulconer, James & Williams, Richard N. (1990b). Reconsidering psychology. In James Faulconer & Richard N. Williams (Eds.), *Reconsidering psychology: Perspectives from continental philosophy* (pp. 9–60). Pittsburgh, PA: Duquesne University Press.

Feldman, S. Shirley, Mont-Reynaud, Randy, & Rosenthal, Doreen. (1992). When east moves west: The acculturation of values of Chinese adolescents in the U.S. and Australia. *Journal of Research on Adolescence, 2*(2), 147–173.

Feng, Hua, & Cartledge, Gwendolyn. (1996). Social skill assessment of inner city Asian, African, and European American students. *School Psychology Review, 25*(2), 228–239.

Fenz, Walter, & Arkoff, Abe. (1962). Comparative need patterns of five ancestry groups in Hawaii. *Journal of Social Psychology, 58,* 67–89.

Ferguson, Susan. (1995). Marriage timing of Chinese American and Japanese American women. *Journal of Family Issues, 16*(3), 314–343.

Feyerabend, Paul. (1970). Against method. *Minnesota Studies for the Philosophy of Science, 4.*

Feyerabend, Paul. (1975). *Against method.* Thetford, UK: Thetford Press.

Finlay, Marike. (1989). Post-modernizing psychoanalysis/Psychoanalysing post-modernity. *Free Associations, 16,* 43–80.

Fontana, Andrea. (1994). Ethnographic trends in the postmodern era. In David R. Dickens & Andrea Fontana (Eds.), *Postmodernism and social inquiry* (pp. 203–223). New York: Guilford.

Forell, Caroline & Matthews, Donna. (1999). *A law of her own: The reasonable woman as a measure of man.* New York: New York University Press.

Foucault, Michel. (1969). *The archaeology of knowledge and the discourse of language.* New York: Harper Colophon.

Fowers, Blaine & Richardson, Frank. (1996). Why is multiculturalism good? *American Psychologist, 51*(6), 609–621.

Fraser, Nancy & Nicholson, Linda. (1990). Social criticism without philosophy: An encounter between feminism and postmodernism. In Linda J. Nicholson (Ed.), *Feminism/postmodernism* (pp. 19–38). New York: Routledge.

Friere, Paulo, & Macedo, Donald. (1995). A dialogue: Culture, language, and race. *Harvard Educational Review, 65*(3), 377–403.

Fugita, Stephen & Fernandez, Marilyn. (1999, March 31–April 3). Religious orientation and the World War II internment of Japanese Americans. Paper presented at the Association of Asian American Studies conference, Philadelphia.

Fujino, Diane C. (1996, June). Race and gender discrimination and coping strategies: A focus on Asian American women. Paper presented at the Association for Asian American Studies conference, Washington, DC.

Fukuyama, Mary A., & Coleman, Nancy C. (1992). A model for bicultural assertion training with Asian Pacific American college students: A pilot study. *Journal for Specialists in Group Work, 17*(4), 210–217.

Fuller, Steve. (1992). Being there with Thomas Kuhn: A parable for postmodern times. *History & Theory, 31*(3), 241–276.

Fuller, Steve. (1995). The voices of rhetoric and politics in social epistemology. *Philosophy of the Social Sciences, 25*(4), 512–523.

Gans, Herbert. (1979). Symbolic ethnicity: The future of ethnic groups and culture. *Ethnic and Racial Studies, 2,* 1–20.

Gavey, Nicola. (1989). Feminist poststructuralism and discourse analysis: Contributions to feminist psychology. *Psychology of Women Quarterly, 13,* 459–475.

Gergen, Kenneth. (1985). The social constructionist movement in modern psychology. *American Psychologist, 40*(3), 266–275.

Gergen, Kenneth. (1988). Feminist critique of science and the challenge of social epistemology. In Mary McCanney Gergen (Ed.), *Feminist thought and the structure of knowledge* (pp. 27–48). New York: New York University Press.

Gergen, Kenneth. (1997). Social psychology as social construction: The emerging vision. In Craig McGarty & Alexander Haslam (Eds.), *The message of social psychology: Perspectives on mind in society* (pp. 113–128). Oxford, UK: Blackwell.

Gergen, Kenneth. (n.d.). When relationships generate realities: Therapeutic communication reconsidered. Retrieved [April 27, 2000] from the World Wide Web: http://www.swarthmore.edu/SocSci/kgergen1/text6.html.

Gergen, Kenneth, Gulerce, Aydan, Lock, Andrew, & Misra, Girishwar. (1996). Psychological science in cultural context. *American Psychologist, 51*(5), 496–503.

Gim Chung, Ruth. (1995). The sites of race and ethnicity in psychological research on Asian Americans. In Gary Okihiro, Marilyn Alquizola, Dorothy Fujita Rony, & K. Scott Wong (Eds.), *Privileging positions: The sites of Asian American studies* (pp. 413–420). Pullman, WA: Washington State University Press.

Glynn, Simon. (1990). The dynamics of alternative realities. In James Faulconer & Richard N. Williams (Eds.), *Reconsidering psychology: Perspectives from continental philosophy* (pp. 175–197). Pittsburgh, PA: Duquesne University Press.

Gordon, Milton. (1964). *Assimilation in American life: The role of race, religion, and national origins.* New York: Oxford University Press.

Gorman, Thomas. (2000). Social class and parental attitudes toward education. *Journal of Contemporary Ethnography, 27*(1), 10–45.

Gottdiener, M. (1993). Ideology, foundationism, and sociological theory. *Sociological Quarterly, 34*(4), 653–672.

Greeley, Andrew M. (1976). The ethnic miracle. *Public Interest, 45,* 20–36.

Griffin, David Ray. (1989). *God and religion in the postmodern world: Essays in postmodern theology.* Albany, NY: State University of New York Press.

Griscom, Joan. (1992). Women and power: Definition, dualism, and difference. *Psychology of Women Quarterly, 16,* 389–414.

Gross, Paul R., & Levitt, Norman. (1994). *Higher superstition: The academic left and its quarrels with science.* Baltimore: Johns Hopkins University Press.

Guba, Egon, & Lincoln, Yvonna. (1998). Competing paradigms in qualitative research. In Norman Denzin & Yvonna Lincoln (Eds.), *The landscape of qualitative research: Theories and issues* (pp. 195–220). Thousand Oaks, CA: Sage.

Gubrium, Jaber & Holstein, James. (1994). Grounding the postmodern self. *Sociological Quarterly, 35*(4), 685–704.

Hamamoto, Darrell. (1994). *Monitored peril: Asian Americans the politics of TV representation.* Minneapolis and London: University of Minnesota Press.

Hamilton, David. (1998). Traditions, preferences, and postures in applied qualitative research. In Norman Denzin & Yvonna Lincoln (Eds.), *The landscape of qualitative research: Theories and issues* (pp. 111–129). Thousand Oaks, CA: Sage.

Handler, Joel. (1992). Postmodernism, protest, and the new social movement. *Law and Society Review, 26*(4), 697–732.

Hare-Mustin, Rachel T., & Marecek, Jeanne. (1990). Beyond difference. In Rachel T. Hare-Mustin & Jeanne Marecek (Eds.), *Making a difference: Psychology and the construction of gender* (pp. 184–201). New Haven, CT: Yale University Press.

Hayano, David. (1981). Ethnic identification and disidentification: Japanese-American views of Chinese Americans. *Ethnic Groups, 3,* 157–171.

Hernadi, Paul. (1987). Literary interpretation and the rhetoric of the human sciences. In John Nelson, Allan Megill, & Donald McCloskey (Eds.), *The rhetoric of the human sciences* (pp. 263–275). Madison, WI: University of Wisconsin Press.

Hobsbawm, Eric. (1983). Introduction: Invention traditions. In Eric Hobsbawm & Terence Ranger (Eds.), *The invention of tradition* (pp. 1–14). Cambridge: Cambridge University Press.

Hollinger, Robert. (1994). *Postmodernism and the social sciences: A thematic approach.* Thousand Oaks, CA: Sage.

Hong, Ying-yi, Morris, Michael, Chiu, Chi-yue, & Benet-Martínez, Verónica. (2000). Multicultural minds: A dynamic constructivist approach to culture and cognition. *American Psychologist, 55*(7), 709–720.

Hoshmand, Lisa Tsoi & Polkinghorne, Donald. (1992). Redefining the science-practice relationship and professional training. *American Psychologist, 47*(1), 55–66.

Hubbard, Ruth. (1988). Some thoughts about the masculinity of the natural sciences. In Mary McCanney Gergen (Ed.), *Feminist thought and the structure of knowledge* (pp. 1–15). New York: New York University Press.

Hune, Shirley. (1997a). Asian-American women and everyday inequities. In Carol R. Ronai, Barbara Zsembik, & Joe Feagin (Eds.), *Everyday sexism in the third millennium* (pp. 181–196). New York: Routledge.

Hune, Shirley. (1997b). Opening the American mind and body: The role of Asian American Studies. In Don Nakanishi and Tina Yamano Nishida (Eds), *The Asian American educational experience* (pp. 322–328). New York: Routledge.

Hune, Shirley, & Chan, Kenyon. (1997). Special Focus: Asian Pacific American demographic and educational trends. In Deborah J. Carter & Reginald Wilson (Eds.), *Minorities in Education, 15.* Washington, DC: American Council on Education.

Hurh, Won Moo, & Kim, Kwang Chung. (1984). *Korean immigrants in America: A structural analysis of ethnic confinement and adhesive adaptation.* Cranbury, NJ: Farleigh Dickinson University Press.

Iwamasa, Gayle, Pai, Shilpa, Hilliard, Kristen, & Lin, Shu-Hui. (1998). Acculturation of Japanese Americans: Use of the SL-ASIA with a community sample. *Asian American and Pacific Islander Journal of Health, 6*(1), 25–34.

Jeong, Gyung Ja & Schumm, Walter. (1990). Family satisfaction in Korean/American marriages: An exploratory story of the perceptions of Korean wives. *Journal of Comparative Family Studies, 21*(3), 325–336.

Johnson, Timothy, Jobe, Jared, O'Rourke, Diane, Sudman, Seymour, Warnecke, Richard, Chavez, Noel, Chapa-Resendez, Gloria, & Golden, Patricia. (1997). Dimensions of self-identification among multicultural and multiethnic respondents in survey reviews. *Evaluation Review, 21*(6), 671–687.

Kagiticbasi, Cigdem. (1989). Family and socialization in cross-cultural perspective: A model of change. In Richard Dienstbier (Ed.), *Nebraska Symposium on motivation, 37: Cross-cultural perspectives* (pp. 135–200). Lincoln, NE: University of Nebraska Press.

Keller, Evelyn Fox. (1985). *Reflections on gender and science.* New Haven, CT: Yale University Press.

Kellner, Douglas. (1988). Postmodernism as social theory: Some challenges and problems. *Theory, Culture and Society, 5*(2–3), 239–269.

Kellner, Douglas. (1998). Zygmunt Bauman's postmodern terms. *Theory, Culture and Society, 15*(1), 73–86.

Kelly, George. (1955). *The psychology of personal constructs.* London: Routledge.

Kiang, Peter. (1991). About face: Recognizing Asian & Pacific American Vietnam veterans in Asian American Studies. *Amerasia Journal, 17*(3), 22–40.

Kibria, Nazli. (1998). The contested meanings of 'Asian American': Racial dilemmas in the contemporary US. *Ethnic and Racial Studies, 21*(5), 939–958.

Kim, Elaine. (1993). Home is where the *Han* is: A Korean American perspective on the Los Angeles upheavals. *Social Justice, 20*(1–2), 1–21.

Kim, Sunah, & Rew, Lynn. (1994). Ethnic identity: Role integration, quality of life, and depression in Korean-American women. *Archives of Psychiatric Nursing, 8*(6), 348–356.

Kim, Yoon-Ock. (1995). Cultural pluralism and Asian-Americans: Culturally sensitive social work practice. *International Social Work, 38*, 69–78.

Kincheloe, Joe. (1999). The struggle to define and reinvent whiteness: A pedagogical analysis. *College Literature, 26*(3), 162–195.

Kincheloe, Joe & McLaren, Peter. (1998). Rethinking critical thinking and qualitative research. In Norman Denzin & Yvonna Lincoln (Eds.), *The landscape of qualitative research: Theories and issues* (pp. 260–299). Thousand Oaks, CA: Sage.

King, Patricia & Hamilton, Kendall. (1997, June 16). Bringing kids all the way home. *Newsweek*, 60–65.

Kitano, Harry. (1970). Mental illness in four cultures. *Journal of Social Psychology*, 80, 121–134.

Kitano, Harry. (1989). A model for counseling Asian Americans. In P. B. Pedersen, J. G. Draguns, Walter J. Lonner, & Joseph E. Trimble (Eds.), *Counseling across cultures* (3rd ed., pp. 139–151). Honolulu, HI: University of Hawaii Press.

Kitano, Harry, & Daniels, Roger. (1996). *Asian Americans: Emerging minorities* (2nd ed.). Englewood Cliffs, NJ: Prentice Hall.

Kockelmans, Joseph. (1990). Some reflections on empirical psychology: Toward an interpretive psychology. In James Faulconer & Richard N. Williams (Eds.), *Reconsidering psychology: Perspectives from continental philosophy* (pp. 75–91). Pittsburgh, PA: Duquesne University Press.

Kuhn, Thomas. (1970). *The structure of scientific revolutions* (2nd ed.). Chicago: University of Chicago Press.

Kupferberg, Feiwel. (1990). Entering the public dialogue the universities, knowledge-society, postmodernity and the Enlightenment project. *Innovation: The European Journal of Social Sciences*, 3(1), 25–40.

LaFromboise, Teresa, Coleman, Hardin, & Gerton, Jennifer. (1993). Psychological impact of biculturalism: Evidence and theory. *Psychological Bulletin*, 114(3), 395–412.

Lakoff, George & Johnson, Mark. (1980). *Metaphors we live by*. Chicago: University of Chicago Press.

Landrine, Hope. (1988). Revising the framework of abnormal psychology. In Phyllis Bronstein & Kathryn Quinna (Eds.), *Teaching a psychology of people* (pp. 37–44). Washington, DC: American Psychological Association.

Landrine, Hope, Klonoff, Elizabeth A., & Brown-Collins, Alice. (1992). Cultural diversity and methodology in feminist psychology. *Psychology of Women Quarterly*, 16, 145–163.

Lee, Evelyn. (1997). *Working with Asian Americans: A guide for clinicians*. New York: Guilford.

Lee, Lee C. (1998). An overview. In Lee C. Lee & Nolan Zane (Eds.), *Handbook of Asian American psychology* (pp. 1–19). Thousand Oaks, CA: Sage.

Lee, Lee C., & Zane, Nolan. (1998). *Handbook of Asian American psychology*. Thousand Oaks, CA: Sage.

Lee, Stacey. (1996). *Unraveling the "model minority" stereotype: Listening to Asian American youth.* New York: Teacher's College Press.

Lemert, Charles. (1991). The end of ideology, really. *Sociological Theory, 9*(2), 164–172.

Lennert, Charles. (1997). *Postmodernism is not what you think.* Malden, MA: Blackwell.

Leong, Fred. (1995). *History of Asian American psychology* [Booklet]. Asian American Psychological Association.

Leong, Frederick & Chou, Elayne, L. (1994). The role of ethnic identity and acculturation in the vocational behavior of Asian Americans: An integrative review. *Journal of Vocational Behavior, 44*, 155–172.

Lester, David. (1994). Differences in the epidemiology of suicide in Asian Americans by nation of origin. *Omega, 29*(2), 89–93.

Lien, Pei-te. (1994). Ethnicity and political participation: A comparison between Asian and Mexican Americans. *Political Behavior, 16*(2), 237–264.

Lincoln, Yvonna & Denzin, Norman. (1998). The fifth movement. In Norman Denzin & Yvonna Lincoln (Eds.), *The landscape of qualitative research: Theories and issues* (pp. 407–430). Thousand Oaks, CA: Sage.

Liu, C., Sue, D., & Dinnel, D. (1992). *Use of the Racial Identity Attitude Scale (RIAS) on Asian Americans.* Unpublished master's thesis, Western Washington University, Bellingham, WA.

Liu, John. (1994, April 7). On going constructions of identity. Paper presented at the annual convention of the Association for Asian American Studies, Ann Arbor, MI.

Liu, Karen & Blila, Susan. (1995). Ethnic awareness and attitudes in young children. *Contemporary Education, 66*(3), 146–153.

Loewen, James. (1995). *Lies my teacher told me.* (1995). New York: Simon & Schuster.

Loo, Chalsa. (1994). Race-related PTSD: The Asian American Vietnam veteran. *Journal of Traumatic Stress, 7*(4) 637–656.

Lowe, Lisa. (1998). The power of culture. *Journal of Asian American Studies, 1*(1), 5–29.

Lyotard, Jean François. (1984). *The postmodern condition: A report on knowledge.* (Geoff Bennington & Brian Massumi, Trans.). Minneapolis, MN: University of Minnesota Press.

Lyotard, Jean François. (1988). *The postmodern explained.* Minneapolis, MN: University of Minnesota Press.

Machado, Paulo & Gonçalves, Óscar. (1999). Introduction: Narrative in psychotherapy: The emerging metaphor. *Journal of Clinical Psychology, 55*(1), 1175–1177.

MacIlwain, Collin. (1997). Campuses ring to a stormy clash over truth and reason. *Nature*, 387, 331–333.

Madison, Gary Brent. (1988). *The hermeneutics of postmodernism*. Bloomington, IN: University of Indiana Press.

Manicas, Peter. (1987). *A history and philosophy of the social sciences*. Oxford, UK: Basil Blackwell.

Mann, Susan, & Kelley, Lori. (1997). Standing at the crossroads of modernist thought. *Gender & Society*, 11(4), 391–401.

Marcia, James. (1980). Identity in adolescence. In Joseph Adelson (Ed.), *Handbook of adolescent psychology* (pp. 159–187). New York: Wiley.

Markus, Hazel Rose & Kitayama, Shinobu. (1998). The cultural psychology of personality. *Journal of Cross-Cultural Psychology*, 29(1), 63–87.

Marsella, Anthony, Johnson, Frank, Johnson, Colleen, & Brennan, Jerry. (1998). Ethnic identity in second- (*nisei*), third- (*sansei*), and fourth (*yonsei*) generation Japanese-Americans in Hawai'i. *Asian American and Pacific Islander Journal of Health*, 6 (1), 46–52.

Martinez-Brawley, Emilia. (1999). Social work, postmodernism and higher education. *International Social Work*, 42(3), 333–346.

Matsuoka, Jon. (1993). Demographic characteristics as determinants in qualitative differences in the adjustment of Vietnamese refugees. *Journal of Social Service Research*, 17(3/4), 1–21.

Matsuoka, Jon K. (1990). Differential acculturation among Vietnamese refugees. *Social Work*, 35(4), 341–345.

Mayeda, David. (1998, June). Ethnic identity and racial formation in Hawai'i: Aspirations and expectations of at-risk Samoan youth. Paper presented at the annual meeting of the Association of Asian American Studies, Honolulu, HI.

McIntosh, Peggy. (2001). White privilege and male privilege: A personal account of coming to see correspondences through work in Women's Studies. In Margaret Andersen & Patricia Hill Collins (Eds.), *Race, class, and gender: An anthology* (4th ed., pp. 95–105). Belmont, CA: Wadsworth.

Meacham, Jack. (1999). Riegel, dialectics, and multiculturalism. *Human Development*, 42, 134–144.

Merton, Robert K. (1938). Social structure and anomie. *American Sociological Review*, 3, 672–682.

Meyerowitz, Beth, Richardson, Jean, Hudson, Sharon, & Leedham, Beth. (1998). Ethnicity and cancer outcomes: Behavioral and psychosocial considerations. *Psychological Bulletin*, 123(1), 47–70.

Mickelson, Rosolyn Arlin, Okazaki, Sumie, National Research Center on Asian American Mental Health, Zheng, Dunchun, & Asian Youth Center. (1993, April). Different tales told at the dinner table: Asian, black, and white adolescents' education attitudes and high school performance. Paper presented at the American Educational Research Association, Atlanta, GA.

Min, Pyong Gap. (1995a). An overview of Asian Americans. In Pyong Gap Min (Ed.), *Asian Americans: Contemporary Trends and Issues* (pp.10–37). Thousand Oaks, CA: Sage.

Min, Pyong Gap. (1995b). Future prospects of Asian Americans. In Pyong Gap Min (Ed.), *Asian Americans: Contemporary Trends and Issues* (pp. 271–281). Thousand Oaks, CA: Sage.

Min, Pyong Gap. (1995c). Korean Americans. In Pyong Gap Min (Ed.), *Asian Americans: Contemporary Trends and Issues* (pp. 199–231). Thousand Oaks, CA: Sage.

Min, Pyong Gap & Choi, Youna. (1993). Ethnic attachment among Korean-American high school students. *Korean Journal of Population and Development, 22,* 167–179.

Moore, Robert. (1988). Racist stereotyping in the English language. In Paula Rothenberg (Ed.), *Racism and sexism: An integrated study* (331–341). New York: St. Martin's Press.

Morawski, Jill G. (1990). Toward the unimagined: Feminism and epistemology in psychology. In Rachel T. Hare-Mustin & Jeanne Marecek (Eds.), *Making a difference: Psychology and the construction of gender* (pp. 150–183). New Haven, CT: Yale University Press.

Morris, Charles. (1998). *Psychology.* New York: Prentice Hall.

Morse, David. (1995). Prejudicial studies: One astounding lesson for the University of Connecticut. In Don Nakanishi & Tina Yamano Nishida (Eds.), *The Asian American educational experience: A source book for teachers and students* (pp. 339–357). New York: Routledge.

Moy, Samuel. (1992). A culturally sensitive, psychoeducational model for understanding and treating Asian-American clients. *Journal of Psychology and Christianity, 11*(4), 358–367.

Munet-Vilaró, Frances & Egan, Maura. (1990). Reliability issues of the Family Environment Scale for cross-cultural research. *Nursing Research, 39*(4), 244–247.

Myers, David. (1998). *Psychology.* (5th ed.). New York: Worth.

Myers, Linda J., Speight, Suzette L., Highlen, Pamela S., Cox, Chikako I., Reynolds, A. L., Adams, E. M., & Hanley, C. P. (1991). Identity development and worldview toward an optimal conceptualization. *Journal of Counseling and Development, 70* 54–63.

Nagata, Donna. (1991). Transgenerational impact of the Japanese American internment: Clinical issues in working with children of former internees. *Psychotherapy*, 28, 121–128.

Nagel, Ernest. (1979). *The structure of science: Problems in the logic of scientific explanation*. Indianapolis, IN: Hackett Publishing.

Nagel, Joane. (1994). Constructing ethnicity: Creating and recreating ethnic identity and culture. *Social Problems*, 41(1), 152–176.

Newbrough, J. R. (1992). Community psychology in the postmodern world. *Journal of Community Psychology*, 20, 10–25.

Nguyen, Huong, Messé, Lawrence, & Stollak, Gary. (1999). Toward a more complex understanding of acculturation and adjustment: Cultural involvements and psychosocial functioning in Vietnamese youth. *Journal of Cross-Cultural Psychology*, 30(1), 5–31.

Nguyen, Viet Thanh & Chen, Tina. (2000). Editor's introduction. *Jouvert*, 4(3). Retrieved [October 3, 2000] from the World Wide Web: http://social.chass. ncsu.edu/jouvert/v4i3/ed43.htm

Nielsen, Harriet. (1999). "Black holes" as sites for self-consciousness. In Ruthellen Josselson & Amia Lieblich (Eds.), *Making meaning of narratives* (pp. 45–76). Thousand Oaks, CA: Sage.

Nuyen, A. T. (1994). Interpretation and understanding in hermeneutics and deconstruction. *Philosophy of the Social Sciences*, 24(1), 426–439.

Oetting, E. R., & Beauvais, Fred. (1990–1991). Orthogonal cultural identification theory: The cultural identification of minority adolescents. *International Journal of the Addictions*, 25, 655–685.

Okazaki, Sumie & Sue, Stanley. (1995). Methodological issues in assessment research with ethnic minorities. *Psychological Assessment*, 7(3), 367–375.

Omi, Michael & Winant, Howard. (1994). *Racial formation in the United States: From the 1960s to the 1990s* (2nd ed.). New York: Routledge & Kegan Paul.

O'Neill, John. (1998). Rhetoric, science, and philosophy. *Philosophy of the Social Sciences*, 28(2), 205–221.

Osajima, Keith. (1995a). Postmodernism and Asian American studies: A critical appropriation. In Gary Okihiro, Marilyn Alquizola, Dorothy Fujita Rony, & K. Scott Wong (Eds.), *Privileging positions: The sites of Asian American studies* (pp. 21–35). Pullman, WA: Washington State University Press.

Osajima, Keith. (1995b). Postmodern possibilities: Theoretical and political directions for Asian American Studies. *Amerasia Journal*, 21(1 & 2), 79–87.

Padilla, Amado. (1980a). *Acculturation: Theory, models, and some new findings*. Boulder, CO: Westview.

Padilla, Amado. (1980b). The role of cultural awareness and ethnic loyalty in acculturation. In Amado Padilla (Ed.), *Acculturation: Theory, models, and some new findings.* (pp. 47–85). Boulder, CO: Westview.

Palinkas, Lawrence & Pickwell, Sheila. (1995). Acculturation as a risk factor for chronic disease among Cambodian refugees in the United States. *Social Science & Medicine, 40*(12), 1643–1653.

Pang, Gin, & Shinagawa, Larry. (1995, August). Interracial relationships and the language of denial. Paper presented at the annual conference of the Association of Asian American Studies, Ann Arbor, MI.

Park, Insook Han & Cho, Lee-Jay. (1995). Confucianism and the Korean family. *Journal of Comparative Family Studies, 26*(1), 117–134.

Parker, Ian. (1997). Discursive psychology. In Dennis Fox & Isaac Prilleltensky (Eds.), *Cultural psychology: An introduction* (pp. 301–317). London: Sage.

Patai, Daphne. (1992). Minority status and the stigma of surplus visibility. *Education Digest, 57*(5), 35–37.

Peacocke, John & Berry, Philippa. (1992). Symposium on Buddhism and modern Western thought. *Asian Philosophy, 2*(2), 211–213.

Pearson, Veronica. (1995). [Review of the book *Asian Americans: Personality patterns, identity, and mental health*]. *Psychiatric Services, 46*(6), 627.

Pepper, Stephen. (1942). *World hypotheses.* Berkeley, CA: University of California Press.

Perlmutter, Philip. (1999). *Legacy of hate: A short history of ethnic, religious, and racial prejudice in America.* Armonk, NY: M.E. Sharpe.

Pinderhughes, Elaine. (1995). Biracial identity—asset or handicap? In Herbert Harris, Howard Blue, & Ezra Griffith (Eds.), *Racial and ethnic identity: Psychological development and creative expression* (pp. 73–93). New York: Routledge.

Polanyi, Michael. (1946/1964). *Science, faith and society.* Chicago: University of Chicago Press.

Polkinghorne, Donald. (1983). *Methodology for the human sciences: Systems of inquiry.* Albany, NY: State University of New York Press.

Polkinghorne, Donald. (1988). *Narrative knowing and the human sciences.* Albany, NY: State University of New York Press.

Polkinghorne, Donald. (1990). Psychology and philosophy. In James Faulconer & Richard N. Williams (Eds.), *Reconsidering psychology: Perspectives from continental philosophy* (pp. 92–115) Pittsburgh, PA: Duquesne University Press.

Polkinghorne, Donald. (1991). Two conflicting calls for methodological reform. *Counseling Psychologist, 19*(1), 103–115.

Popper, Karl. (1968). *The logic of scientific discovery.* New York: Harper & Row.

Porter, J. R., & Washington, R. E. (1993). Minority identity and self-esteem. *Annual Review of Sociology, 19,* 139–161.

Powlishta, K. (1995). Ingroup processes in childhood: Social categorization and sex role development. *Developmental Psychology, 31,* 781–788.

Prohaska, Thomas, Albrecht, Gary, Levy, Judith, Sugrue, Noreen, & Kim, Joung-Hwa. (1990). Determinants of self-perceived risk for AIDS. *Journal of Health and Social Behavior, 31*(4), 384–394.

Racevskis, Karlis. (1993). *Postmodernism and the search for enlightenment.* Charlottesville, VA: University Press of Virginia.

Renteln, Alison. (1995). A psychohistorical analysis of the Japanese American internment. *Human Rights Quarterly, 17,* 618–648.

Richardson, Frank & Fowers, Blaine. (1998). Interpretive social science: An overview. *American Behavioral Scientist, 41*(4), 465–496.

Ritzer, George. (1997). *Postmodern social theory.* New York: McGraw-Hill.

Roberts, Robert, & Phinney, Jean. (1999). The structure of ethnic identity of young adolescents from diverse ethnocultural groups. *Journal of Early Adolescence, 19*(3), 301–322.

Robinson, Daniel N. (1976). *An intellectual history of psychology.* New York: Macmillan.

Roffey, Arthur. (1993). Existentialism in a post-modern world: Meaningful lessons for the counselor. *Counseling and Values, 37*(3), 129–149.

Rohmann, Chris. (1999). *A world of ideas.* New York: Ballantine.

Rogers, Annie, Casey, Mary, Ekert, Jennifer, Hollands, James, Nakkula, Victoria, & Sheinberg, Nurit. (1999). An interpretive poetics of language of the unsayable. In Ruthellen Josselson & Amia Lieblich (Eds.), *Making meaning of narratives* (pp. 77–106). Thousand Oaks, CA: Sage.

Root, Maria. (1992). Reconstructing the impact of trauma on personality. In Laura Brown & Mary Ballou (Eds.), *Personality and psychopathology: Feminist appraisals* (pp. 229–265). New York: Guilford.

Root, Maria. (1998). Multiracial Americans. In Lee Lee & Nolan Zane (Eds.), *Handbook of Asian American psychology* (pp. 261–287). Thousand Oaks, CA: Sage.

Rosenau, Pauline. (1992). *Post-modernism and the social sciences: Insights, inroads, and intrusions.* Princeton, NJ: Princeton University Press.

Rosenthal, Doreen & Feldman, S. Shirley. (1992). The nature and stability of ethnic identity in Chinese youth: Effects of length of residence in two cultural contexts. *Journal of Cross-Cultural Psychology, 23*(2), 214–227.

Rychlak, Joseph. (1975). Psychological science as a humanist views it. *Nebraska Symposium on Motivation, 23,* 205–279.

Said, Edward. (1978). *Orientalism.* New York: Pantheon.

Sampson, Edward. (1999). The romantic and the postmodern. *Journal of Humanistic Psychology, 39*(3), 47–55.

San Juan, E., Jr. (1992). *Racial formations/critical transformations: Articulations of power in ethnic and racial studies in the United States.* Atlantic Highlands, NJ: Humanities Press.

Sarup, Madan. (1989). *An introductory guide to post-structuralism and postmodernism.* Athens, GA: University of Georgia Press.

Schneider, Barbara, & Lee, Yongsook. (1990). A model for academic success: The schools and home environment of East Asian students. *Anthropology and Education Quarterly, 21,* 358–377.

Schneider, Kirk. (1999). The revival of the romantic means a revival of psychology. *Journal of Humanistic Psychology, 39*(2), 13–29.

Schrag, Calvin O. (1990). Explanation and understanding in the science of human behavior. In James Faulconer & Richard N. Williams (Eds.), *Reconsidering psychology: Perspectives from continental philosophy* (pp. 61–74). Pittsburgh, PA: Duquesne University Press.

Scott, Joan W. (1988). Deconstructing equality-versus-difference: Or, the uses of poststructuralist theory for feminism. *Feminist Studies, 14*(1), 33–65.

Segal, Daniel A., & Handler, Richard. (1995). U.S. multiculturalism and the concept of culture. *Identities, 1*(4), 391–407.

Shah, Hemant. (1991). Communication and cross-cultural adaptation patterns among Asian Indians. *International Journal of Intercultural Relations, 15,* 311–321.

Sheth, Manju. (1995). Asian Indian Americans. In Pyong Gap Min (Ed.), *Asian Americans: Contemporary trends and issues* (pp. 169–198). Thousand Oaks, CA: Sage.

Shinagawa, Larry, & Pang, Gin. (1996). Asian American pan-ethnicity and intermarriage. *Amerasia Journal, 22*(2), 127–153.

Shrake, Eunai Kim. (1998, June). Korean American parenting styles and adolescent problems. Paper presented at the annual Association of Asian American Studies meeting, Honolulu, HI.

Silbey, Susan. (1997). "Let them eat cake": Globalization, postmodern colonialism, and the possibilities of justice. *Law and Society Review, 31*(2), 207–231.

Slife, Brent, & Gantt, Edwin. (1999). Methodological pluralism: A framework for psychotherapy research. *Journal of Clinical Psychology, 55*(12), 1453–1485.

Slife, Brent D., & Williams, Richard N. (1995). *What's behind the research? Discovering hidden assumptions in the behavioral sciences.* Thousand Oaks, CA: Sage.

Sloan, Douglas. (1992). Imagination, education, and our postmodern possibilities. *ReVision, 15*(2), 42–53.

Smith, M. Brewster. (1994). Selfhood at risk: Postmodern perils and the perils of postmodernism. *American Psychologist, 49*, 405–411.

Sorenson, Susan. (1996). Violence against women: Examining ethnic differences and commonalities. *Evaluation Review, 20*(2), 123–145.

Spivak, Gayatri. (1974). Translator's preface. In Jacques Derrida, *Of grammatology.* Baltimore: Johns Hopkins University Press.

Spretnak, Charlene. (1997). *The resurgence of the real: Body, nature, and place in a hypermodern world.* New York: Addison Wesley.

Steele, Claude, & Aronson, Joshua. (1995). Stereotype threat and the intellectual test performance of African Americans. *Journal of Personality and Social Psychology, 69*, 797–811.

Sue, David, Mak, Winnie, & Sue, Derald. (1998). Ethnic identity. In Lee C. Lee & Nolan Zane (Eds.), *Handbook of Asian American Psychology* (pp. 289–323). Thousand Oaks, CA: Sage.

Sue, Stanley. (1991). Ethnicity and culture in psychological research and practice. In Jacqueline Goodchilds (Ed.), *Psychological perspectives on human diversity in America* (pp. 51–85). Washington, DC: American Psychological Association.

Sue, Stanley. (1999). Science, ethnicity, and bias: Where have we gone wrong? *American Psychologist, 54*(12), 1070–1077.

Sue, Stanley, & Morishima, James. (1982). *The mental health of Asian Americans.* San Francisco: Jossey-Bass.

Sue, Stanley, & Sue, Derald W. (1971). Chinese American personality and mental health. *Amerasia Journal, 1*, 36–49.

Suinn, Richard. (1998). Measurement of acculturation of Asian Americans. *Asian American and Pacific Islander Journal of Health, 6*(1), 7–12.

Suinn, Richard, Khoo, Gillian, & Ahuna, Carol. (1995). The Suinn-Lew Asian Self-Identity Acculturation Scale: Cross-cultural information. *Journal of Multicultural Counseling and Development, 23* 139–148.

Sumida, Stephen. (1998). East of California: Points of origin in Asian American Studies. *Journal of Asian American Studies, 1* (1), 83–100.

Takagi, Dana. (1993). Asian Americans and racial politics: A postmodern paradox. *Social Justice, 20*(1–2), 115–128.

Takagi, Dana. (1995). Postmodernism from the edge: Asian American identities. In Gary Okihiro, Marilyn Alquizola, Dorothy F. Fujita Rony, & K. Scott Wong

(Eds.), *Privileging positions: The sites of Asian American studies* (pp. 37–45). Pullman, WA: Washington State University Press.

Tan, David. (1994). Uniqueness of the Asian-American experience in higher education. *College Student Journal, 28*(4), 412–421.

Tanaka, Jeffrey, Ebrero, Angela, Linn, Nancy, & Morera, Osvaldo. (1998). *Research methods: The construct validity of self-identity and its psychological implications.* In Lee C. Lee & Nolan Zane (Eds.), *Handbook of Asian American psychology* (pp. 21–79). Thousand Oaks, CA: Sage.

Tavris, Carol. (1991). The mismeasure of woman: Paradoxes and perspectives in the study of gender. In Jacqueline Goodchilds (Ed.), *Psychological perspectives on human diversity in America* (pp. 91–136). Washington, DC: American Psychological Association.

Taylor, Daniel M. (1970). *Explanation & meaning: An introduction to philosophy.* London: Cambridge University Press.

Torres, Rodolfo & Ngin, ChorSwang. (1995). Racialized boundaries, class relations, and cultural politics: The Asian-American and Latino experience. In Antonia Darder (Ed.), *Culture and difference: Cultural perspectives on the bicultural experience in the United States* (pp.55–69). Westport, CT: Bergin and Garvey.

Toulmin, Stephen. (1951). *The philosophy of science: An introduction.* NY: Hutchinson's University Library.

Toulmin, Stephen. (1961). *Foresight and understanding.* Bloomington, IN: Indiana University Press.

Toulmin, Stephen. (1972). *Human understanding: The collective use and evolution of concepts.* Princeton, NJ: Princeton University Press.

Toulmin, Stephen. (1990). *Cosmopolis: The hidden agenda of modernity.* New York: Free Press.

Tropp, Linda, Erkut, Sumru, García Coll, Cynthia, Alarcón, Odette, & Vázquez García, Heide A. (1999). Psychological acculturation: Development of a new measure for Puerto Ricans on the U.S. mainland. *Educational and Psychological Measurement, 59*(2), 351–367.

Uba, Laura. (1994a). *Asian Americans: Personality patterns, identity, and mental health.* New York: Guilford.

Uba, Laura. (1994b). The supply of Asian/Pacific Islanders in the health-care professions. In Nolan Zane & David Takeuchi (Eds.), *Asian and Pacific Islander health issues in the United States: Current research and future directions.* Newbury Park, CA: Sage.

Uehara, Edwina, Takeuchi, David, & Smukler, Michael. (1994). Effects of combining disparate groups in the analysis of ethnic differences: Variations among Asian American mental health service consumers in level of community functioning. *American Journal of Community Psychology, 22*(1), 83–99.

Unger, Rhoda K. (1988). Psychological, feminist, and personal epistemology: Transcending contradictions. In Mary McCanney Gergen (Ed.), *Feminist thought and the structure of knowledge* (pp. 124–141). New York: New York University Press.

Vaihinger, Hans. (1924). *The philosophy of "as if"*. Berlin: Springer.

Wade, Carole & Tavris, Carol (1995). *Psychology* (4th ed.). New York: HarperCollins.

Walton, Douglas. (1992). *One-sided arguments*. Albany, NY: State University of New York Press.

Ward, Steven. (1995). The revenge of the humanities: Reality, rhetoric, and the politics of postmodernism. *Sociological Perspectives, 38*(2), 109–129.

Waters, Mary. (2001). Optional ethnicities: For whites only? In Margaret Andersen & Patricia Hill Collins (Eds.), *Race, class, and gender: An anthology* (4th ed., pp. 430–439). Belmont, CA: Wadsworth.

Watson, Graham. (1992). *The place of emotion in argument*. University Park, PA: Pennsylvania State University Press.

Weisz, John. (1989). Culture and the development of child psychopathology: Lessons from Thailand. In Dante Cicchetti (Ed.), *The emergence of a discipline: Rochester Symposium on Developmental Psychopathology Vol. 1* (pp. 89–117). Hillsdale, NJ: Erlbaum.

Werner, Heinz. (1948). *Comparative psychology of mental development*. New York: International Universities Press.

West, Cornel. (1992). Black leadership and the pitfalls of racial reasoning. In Toni Morrison (Ed.), *Race–ing justice, en-gendering power: Essays on Anita Hill, Clarence Thomas, and the construction of social reality* (pp. 390–401). New York: Pantheon.

West, Cornel. (2001). Race matters. In Margaret Andersen & Patricia Hill Collins (Eds.), *Race, class, and gender: An anthology* (4th ed., pp. 119–124). Belmont, CA: Wadsworth.

Williams, Carolyn L., & Berry, John. (1991). Primary prevention of acculturative stress among refugees: Application of psychological theory and practice. *American Psychologist, 46,* 632.

Williams, Patricia. (2001). Of race and risk. In Margaret Andersen & Patricia Hill Collins (Eds.), *Race, class, and gender: An anthology*. (4th ed., pp. 106–108). Belmont, CA: Wadsworth.

Williams, Richard N. (1990). The metaphysics of things and discourse about them. In James Faulconer & Richard N. Williams (Eds.), *Reconsidering psychology: Perspectives from continental philosophy* (pp. 136–150). Pittsburgh, PA: Duquesne University Press.

Winter, Steven. (1992). For what it's worth: Comment on Presidential Address. *Law and Society Review*, 26(4), 789–810.

Wittgenstein, Ludwig. (1963). *Philosophical investigations*. (G. Anscombe, trans.) New York: Macmillan.

Wong, K. Scott. (1995). The site of race and ethnicity: Social constructions of consequence. In Gary Okihiro, Marilyn Alquizola, Dorothy Fujita Rony, & K. Scott Wong (Eds.), *Privileging positions: The sites of Asian American studies* (pp. 309–313). Pullman, WA: Washington State University Press.

Wong, Roger R. (1995). Divorce mediation among Asian Americans: Bargaining in the shadow of diversity. *Family and Conciliation Courts Review*, 133(1), 110–128.

Wong-Rieger, Durhane & Quintana, Diana. (1987). Comparative acculturation of Southeast Asian and Hispanic immigrants and sojourners. *Journal of Cross-Cultural Psychology*, 18(3), 345–362.

Woo, Deborah. (2000). The inventing and reinventing of "Model Minorities": The cultural veil obscuring structural sources of inequality. In Timothy Fong & Larry Shinagawa (Eds.), *Asian Americans: Experiences and perspectives* (pp. 193–212). Upper Saddle River, NJ: Prentice Hall.

Wood, Samuel & Wood, Ellen. (1999). *The world of psychology* (3rd ed.). Boston: Allyn & Bacon.

Woollett, Anne, Marshall, Hariette, Nicolson, Paula, & Dosanjh, Neelam. (1994). Asian women's ethnic identity: The impact of gender and context in the accounts of women bringing up children in East London. *Feminism and Psychology*, 4(1), 119–132.

Xiaojing, Zhou. (2000). Denaturalizing identities, decolonizing desire: Videos by Richard Fung and Ming-Yuen Ma. *Jouavert: A Journal of Postcolonial Studies*, 4(3). Retrieved [September 26, 2000] from the World Wide Web: http://social.chass.ncsu.edu/jouvert/v4ia/zhou.htm

Xu, Wu & Leffler, Ann. (1996). Gender and race effects on occupational prestige, segregation, and earnings. In Esther Ngan-ling Chow, Doris Wilkinson, & Maxine Baca Zinn (Eds.), *Race, class, and gender: Common bonds, different voices* (pp. 107–124). Thousand Oaks, CA: Sage.

Yau, Jenny & Smetana, Judith. (1993). Chinese-American adolescents' reasoning about cultural conflicts. *Journal of Adolescent Research*, 8(4), 419–438.

Ying, Yu-Wen. (1989). Nonresponse on the Center for Epidemiological Studies-Depression Scale in Chinese Americans. *International Journal of Social Psychiatry*, 35(2), 156–163.

Young, Robert. (1994). Egypt in America. In Ali Rattansi & Sallie Westwood (Eds.), *Racism, modernity and identity on the western front* (pp. 150–169). Cambridge, U.K.: Polity.

Young, T. R. (1991). Chaos and social change: Metaphysics of the postmodern. *Social Science Journal, 28*(3), 238–306.

Zane, Nolan, & Sasao, Toshiaki. (1992). Research on drug abuse among Asian Pacific Americans. *Drugs and Society, 6*(3–4), 181–209.

Zelditch, Morris, Jr. (1992). Problems and progress in sociological theory. *Sociological Perspectives, 35*(3), 415–433.

Zeller, Nancy & Farmer, Frank. (1999). "Catchy, clever titles are not acceptable": Style, APA, and qualitative reporting. *International Journal of Qualitative Studies in Education, 12*(1), 3–20.

Zhou, Min. (1998, June). Coming of age: The current situation of Asian American children. Paper presented at the annual meeting of the Association of Asian American Studies, Honolulu, HI.

Zoreda, Margaret. (1997). Cross-cultural relations and pedagogy. *American Behavioral Scientists, 40*(7), 923–936.

Name Index

Subject Index